Graphic Classics:
EDGAR ALLAN POE

Graphic Classics Volume One
Second Edition
2004

Edited by Tom Pomplun

EUREKA PRODUCTIONS

8778 Oak Grove Road, Mount Horeb, Wisconsin 53572
www.graphicclassics.com

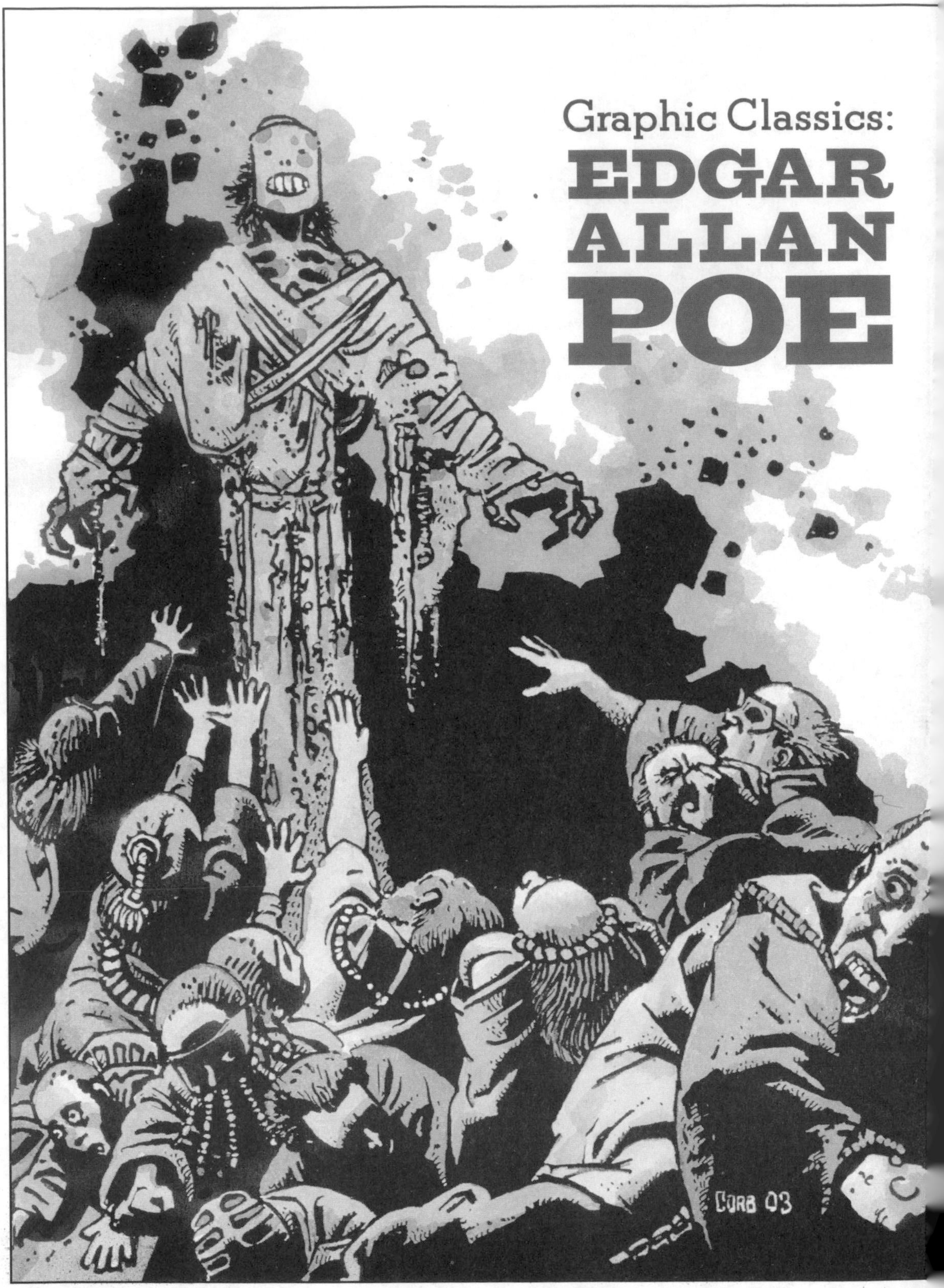
Graphic Classics:
EDGAR
ALLAN
POE
CORB 03

YAP

CONTENTS

Cover illustration by Skot Olsen
Additional illustrations by Richard Corben, Maxon Crumb and Spencer Walts

Graphic Classics: Edgar Allan Poe (Second Edition, ISBN 0-9712464-9-1) is published by Eureka Productions. Price US $9.95. Available from Eureka Productions, 8778 Oak Grove Road, Mount Horeb, WI 53572. Tom Pomplun, editor and designer, tom@graphicclassics.com. Eileen Fitzgerald, editorial assistant. The Graphic Classics website is at http://www.graphicclassics.com. **The East Texas Po' Kid Finds Poe** ©2001 Joe R. Lansdale. **The Bells** was published by Tome Press 1999. Reprinted by permission of the creators. **The Raven** originally appeared in **Star★Reach #17**, 1979. Reprinted by permission of the artist. **The Inheritance of Rufus Griswold** appeared in **Arcade #7**, 1976. Reprinted by permission of the artist. This compilation and all original works ©2004 Eureka Productions. All rights revert to creators after publication. Graphic Classics is a trademark of Eureka Productions. Printed in Canada.

ILLUSTRATION ©2003 RICHARD CORBEN

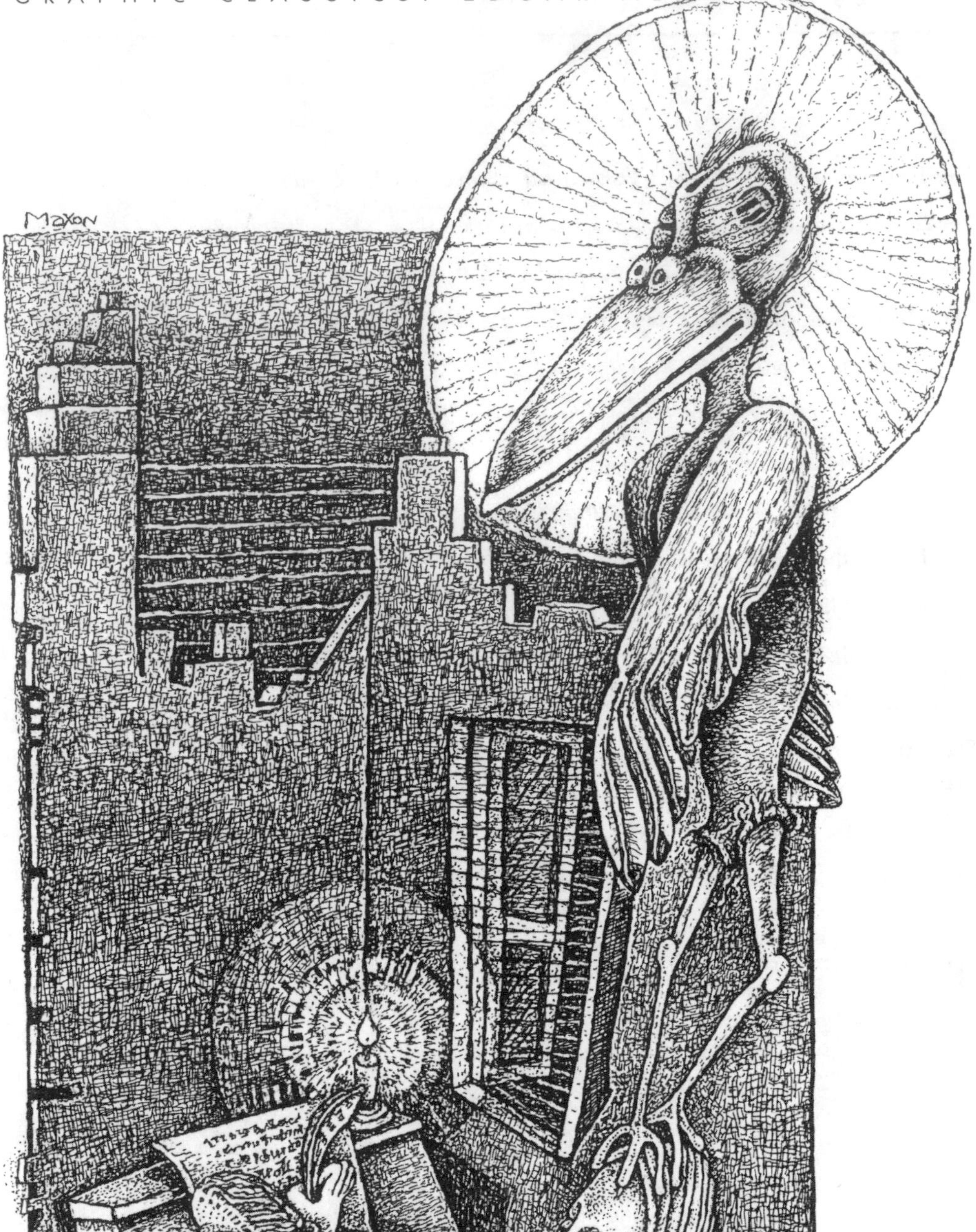
MAXON

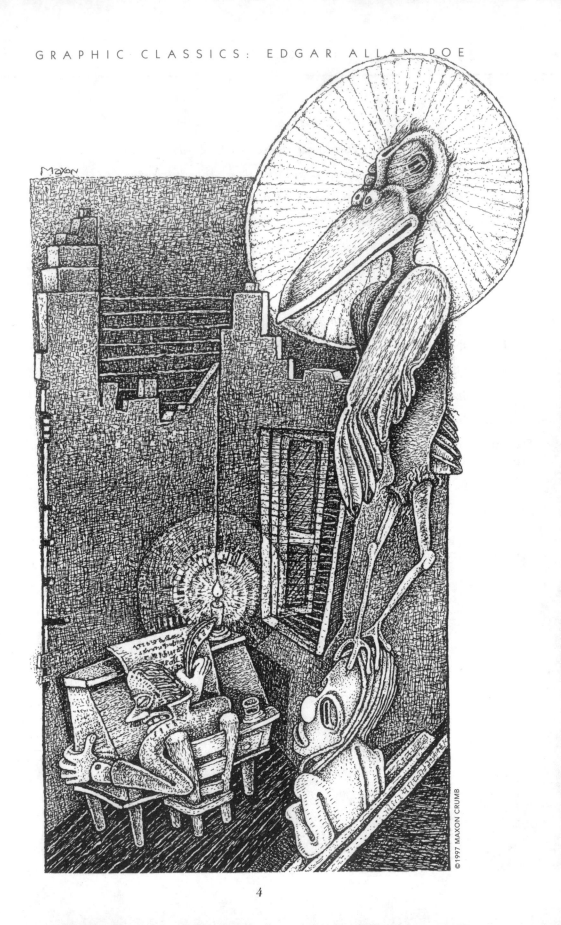

The East Texas Po' Kid Finds Poe and Hopes You Will Too

by Joe R. Lansdale

WHEN I WAS A KID IN EAST TEXAS, early on, before I outgrew it and became healthy as the proverbial horse, I was sickly and therefore spent a lot of time indoors, away from Texas heat.

You have to realize this was before air conditioning was readily available. I remember when air conditioning first appeared in a local store, me and my nephew and niece—they were about my age, as my brother was seventeen when I was born—used to go to the grocery store, Philip's Grocery to be exact, so we could stand inside and feel the cool and we'd buy these big soda pops called Top Colas and candy bars of mixed denominations, then we'd go over to Green's, which was a kind of catch-all store, buy comics and walk home in hellish heat that threatened to melt you.

It was this kind of weather that kept me inside, especially mid-day, mid-summer, and when my nephew and niece were not visiting, I liked to lay up in my bed with the window fan on, the wet straw backing fueled by the water hose, and read comics. And when I wanted something stronger, well, I read Edgar Allan Poe.

Let me tell you, Poe was nothing like East Texas. His world was dark and full of dusty rooms and old deeds, mad men and dead folks. Poe's tales twisted my little gourd like an old-fashioned wash ringer twists a wet rag.

His was a world full of men on the edge, about to go off and go crazy. A world of beating hearts beneath floor boards, squawking black ravens that signaled doom, horrid red plagues, nasty black cats, and deformed men who wore jester outfits and hopped like frogs.

For my taste, this was highly superior to a goat roping or a rodeo or some school function. Here was a world where some really nasty business went on that was interesting, and when you wanted to, all you had to do was close the book, and it went away.

Well, you wanted it to go away.

That was what was unique about Poe. Like Edgar Rice Burroughs, but in a totally different way, his worlds did not go away, they lingered. They were real. And maybe, just maybe, not really that far away.

Add to this the Roger Corman films. With the assistance of such fantasy greats as Richard Matheson and Charles Beaumont, more noted for their work on the classic *Twilight Zone* television show, Corman was making a series of movies based on Poe stories. Well, loosely based. Very loosely. And there was a reason for this. Most of the Poe stories, like *The Pit and the Pendulum*, were brief, and what made them horrifying was the way the characters perceived the events, as well as mood and atmosphere. This was not enough for a full-length feature, so the stories were modified to make entertaining screen plays.

I loved them.

I loved a number of films based on Poe stories.

But... they were not Poe.

Poe was darker, and far more savage, and so far ahead of his time. I believe it is only now that we are beginning to catch up to and understand more fully the savage psychological impact of his tales, as opposed to more simplistic stories of monsters and booger bears.

Poe was a madman, and he shared his madness with us through a series of tales and sketches and poems. The off-the-wall nature of his stories and the uncertainty of his characters' perceptions were a great influence on me as a writer, and I thank Poe for that. Most of his stories were horrors of the mind, or physical horrors, like the plague in *Masque of the Red Death*.

Yes, he was a great teacher to so many of us.

But no one, absolutely no one, has come close to bearding Poe in his own den.

No one can do what he did. No one can generate that absolute darkness better than he.

As a kid in East Texas, lying there on my bed, mid-day, the window fan beating a numbing rhythm, my mind lost inside a Poe story, the world was a stranger and darker place, the atmosphere foggy and cold; odd things moved inside my head, needled little areas of my brain I had never purposely explored, and at that age, did not understand.

I'm not sure I understand them now.

But Poe did. Somewhere inside of him, and inside of those stories, he understood what some of us have felt. Not understood, but felt.

Maybe it's best not to understand. Not to look too long into the abyss.

Understanding drove Poe to drink, and maybe madness.

This volume of *Graphic Classics* is dedicated to the work of that genteel mad man, Poe, and is illustrated by artists who, like me, love Poe.

They get it.

Poe, though well known, is not as appreciated today as he was when I was growing up. He was considered a major writer and his work was the first horror I ever remember reading, and it was given to me gladly by a librarian. His work was thought to be literature, and therefore good for you.

And it is good for you. Disturbing. But good for you.

For what it's worth, his work influenced me and many others who are currently acknowledged as writers of horror and/or suspense. He may be the reason I come back again and again to non-supernatural horror, to the horrors of the mind. It's probably all Poe's fault.

Damn he was good.

I recommend everything he ever wrote.

So, from all of us, this love letter to the man who gave America true horror, detective stories, and a literary legacy.

We give you Edgar Allan Poe, the master. Enjoy.

Award-winning author Joe R. Lansdale has written over thirty books in the horror, western, fantasy and mystery genres. Bubba Ho-Tep, a film based on his novella of the same name, is currently making the rounds of arthouses throughout America.

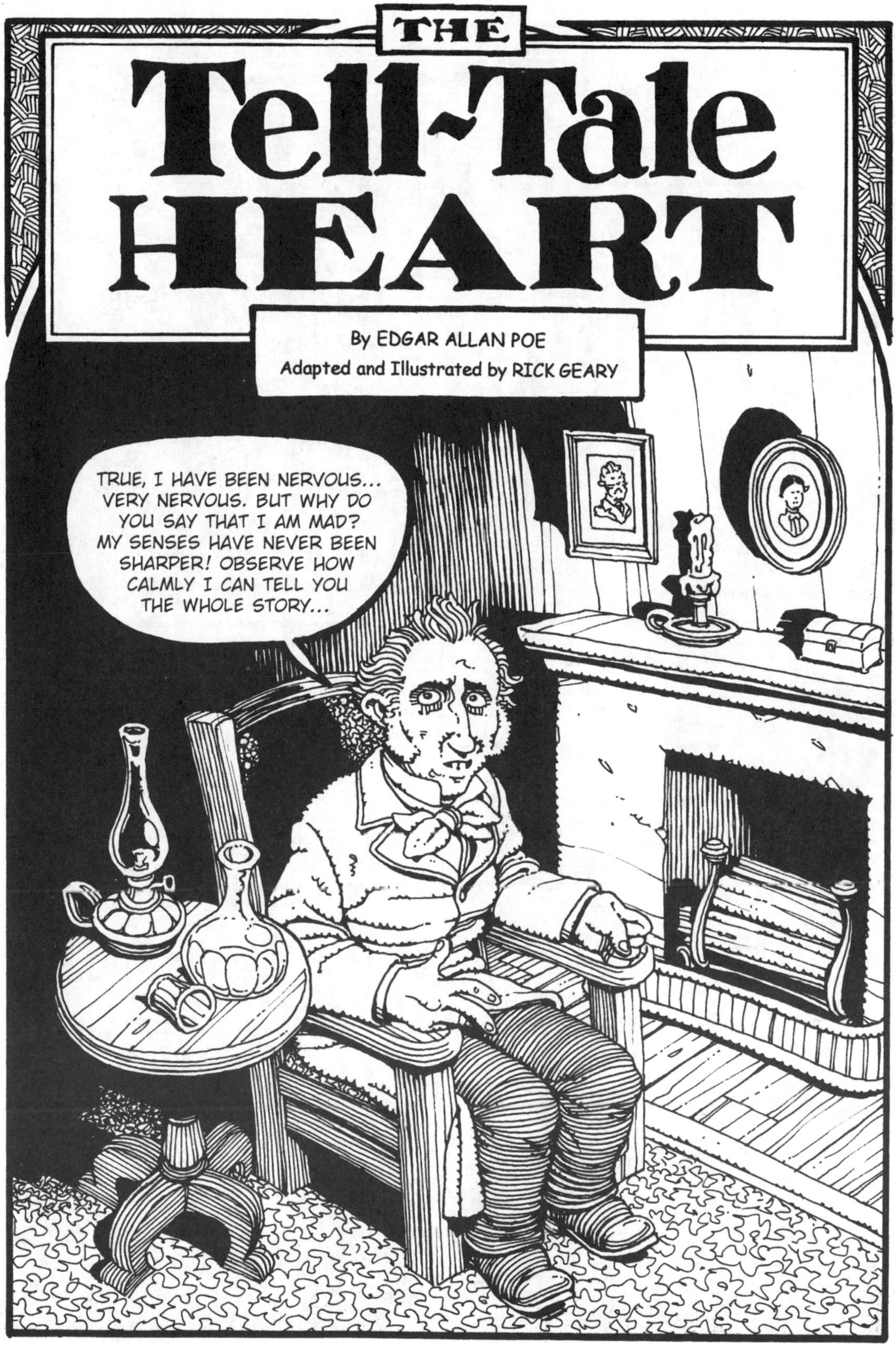
THE
Tell-Tale
HEART
By EDGAR ALLAN POE
Adapted and Illustrated by RICK GEARY
TRUE, I HAVE BEEN NERVOUS... VERY NERVOUS. BUT WHY DO YOU SAY THAT I AM MAD? MY SENSES HAVE NEVER BEEN SHARPER! OBSERVE HOW CALMLY I CAN TELL YOU THE WHOLE STORY...

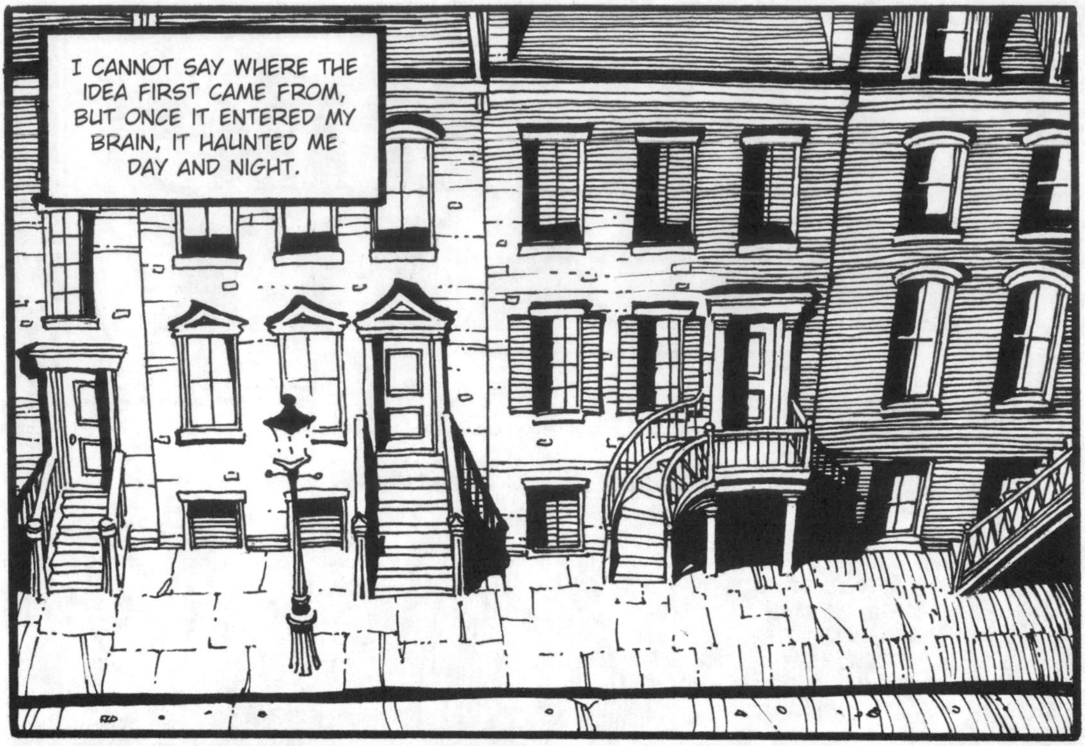
I CANNOT SAY WHERE THE IDEA FIRST CAME FROM, BUT ONCE IT ENTERED MY BRAIN, IT HAUNTED ME DAY AND NIGHT.

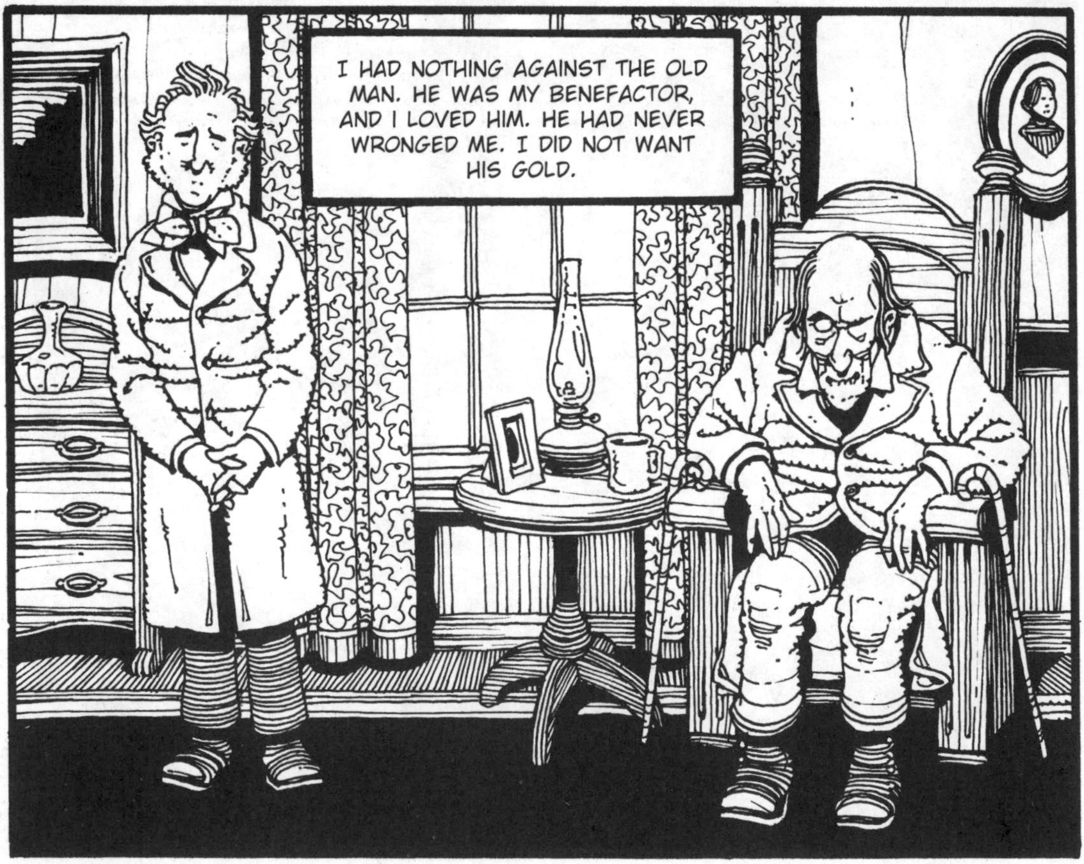
I HAD NOTHING AGAINST THE OLD MAN. HE WAS MY BENEFACTOR, AND I LOVED HIM. HE HAD NEVER WRONGED ME. I DID NOT WANT HIS GOLD.

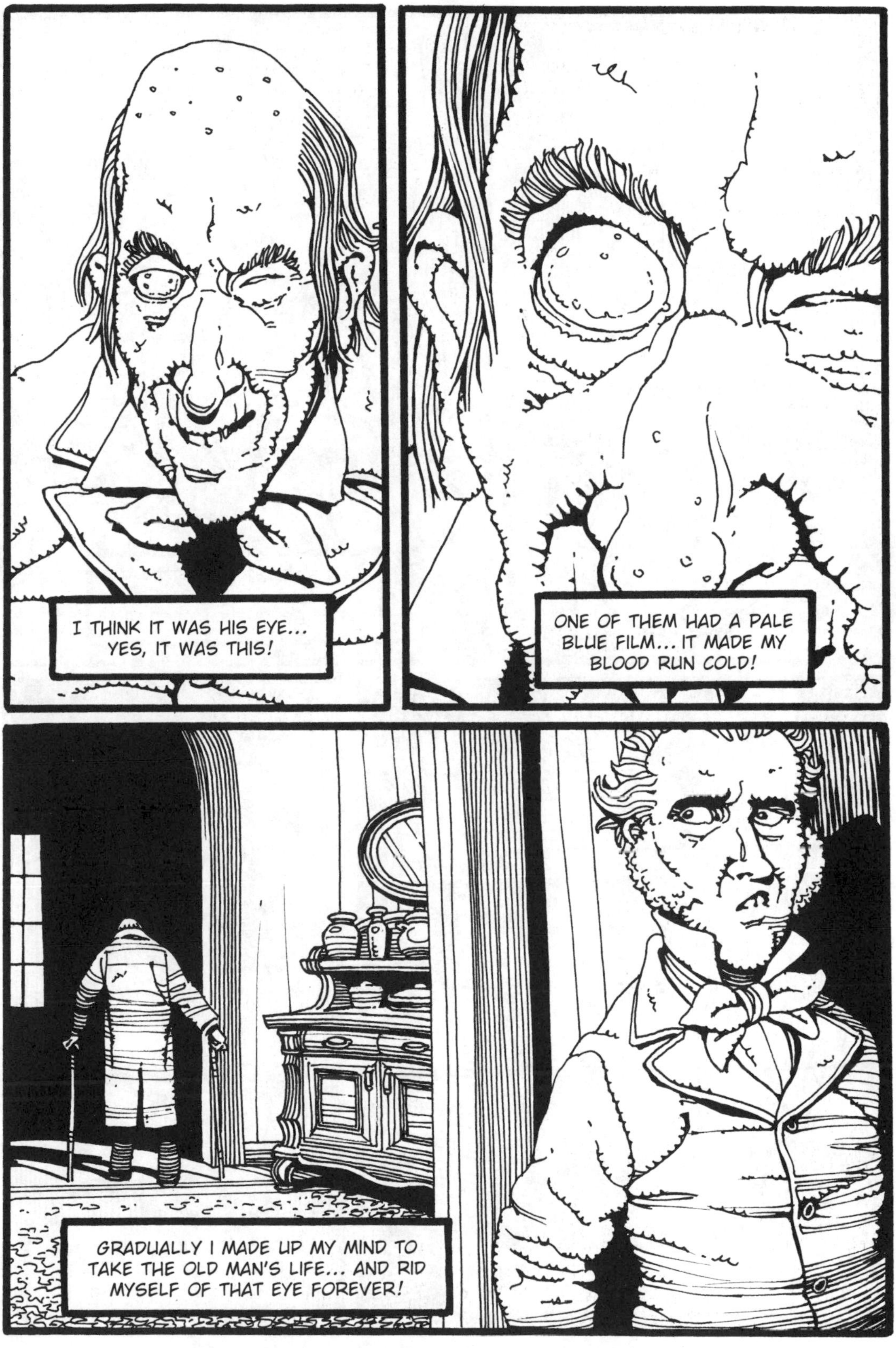
I THINK IT WAS HIS EYE... YES, IT WAS THIS!
ONE OF THEM HAD A PALE BLUE FILM... IT MADE MY BLOOD RUN COLD!
GRADUALLY I MADE UP MY MIND TO TAKE THE OLD MAN'S LIFE... AND RID MYSELF OF THAT EYE FOREVER!

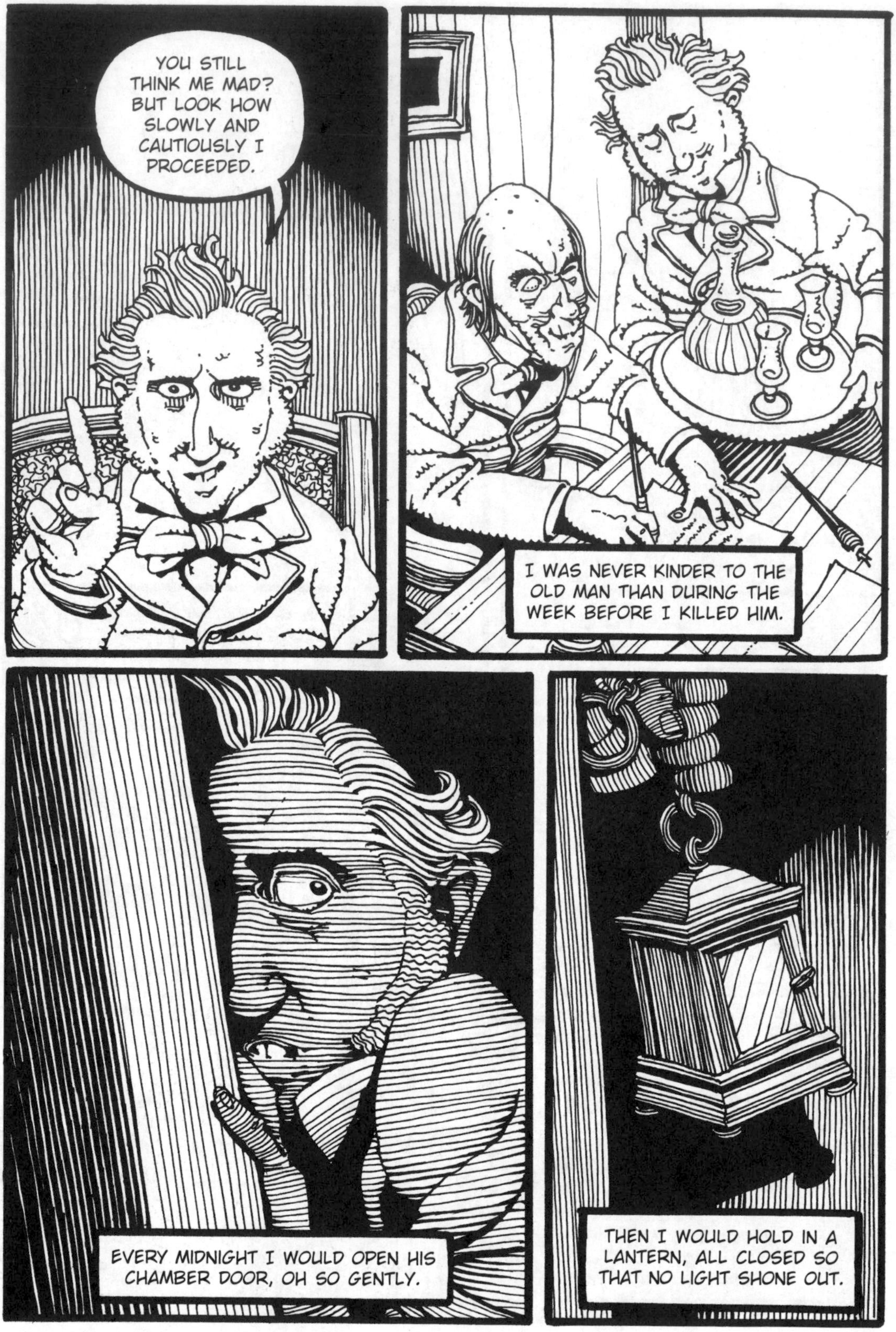
YOU STILL THINK ME MAD? BUT LOOK HOW SLOWLY AND CAUTIOUSLY I PROCEEDED.
I WAS NEVER KINDER TO THE OLD MAN THAN DURING THE WEEK BEFORE I KILLED HIM.
EVERY MIDNIGHT I WOULD OPEN HIS CHAMBER DOOR, OH SO GENTLY.
THEN I WOULD HOLD IN A LANTERN, ALL CLOSED SO THAT NO LIGHT SHONE OUT.

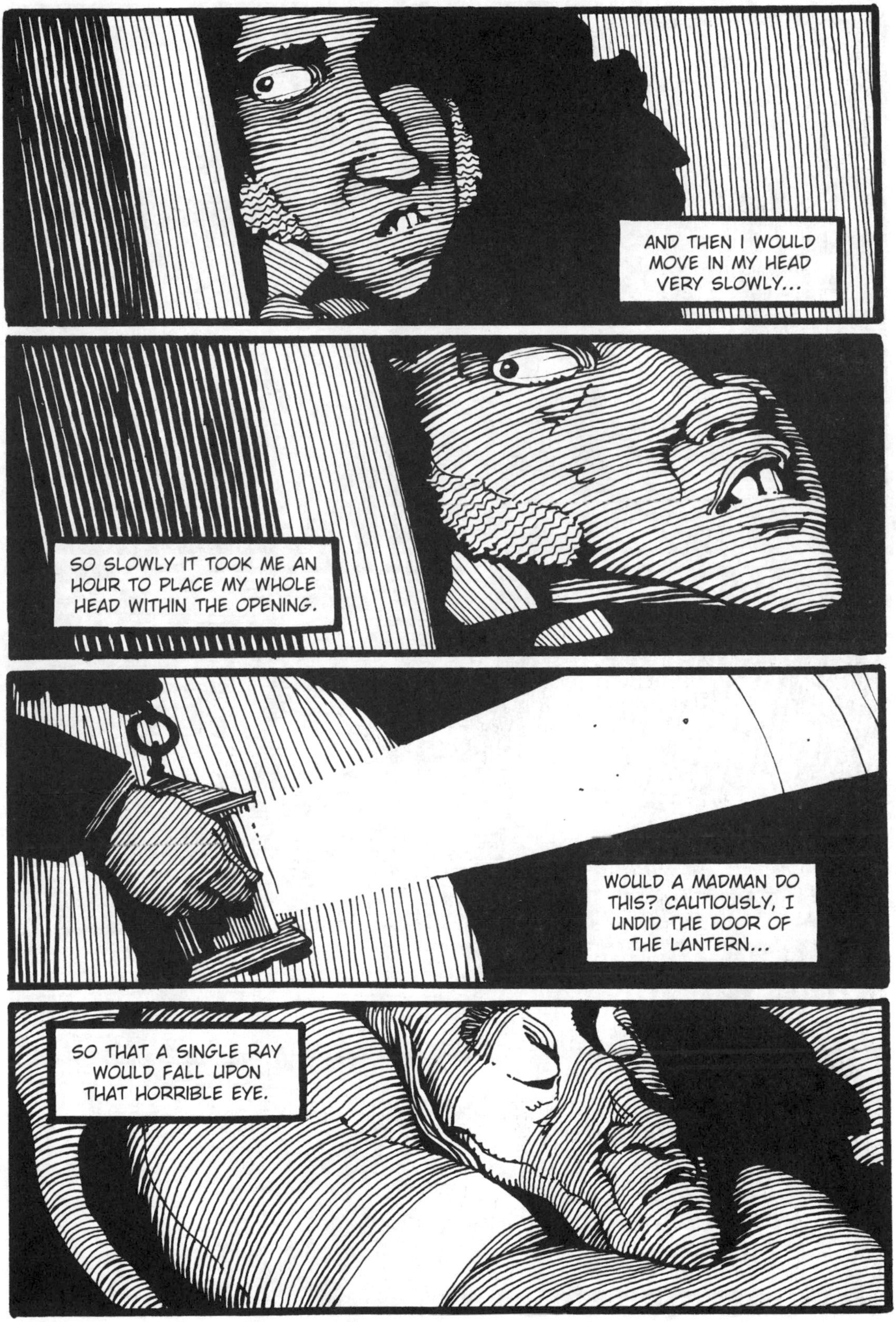
AND THEN I WOULD MOVE IN MY HEAD VERY SLOWLY...
SO SLOWLY IT TOOK ME AN HOUR TO PLACE MY WHOLE HEAD WITHIN THE OPENING.
WOULD A MADMAN DO THIS? CAUTIOUSLY, I UNDID THE DOOR OF THE LANTERN...
SO THAT A SINGLE RAY WOULD FALL UPON THAT HORRIBLE EYE.

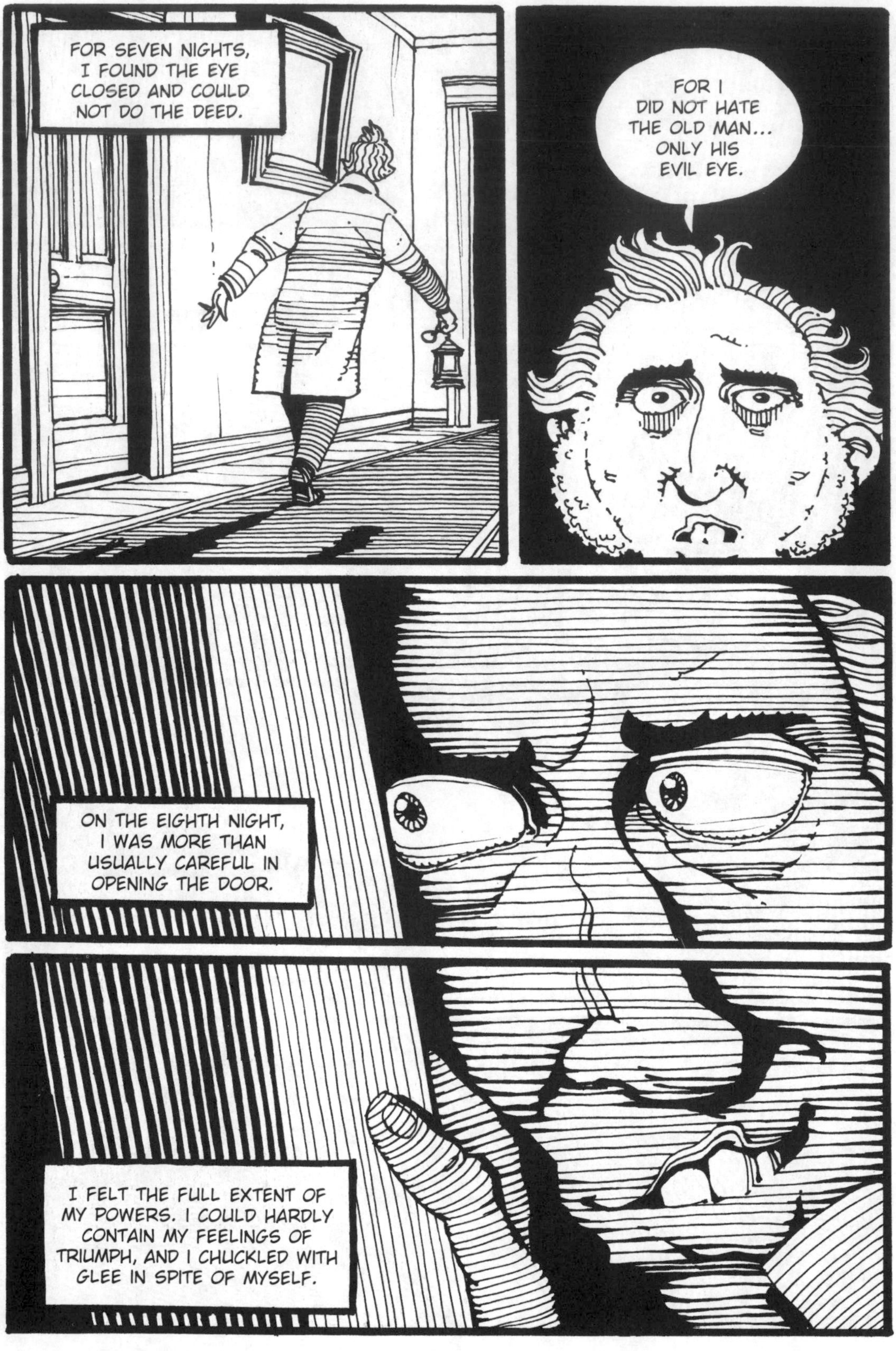
FOR SEVEN NIGHTS, I FOUND THE EYE CLOSED AND COULD NOT DO THE DEED.
FOR I DID NOT HATE THE OLD MAN... ONLY HIS EVIL EYE.
ON THE EIGHTH NIGHT, I WAS MORE THAN USUALLY CAREFUL IN OPENING THE DOOR.
I FELT THE FULL EXTENT OF MY POWERS. I COULD HARDLY CONTAIN MY FEELINGS OF TRIUMPH, AND I CHUCKLED WITH GLEE IN SPITE OF MYSELF.

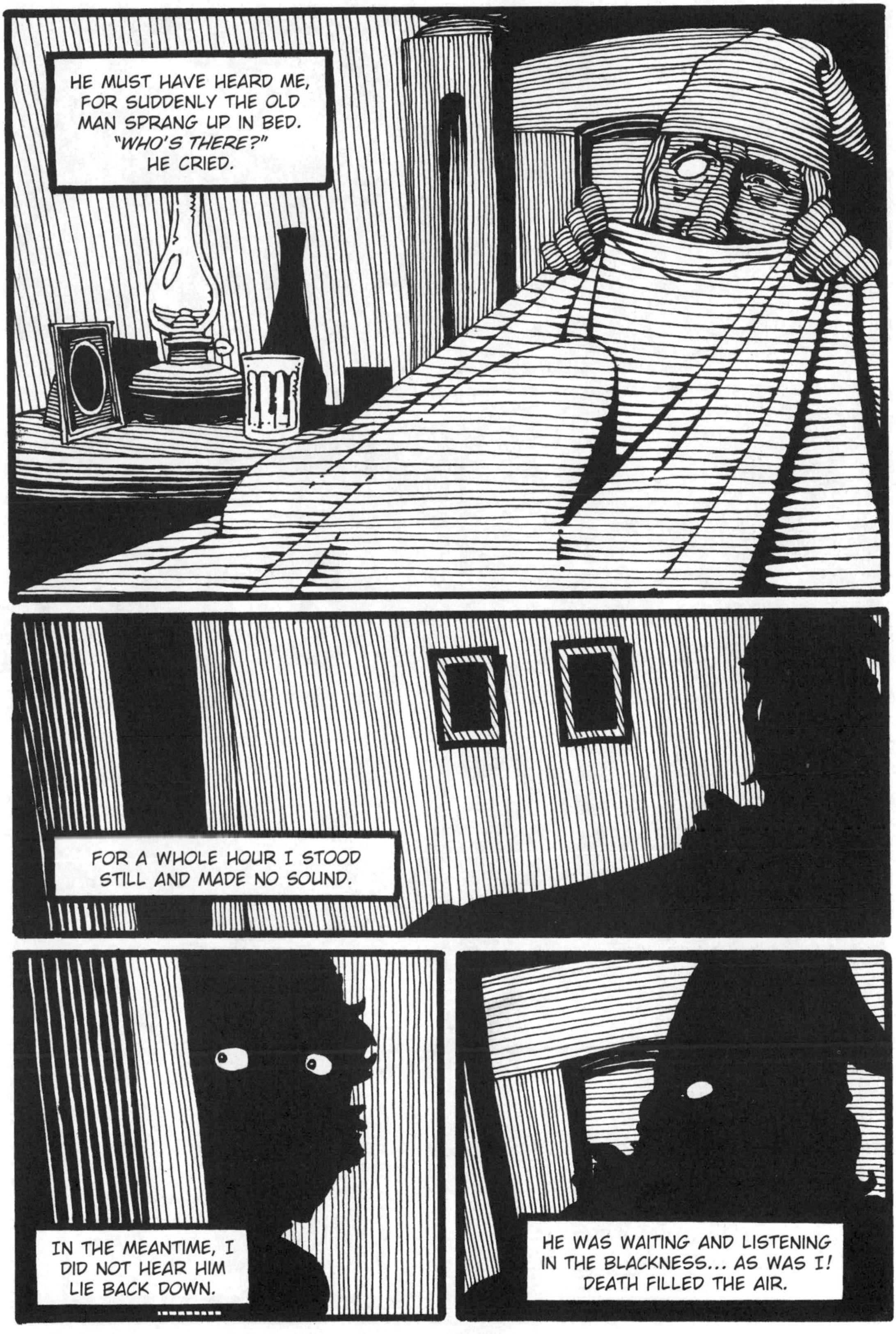
HE MUST HAVE HEARD ME, FOR SUDDENLY THE OLD MAN SPRANG UP IN BED. *"WHO'S THERE?"* HE CRIED.
FOR A WHOLE HOUR I STOOD STILL AND MADE NO SOUND.
IN THE MEANTIME, I DID NOT HEAR HIM LIE BACK DOWN.
HE WAS WAITING AND LISTENING IN THE BLACKNESS... AS WAS I! DEATH FILLED THE AIR.

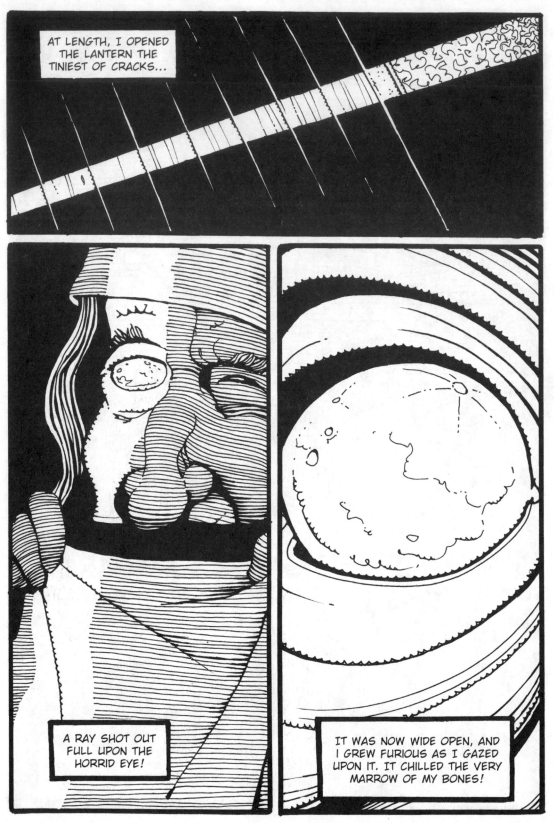

AT LENGTH, I OPENED THE LANTERN THE TINIEST OF CRACKS...

A RAY SHOT OUT FULL UPON THE HORRID EYE!

IT WAS NOW WIDE OPEN, AND I GREW FURIOUS AS I GAZED UPON IT. IT CHILLED THE VERY MARROW OF MY BONES!

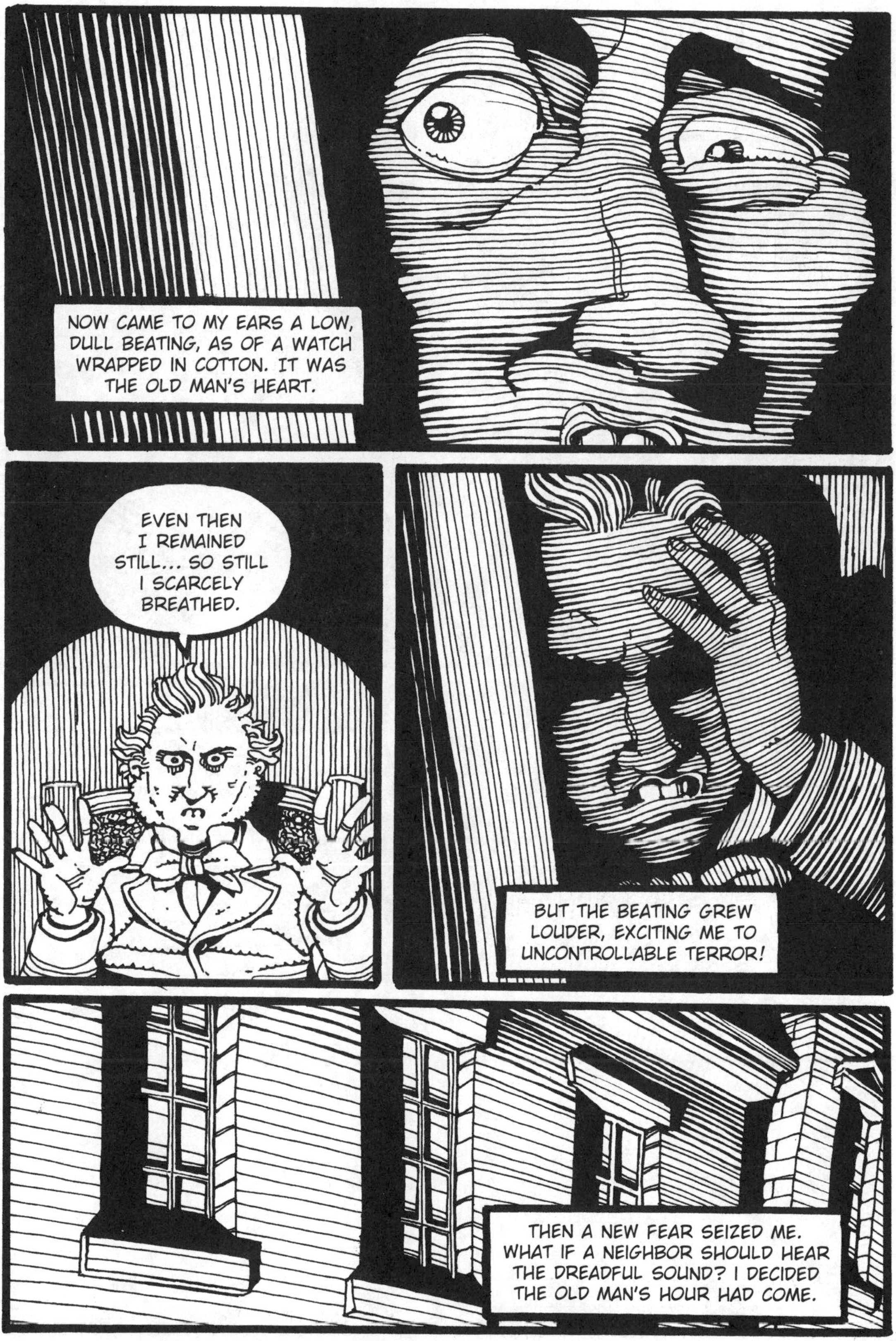
NOW CAME TO MY EARS A LOW, DULL BEATING, AS OF A WATCH WRAPPED IN COTTON. IT WAS THE OLD MAN'S HEART.
EVEN THEN I REMAINED STILL... SO STILL I SCARCELY BREATHED.
BUT THE BEATING GREW LOUDER, EXCITING ME TO UNCONTROLLABLE TERROR!
THEN A NEW FEAR SEIZED ME. WHAT IF A NEIGHBOR SHOULD HEAR THE DREADFUL SOUND? I DECIDED THE OLD MAN'S HOUR HAD COME.

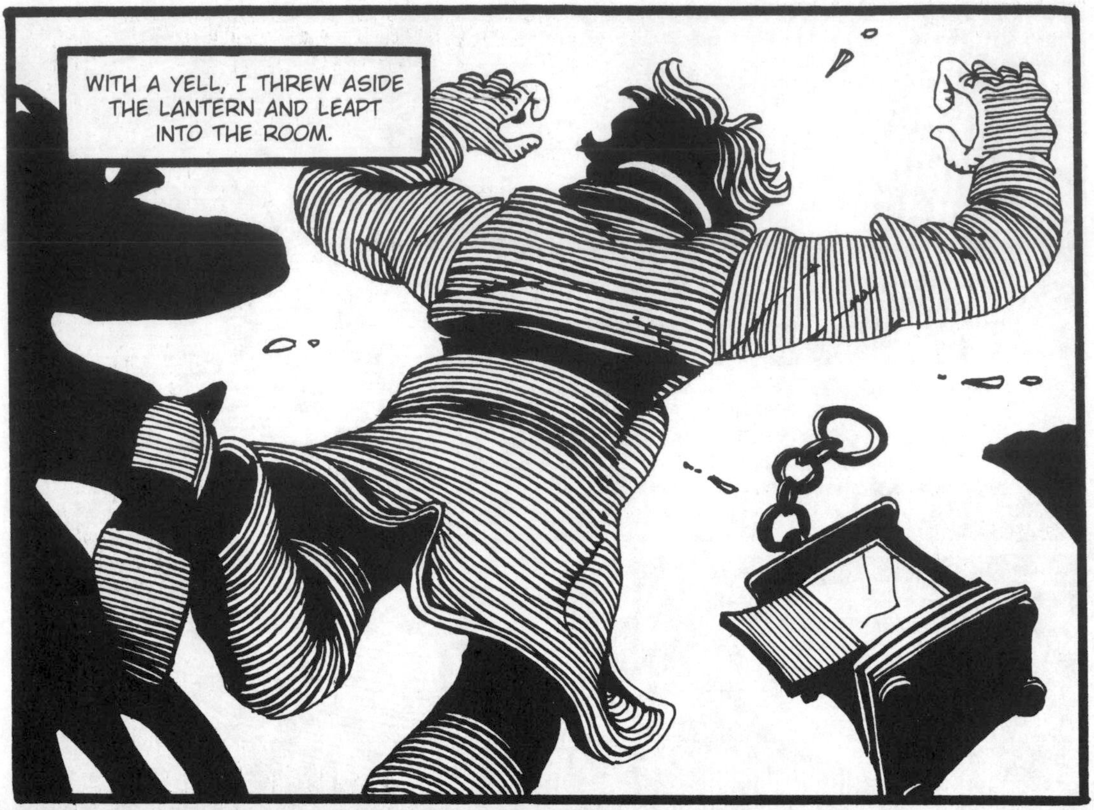
WITH A YELL, I THREW ASIDE THE LANTERN AND LEAPT INTO THE ROOM.

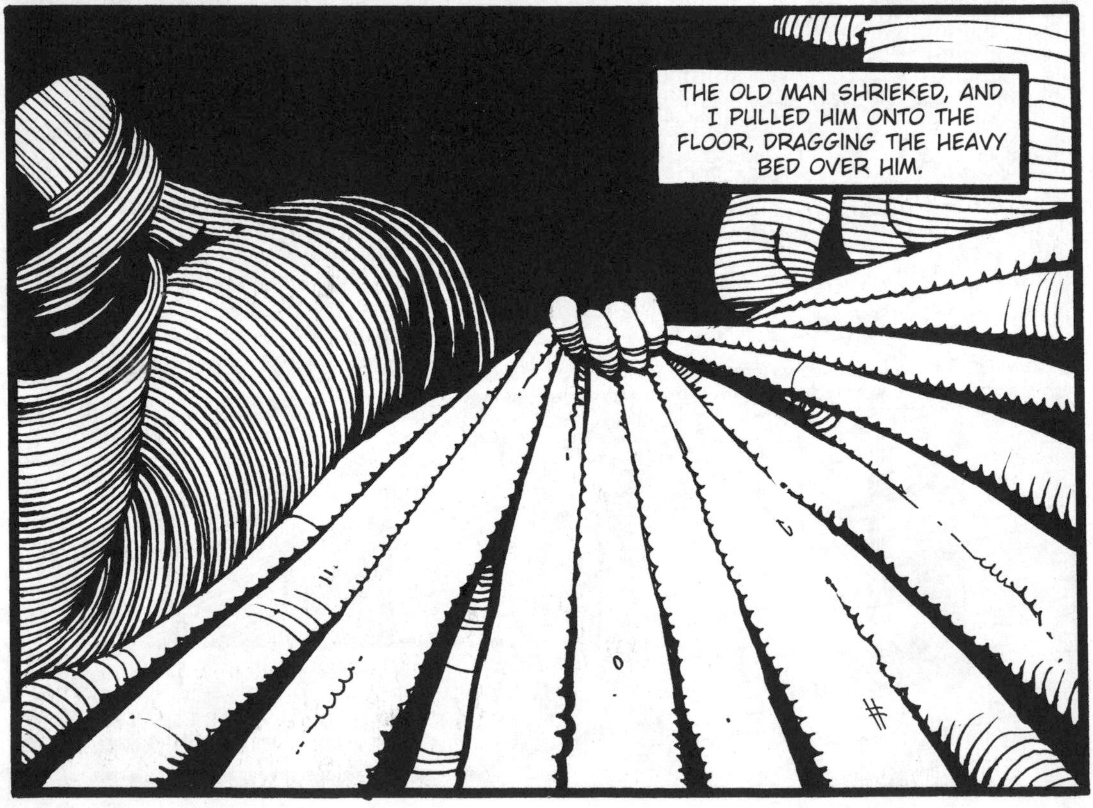
THE OLD MAN SHRIEKED, AND I PULLED HIM ONTO THE FLOOR, DRAGGING THE HEAVY BED OVER HIM.

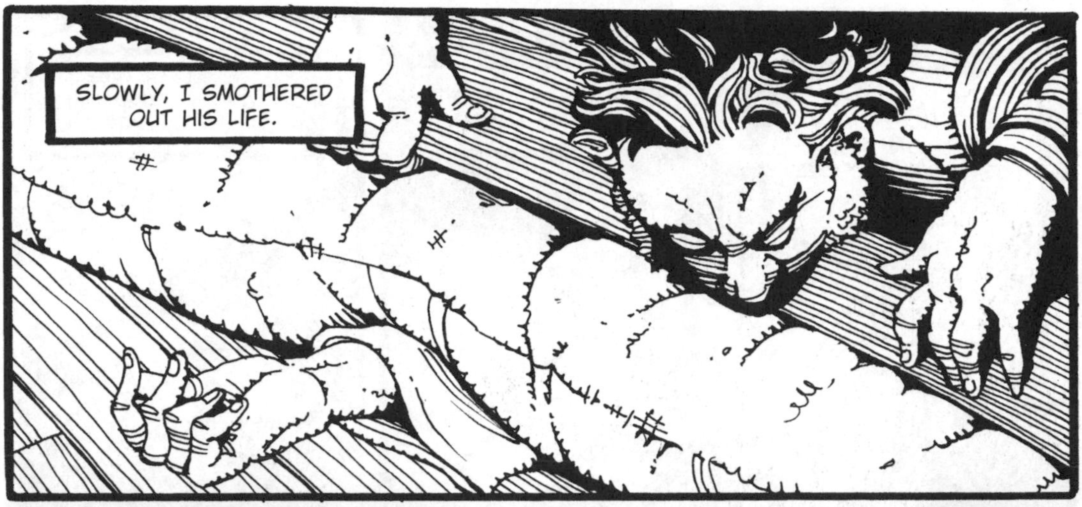
SLOWLY, I SMOTHERED OUT HIS LIFE.

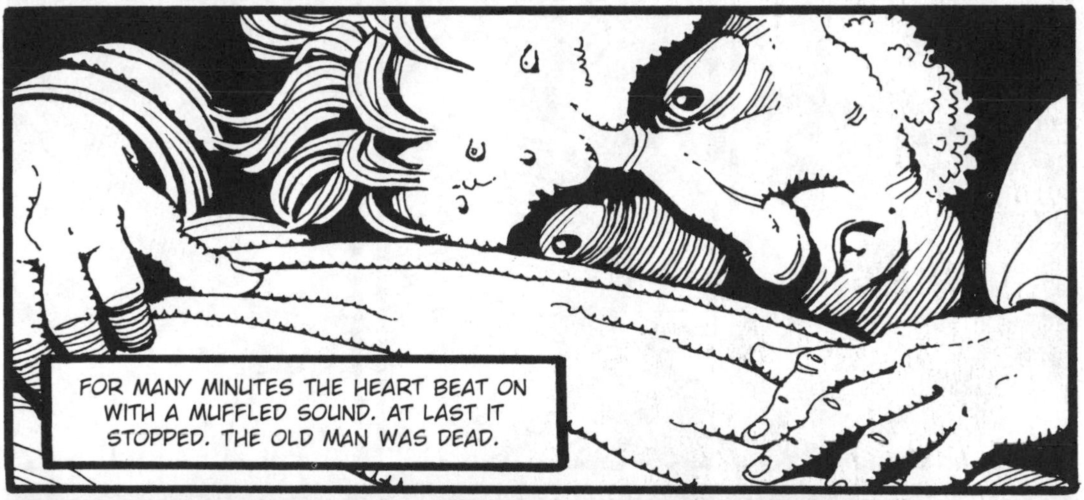
FOR MANY MINUTES THE HEART BEAT ON WITH A MUFFLED SOUND. AT LAST IT STOPPED. THE OLD MAN WAS DEAD.

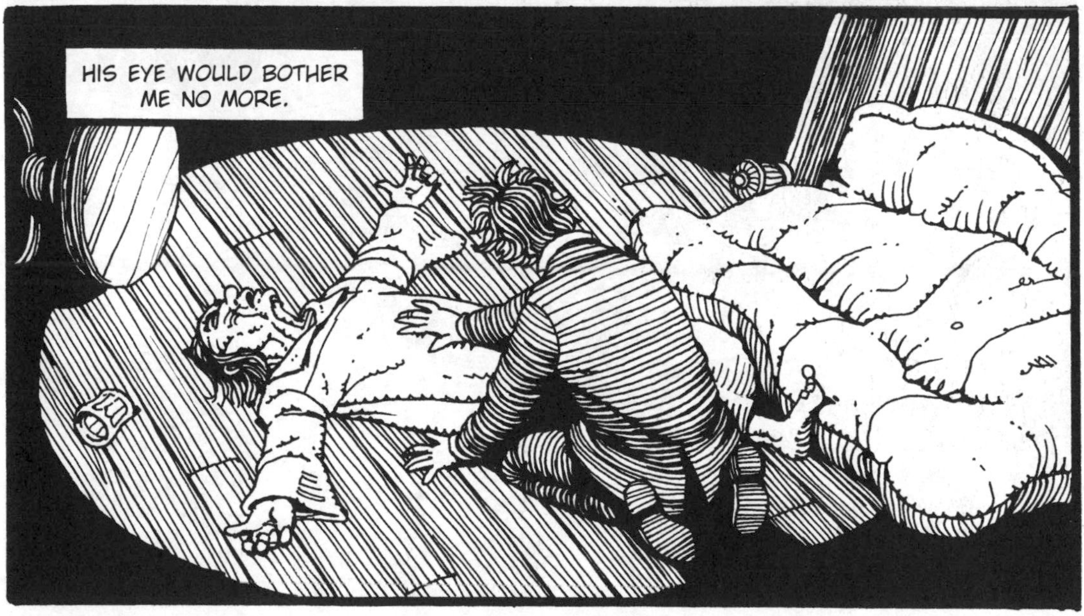
HIS EYE WOULD BOTHER ME NO MORE.

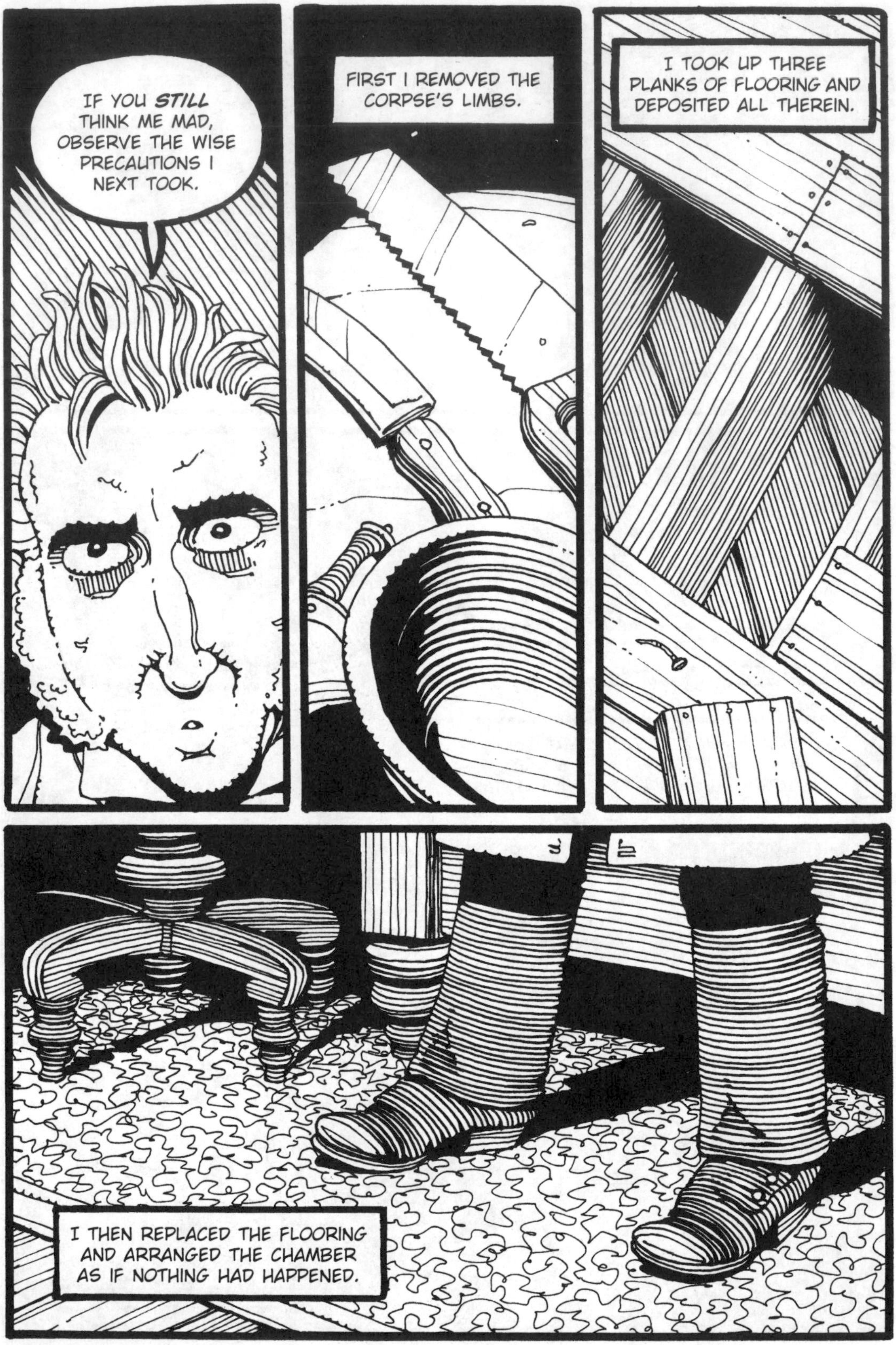
IF YOU ***STILL*** THINK ME MAD, OBSERVE THE WISE PRECAUTIONS I NEXT TOOK.
FIRST I REMOVED THE CORPSE'S LIMBS.
I TOOK UP THREE PLANKS OF FLOORING AND DEPOSITED ALL THEREIN.
I THEN REPLACED THE FLOORING AND ARRANGED THE CHAMBER AS IF NOTHING HAD HAPPENED.

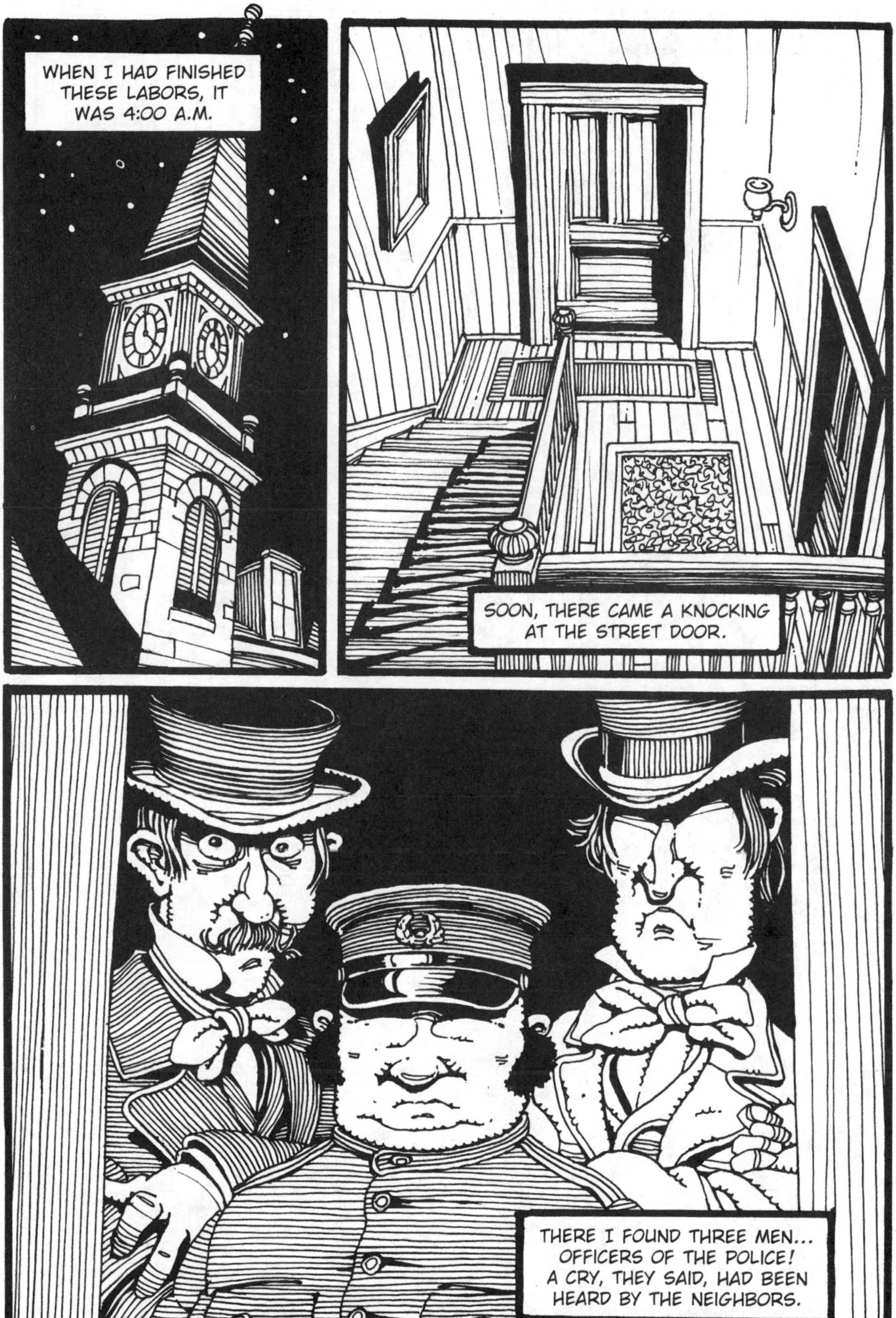
WHEN I HAD FINISHED THESE LABORS, IT WAS 4:00 A.M.
SOON, THERE CAME A KNOCKING AT THE STREET DOOR.
THERE I FOUND THREE MEN... OFFICERS OF THE POLICE! A CRY, THEY SAID, HAD BEEN HEARD BY THE NEIGHBORS.

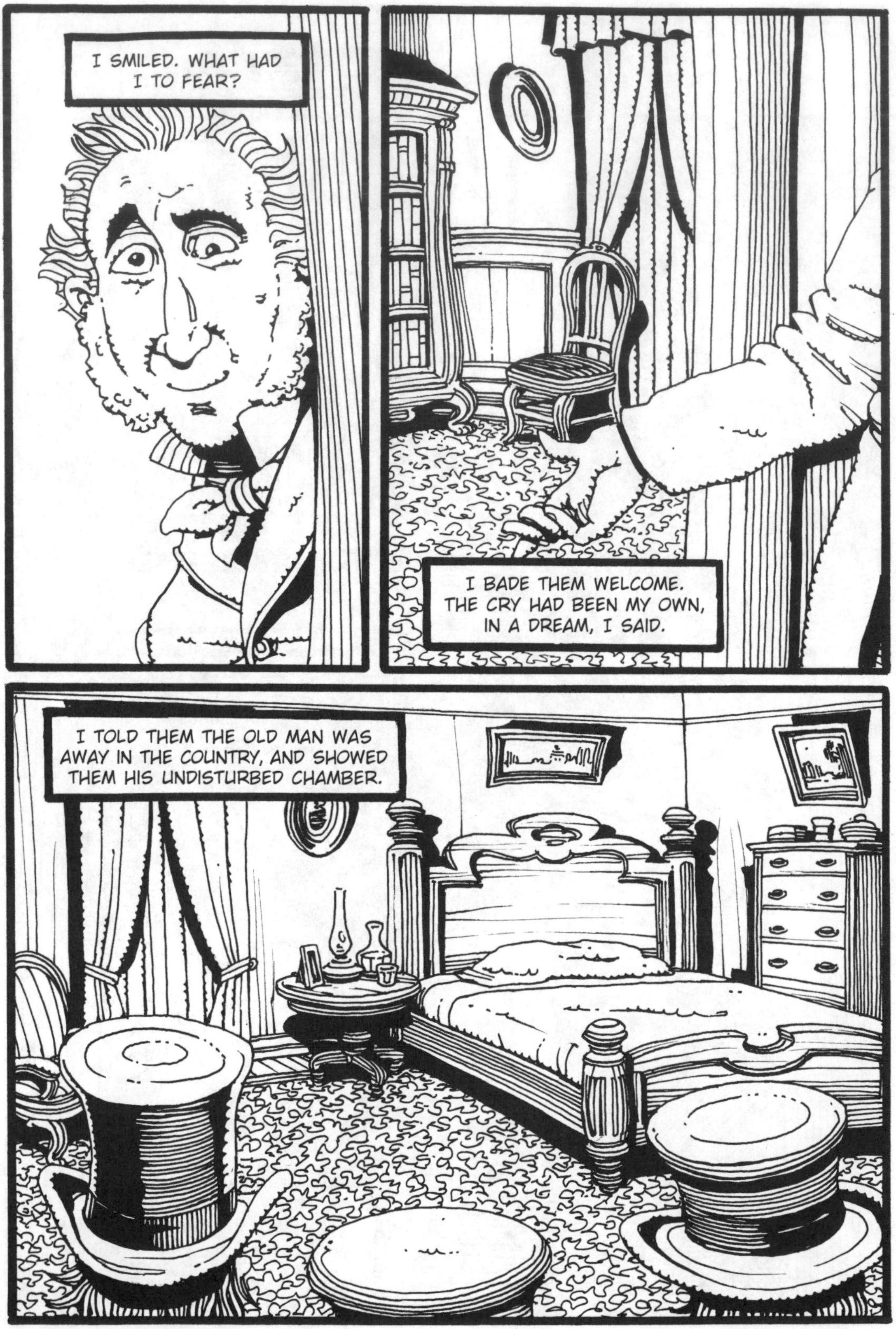
I SMILED. WHAT HAD I TO FEAR?
I BADE THEM WELCOME. THE CRY HAD BEEN MY OWN, IN A DREAM, I SAID.
I TOLD THEM THE OLD MAN WAS AWAY IN THE COUNTRY, AND SHOWED THEM HIS UNDISTURBED CHAMBER.

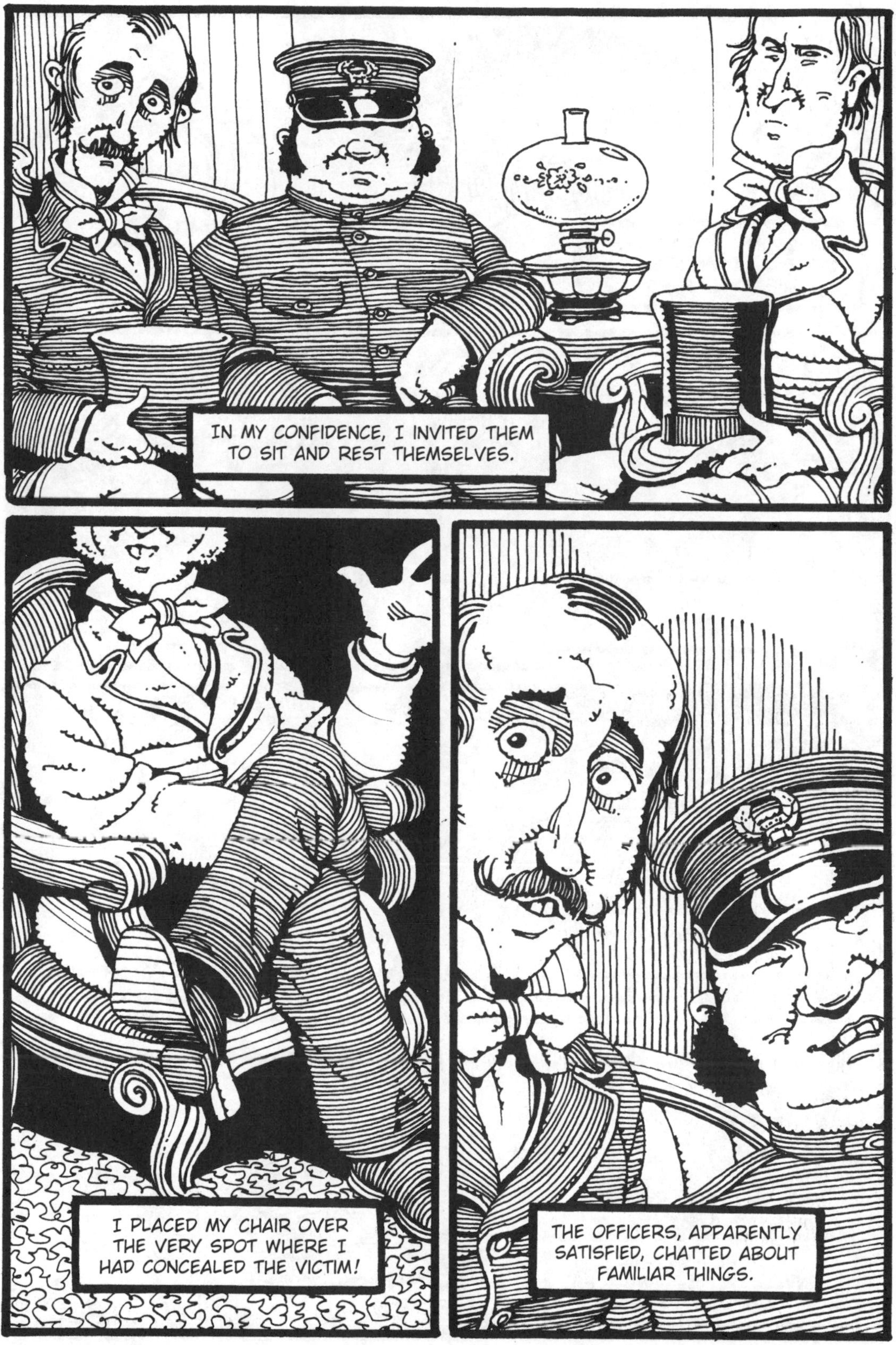
IN MY CONFIDENCE, I INVITED THEM TO SIT AND REST THEMSELVES.
I PLACED MY CHAIR OVER THE VERY SPOT WHERE I HAD CONCEALED THE VICTIM!
THE OFFICERS, APPARENTLY SATISFIED, CHATTED ABOUT FAMILIAR THINGS.

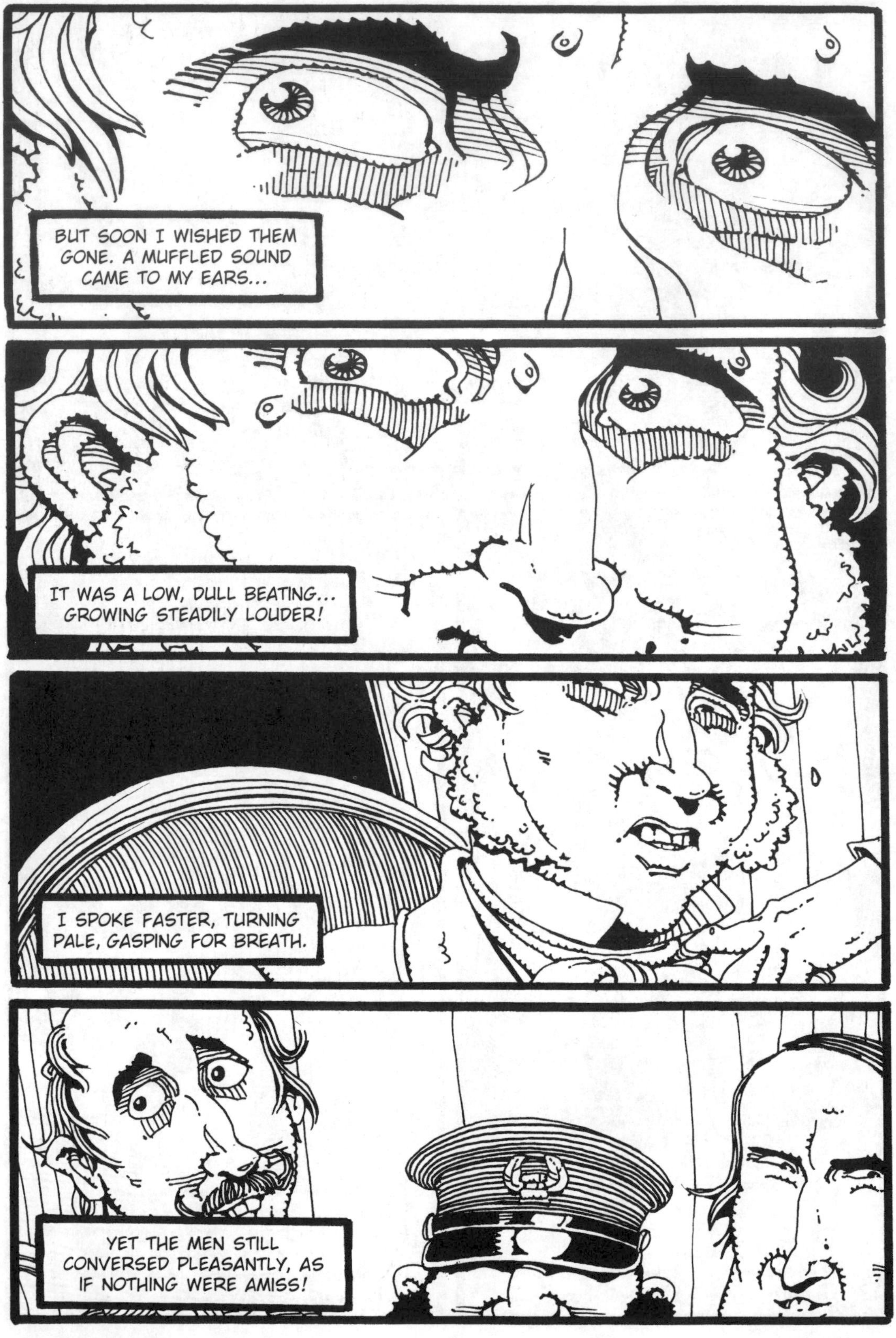
BUT SOON I WISHED THEM GONE. A MUFFLED SOUND CAME TO MY EARS...
IT WAS A LOW, DULL BEATING... GROWING STEADILY LOUDER!
I SPOKE FASTER, TURNING PALE, GASPING FOR BREATH.
YET THE MEN STILL CONVERSED PLEASANTLY, AS IF NOTHING WERE AMISS!

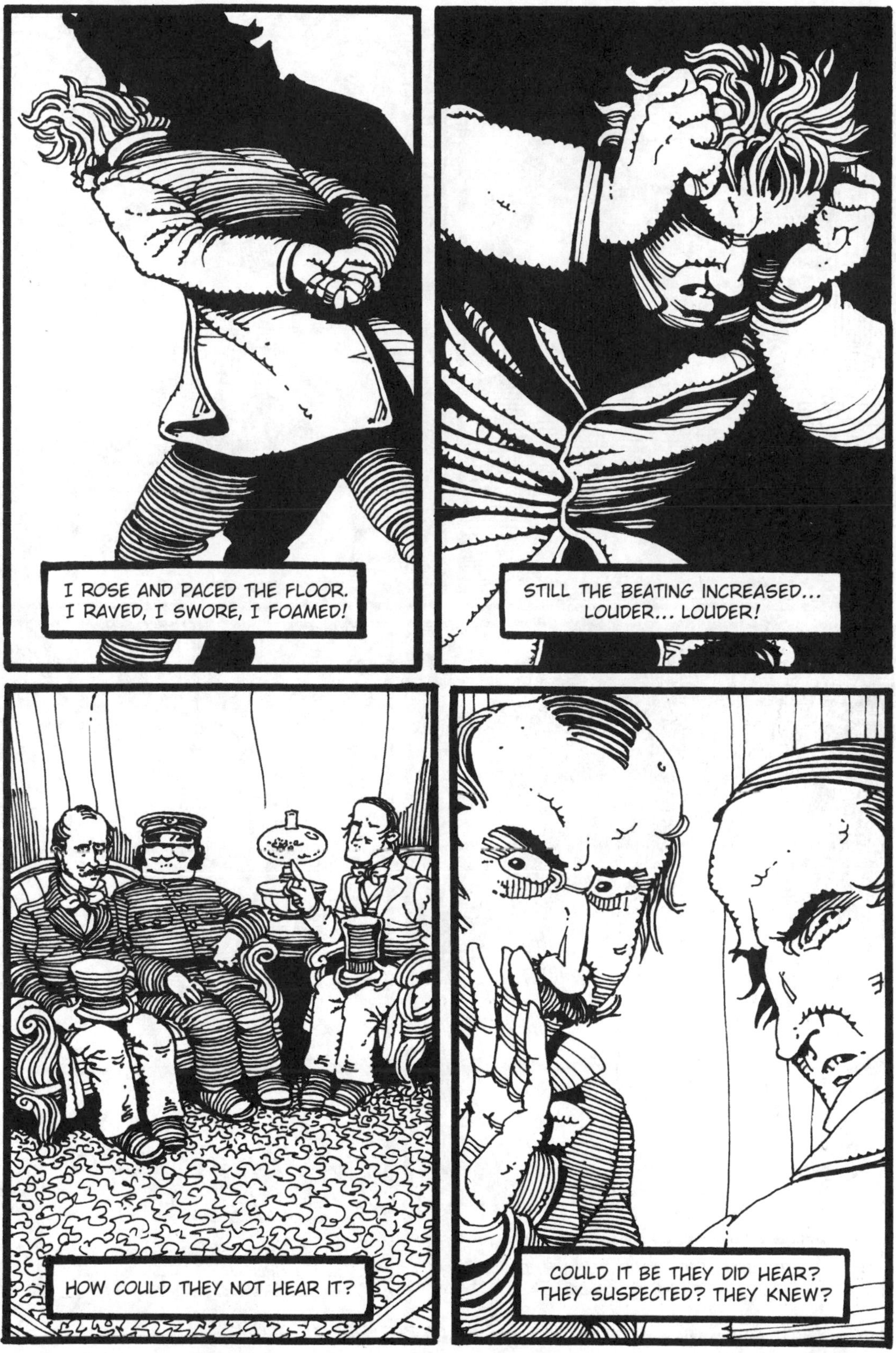
I ROSE AND PACED THE FLOOR.
I RAVED, I SWORE, I FOAMED!
STILL THE BEATING INCREASED...
LOUDER... LOUDER!
HOW COULD THEY NOT HEAR IT?
COULD IT BE THEY DID HEAR?
THEY SUSPECTED? THEY KNEW?

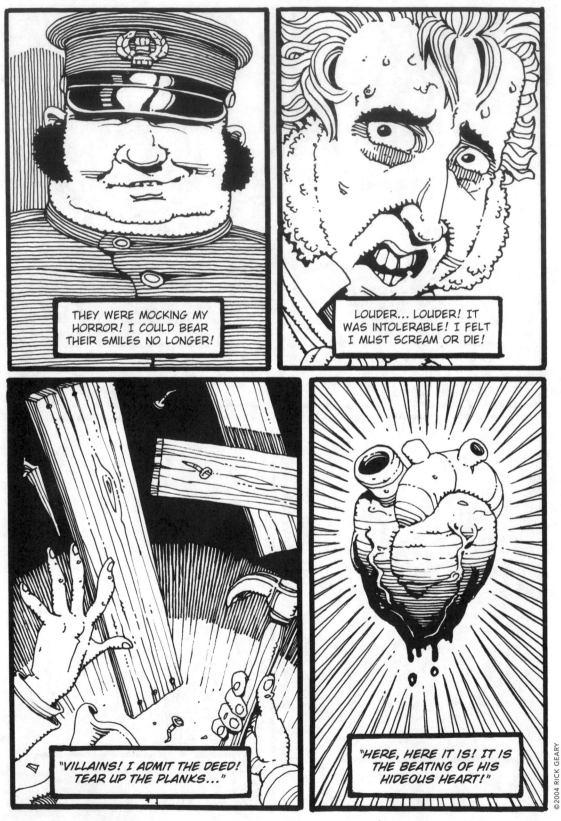

THEY WERE MOCKING MY HORROR! I COULD BEAR THEIR SMILES NO LONGER!

LOUDER... LOUDER! IT WAS INTOLERABLE! I FELT I MUST SCREAM OR DIE!

"VILLAINS! I ADMIT THE DEED! TEAR UP THE PLANKS..."

"HERE, HERE IT IS! IT IS THE BEATING OF HIS HIDEOUS HEART!"

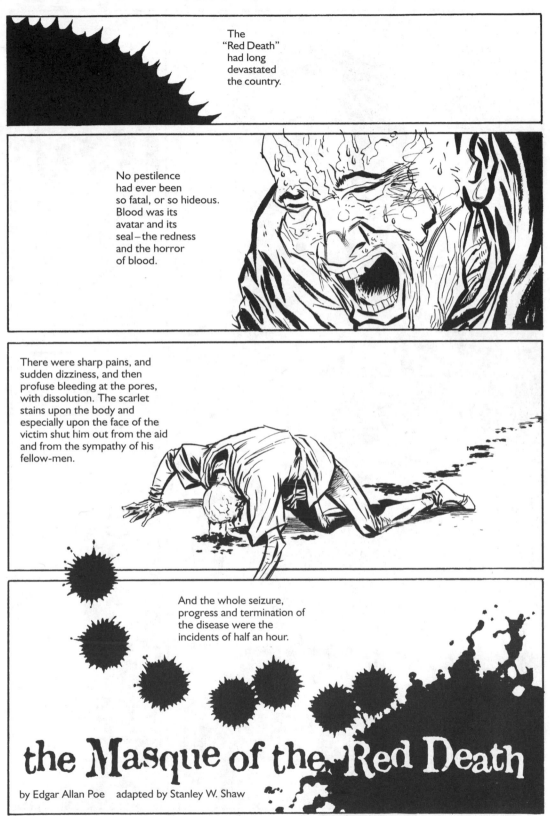

The "Red Death" had long devastated the country.

No pestilence had ever been so fatal, or so hideous. Blood was its avatar and its seal—the redness and the horror of blood.

There were sharp pains, and sudden dizziness, and then profuse bleeding at the pores, with dissolution. The scarlet stains upon the body and especially upon the face of the victim shut him out from the aid and from the sympathy of his fellow-men.

And the whole seizure, progress and termination of the disease were the incidents of half an hour.

the Masque of the Red Death

by Edgar Allan Poe   adapted by Stanley W. Shaw

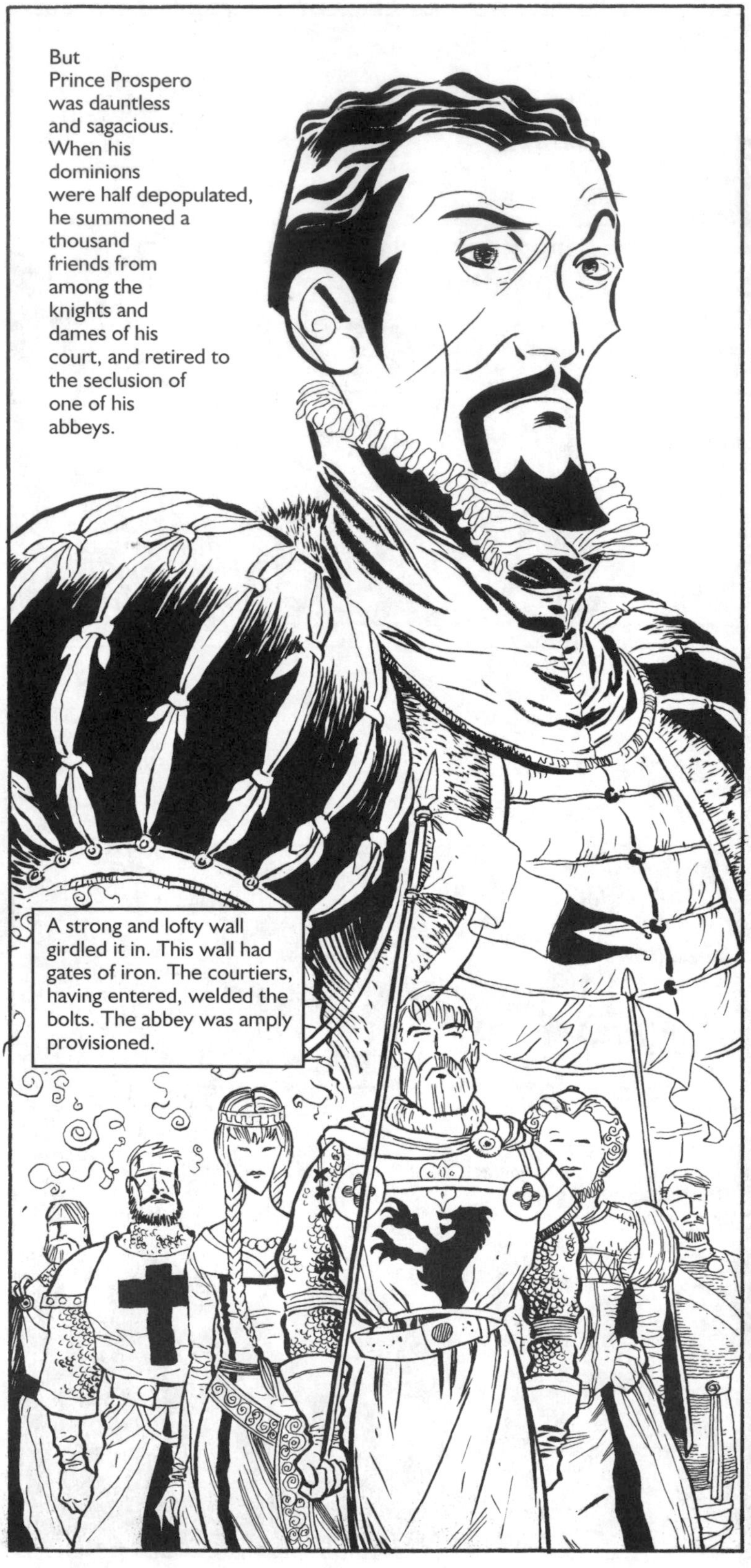
But Prince Prospero was dauntless and sagacious. When his dominions were half depopulated, he summoned a thousand friends from among the knights and dames of his court, and retired to the seclusion of one of his abbeys.
A strong and lofty wall girdled it in. This wall had gates of iron. The courtiers, having entered, welded the bolts. The abbey was amply provisioned.

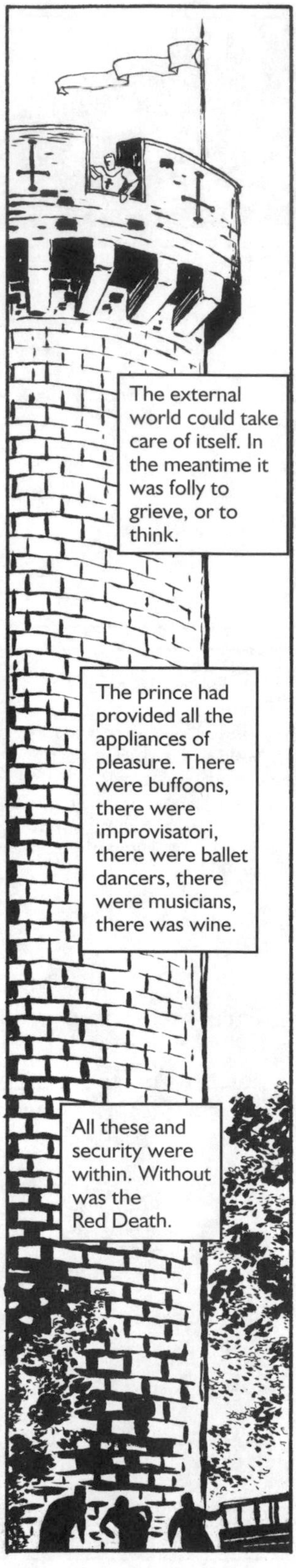
The external world could take care of itself. In the meantime it was folly to grieve, or to think.
The prince had provided all the appliances of pleasure. There were buffoons, there were improvisatori, there were ballet dancers, there were musicians, there was wine.
All these and security were within. Without was the Red Death.

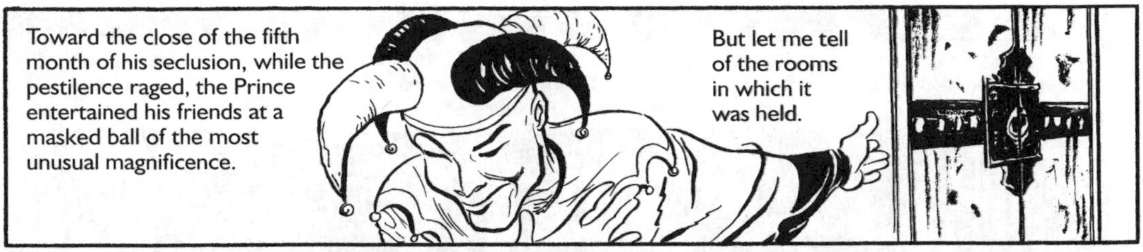
Toward the close of the fifth month of his seclusion, while the pestilence raged, the Prince entertained his friends at a masked ball of the most unusual magnificence.
But let me tell of the rooms in which it was held.

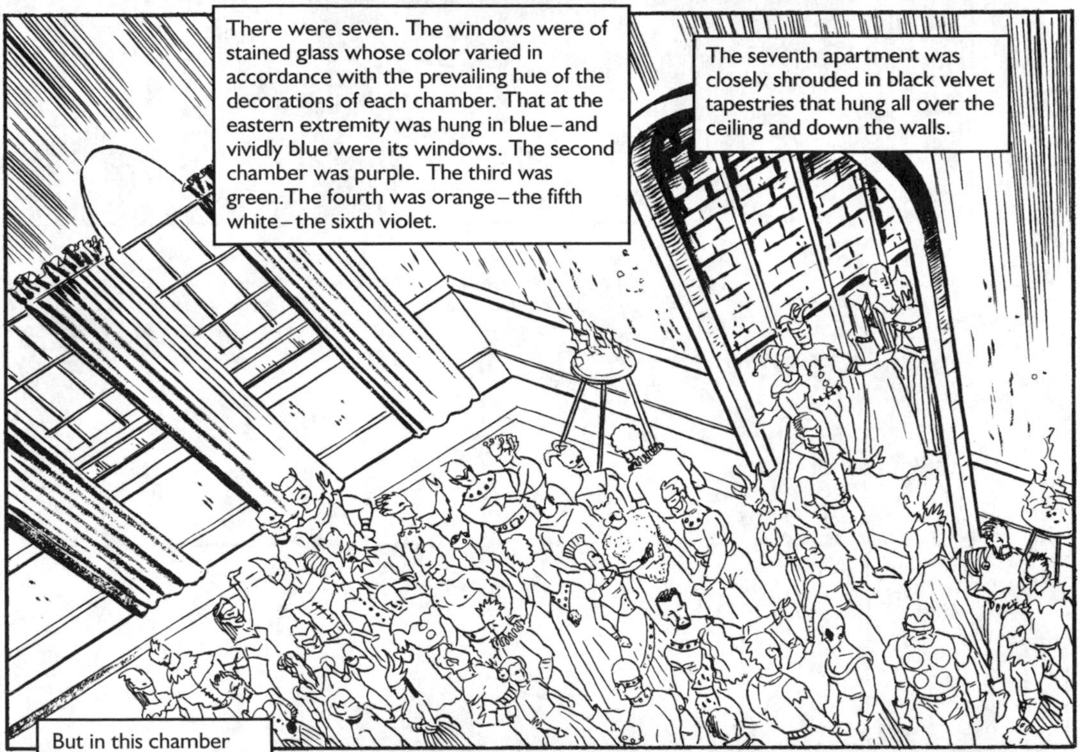
There were seven. The windows were of stained glass whose color varied in accordance with the prevailing hue of the decorations of each chamber. That at the eastern extremity was hung in blue–and vividly blue were its windows. The second chamber was purple. The third was green. The fourth was orange–the fifth white–the sixth violet.
The seventh apartment was closely shrouded in black velvet tapestries that hung all over the ceiling and down the walls.

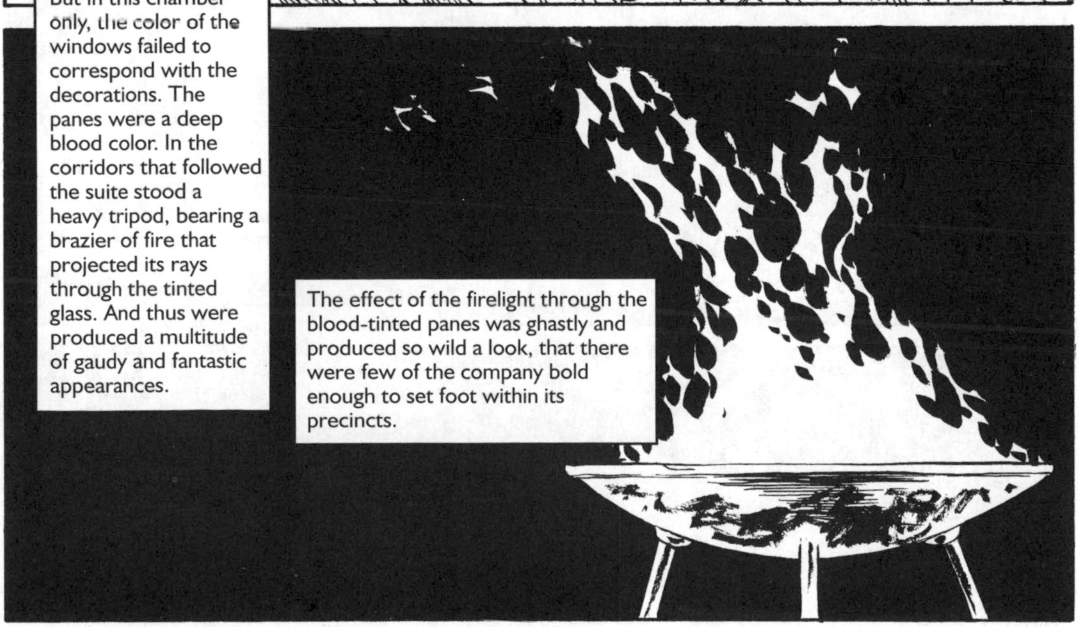
But in this chamber only, the color of the windows failed to correspond with the decorations. The panes were a deep blood color. In the corridors that followed the suite stood a heavy tripod, bearing a brazier of fire that projected its rays through the tinted glass. And thus were produced a multitude of gaudy and fantastic appearances.
The effect of the firelight through the blood-tinted panes was ghastly and produced so wild a look, that there were few of the company bold enough to set foot within its precincts.

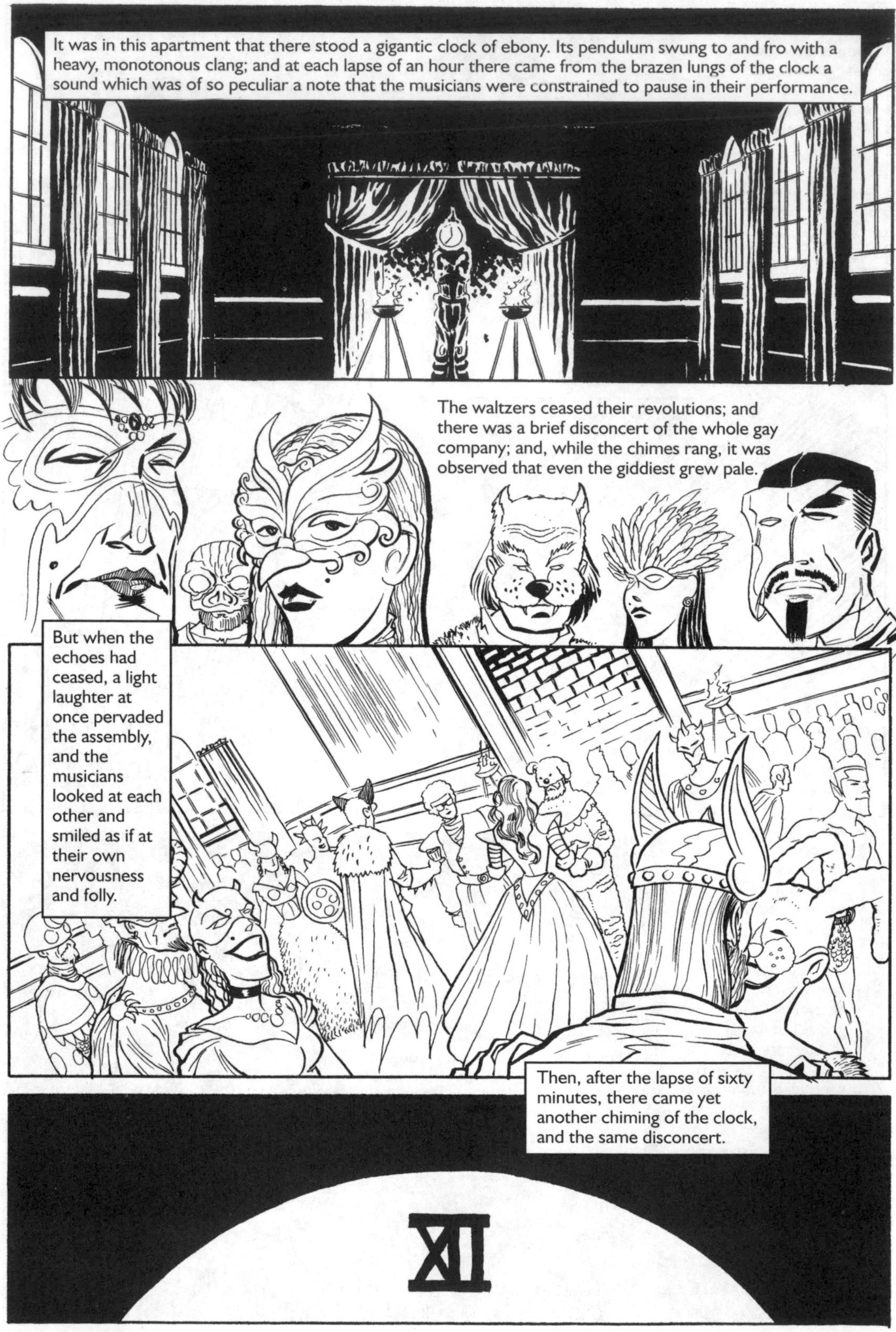
It was in this apartment that there stood a gigantic clock of ebony. Its pendulum swung to and fro with a heavy, monotonous clang; and at each lapse of an hour there came from the brazen lungs of the clock a sound which was of so peculiar a note that the musicians were constrained to pause in their performance.
The waltzers ceased their revolutions; and there was a brief disconcert of the whole gay company; and, while the chimes rang, it was observed that even the giddiest grew pale.
But when the echoes had ceased, a light laughter at once pervaded the assembly, and the musicians looked at each other and smiled as if at their own nervousness and folly.
Then, after the lapse of sixty minutes, there came yet another chiming of the clock, and the same disconcert.
XII

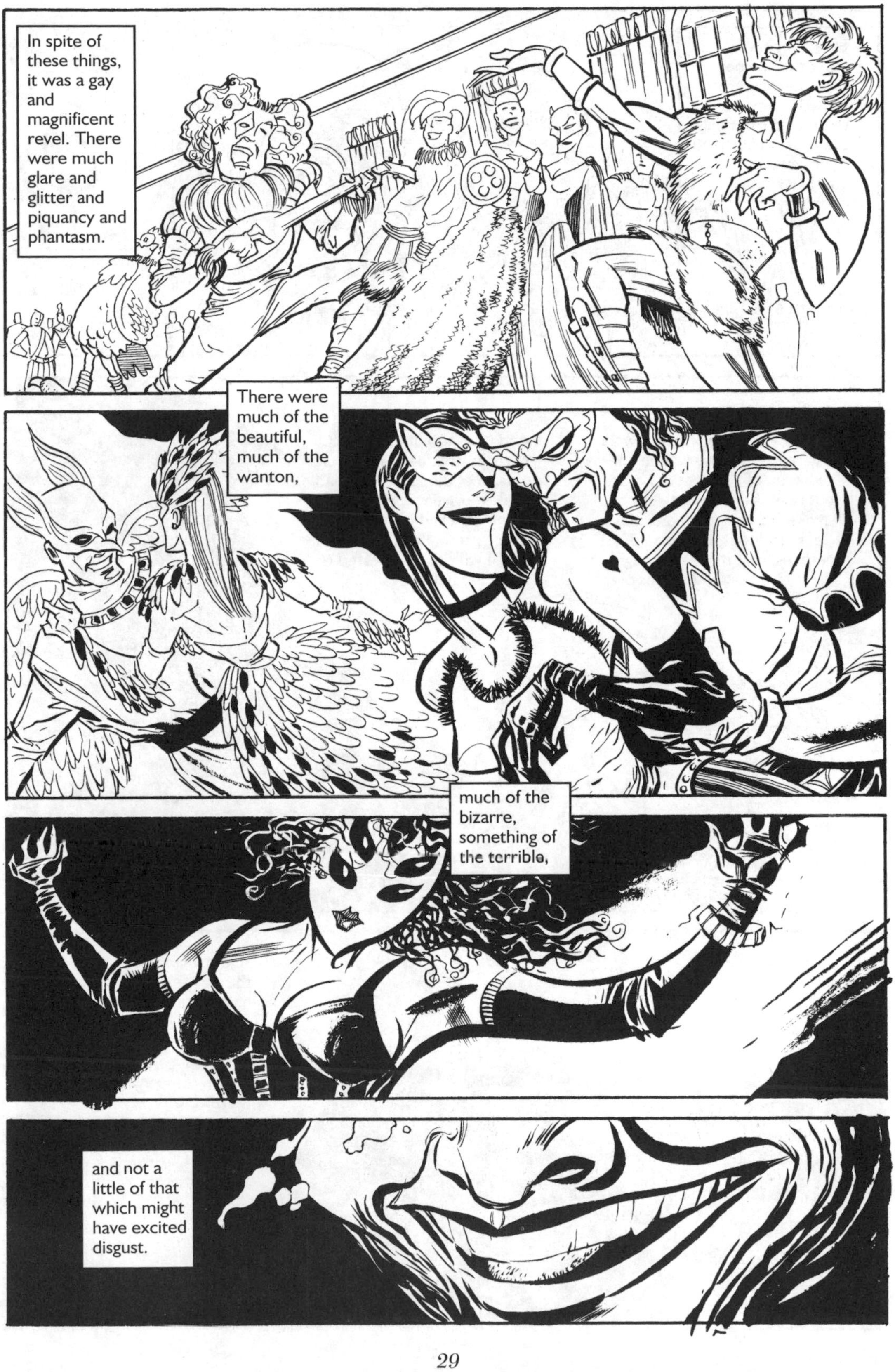
In spite of these things, it was a gay and magnificent revel. There were much glare and glitter and piquancy and phantasm.
There were much of the beautiful, much of the wanton,
much of the bizarre, something of the terrible,
and not a little of that which might have excited disgust.

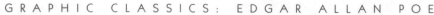

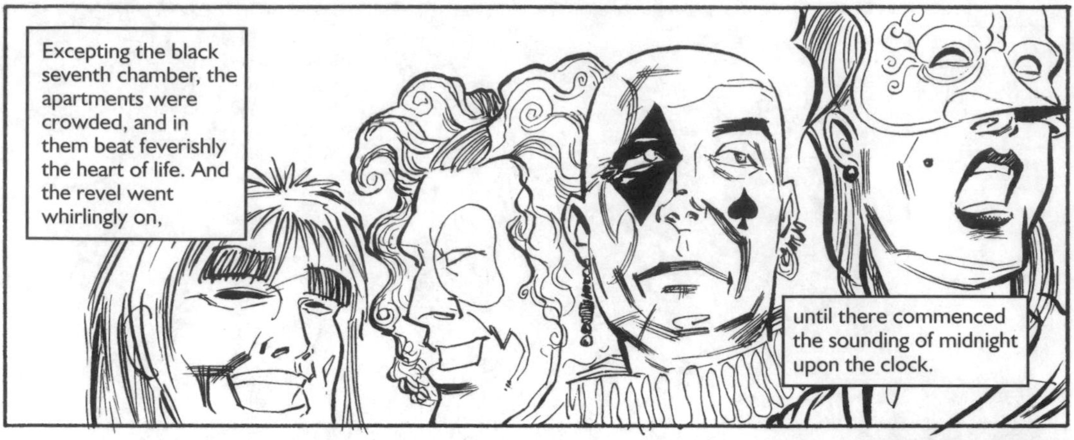
Excepting the black seventh chamber, the apartments were crowded, and in them beat feverishly the heart of life. And the revel went whirlingly on,
until there commenced the sounding of midnight upon the clock.

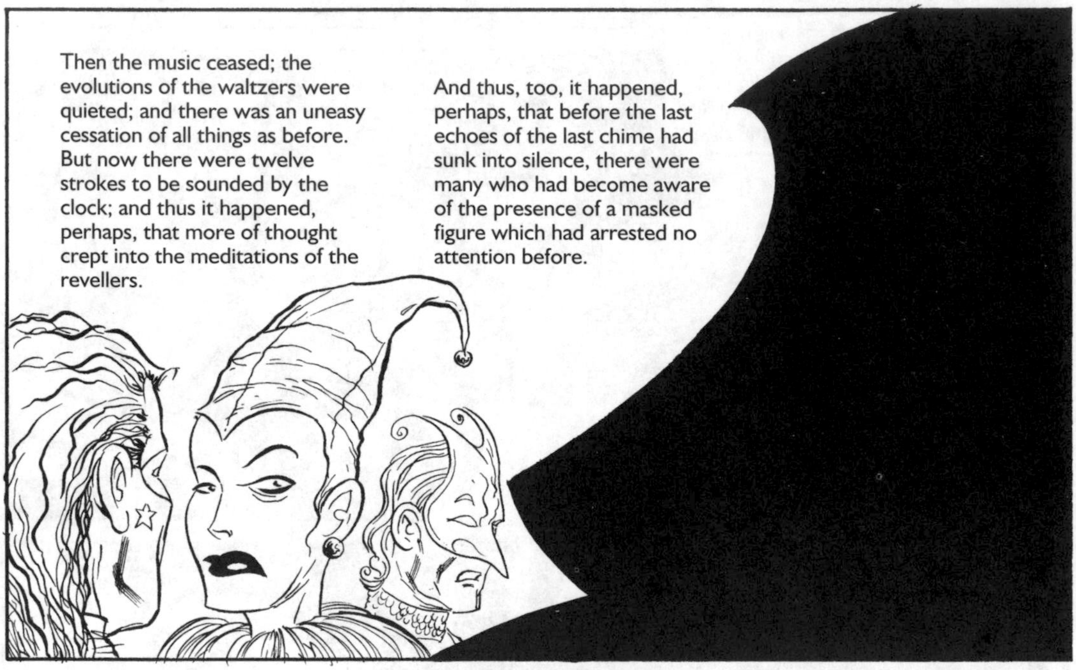
Then the music ceased; the evolutions of the waltzers were quieted; and there was an uneasy cessation of all things as before. But now there were twelve strokes to be sounded by the clock; and thus it happened, perhaps, that more of thought crept into the meditations of the revellers.
And thus, too, it happened, perhaps, that before the last echoes of the last chime had sunk into silence, there were many who had become aware of the presence of a masked figure which had arrested no attention before.

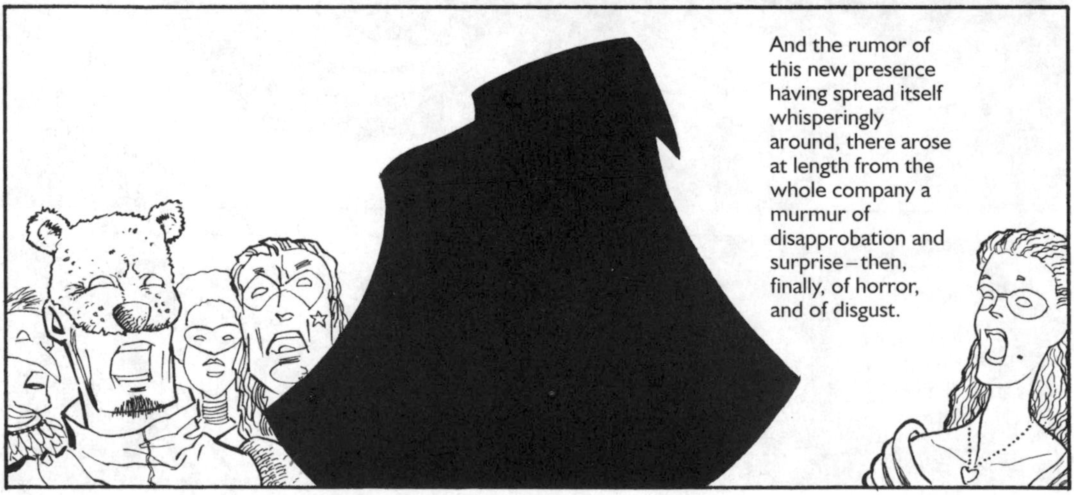
And the rumor of this new presence having spread itself whisperingly around, there arose at length from the whole company a murmur of disapprobation and surprise – then, finally, of horror, and of disgust.

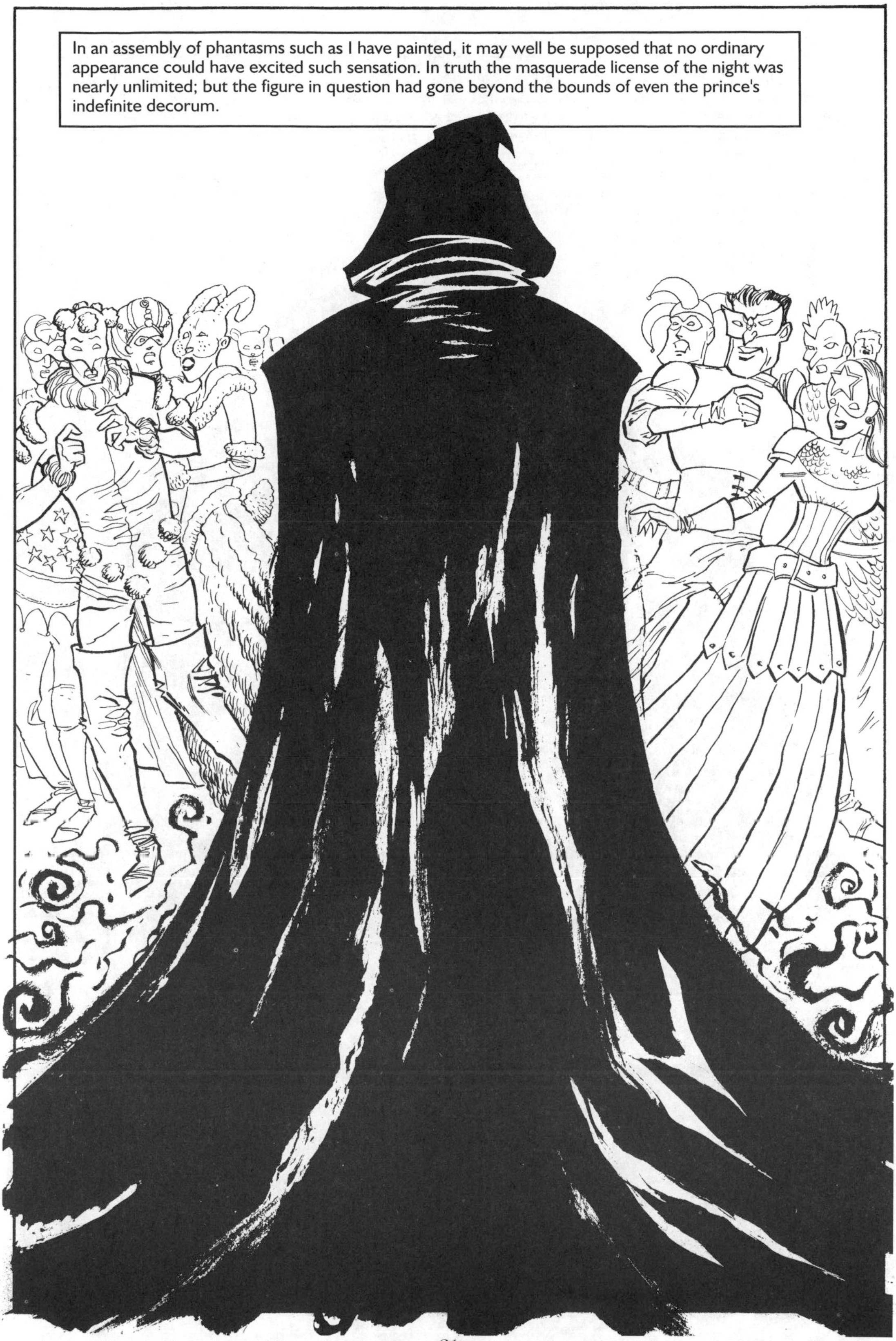
In an assembly of phantasms such as I have painted, it may well be supposed that no ordinary appearance could have excited such sensation. In truth the masquerade license of the night was nearly unlimited; but the figure in question had gone beyond the bounds of even the prince's indefinite decorum.

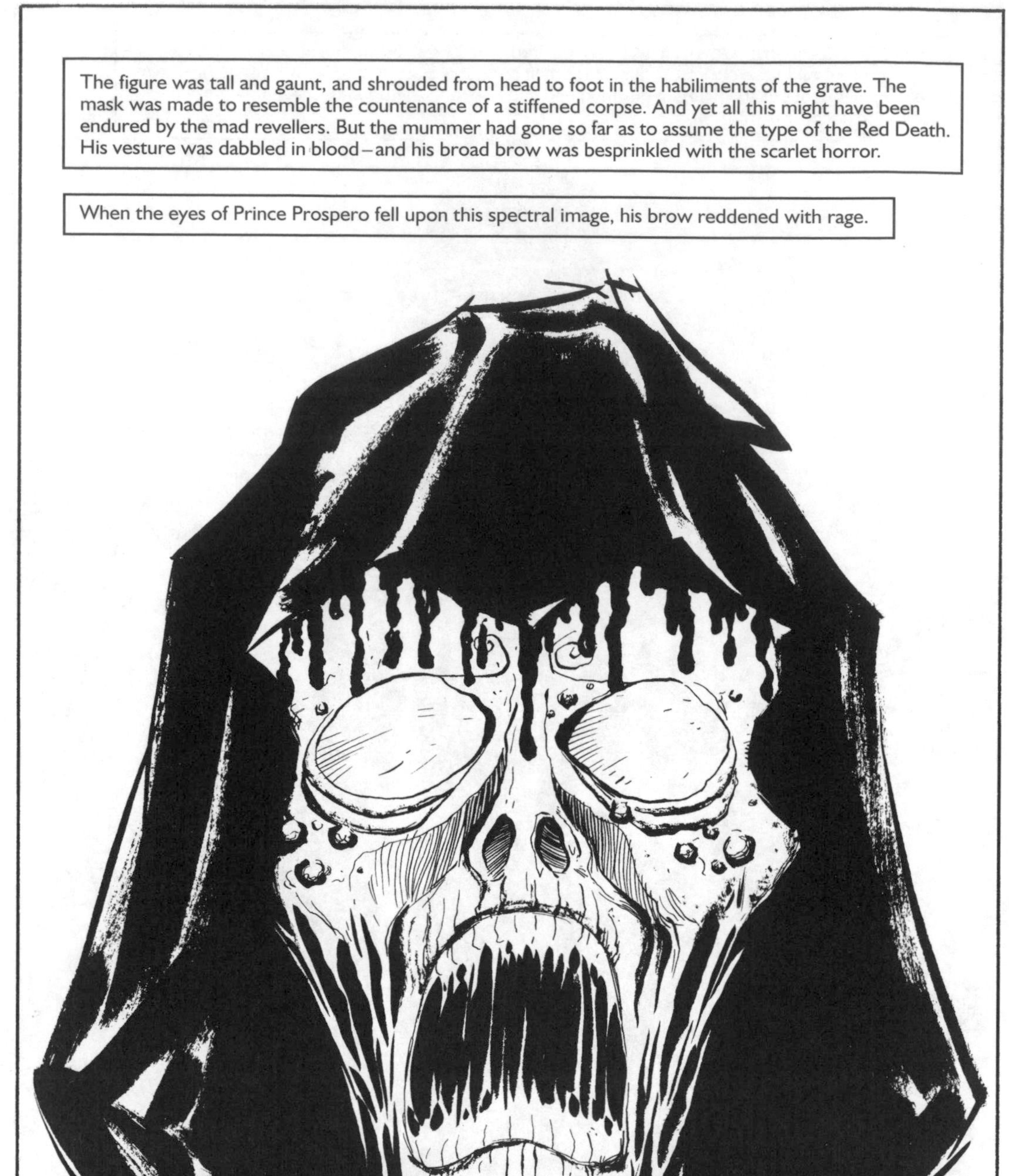
The figure was tall and gaunt, and shrouded from head to foot in the habiliments of the grave. The mask was made to resemble the countenance of a stiffened corpse. And yet all this might have been endured by the mad revellers. But the mummer had gone so far as to assume the type of the Red Death. His vesture was dabbled in blood—and his broad brow was besprinkled with the scarlet horror.
When the eyes of Prince Prospero fell upon this spectral image, his brow reddened with rage.

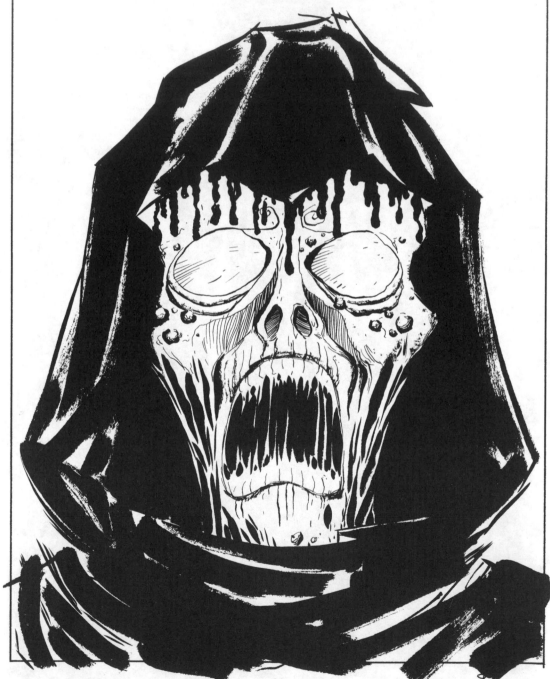

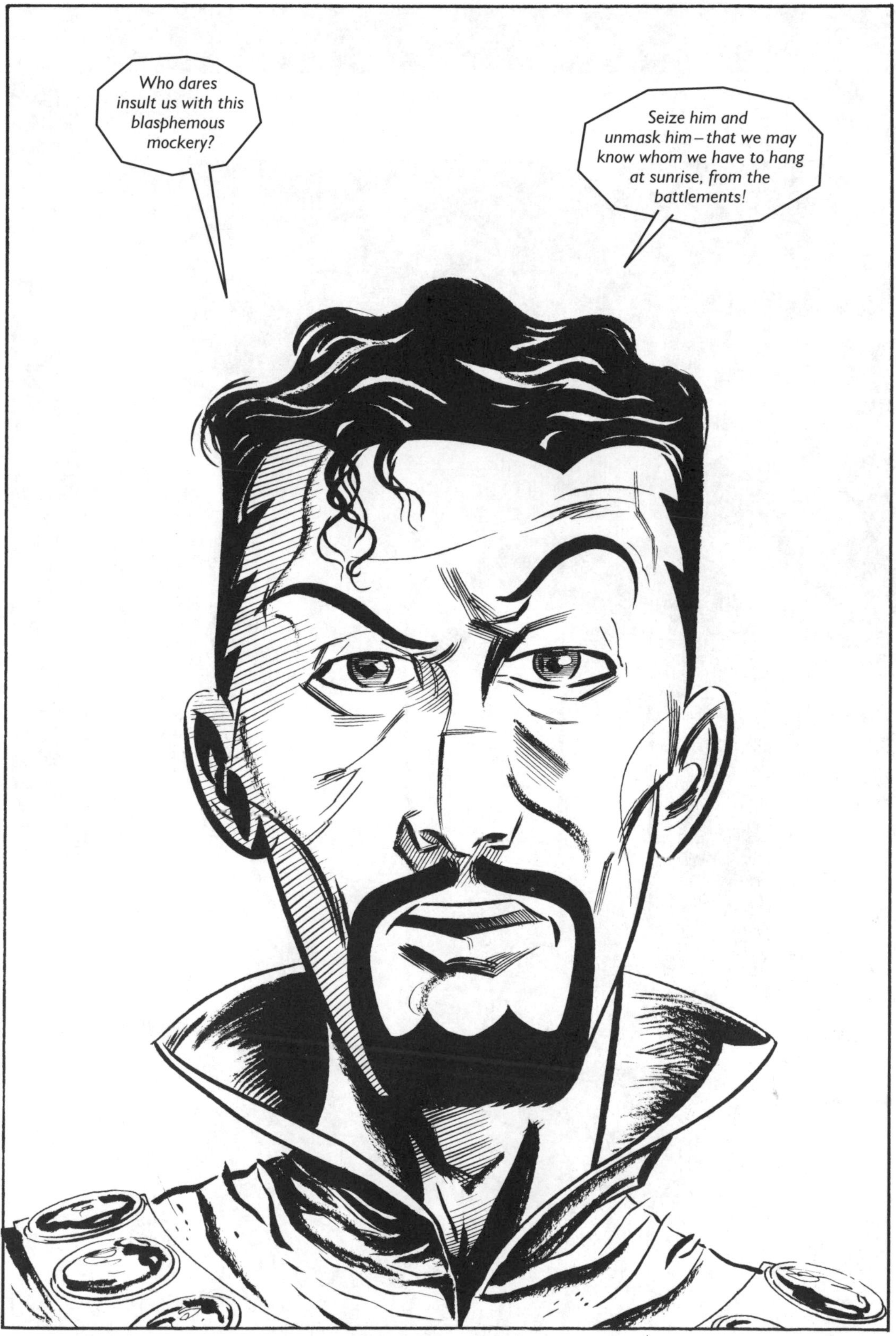
Who dares insult us with this blasphemous mockery?
Seize him and unmask him–that we may know whom we have to hang at sunrise, from the battlements!

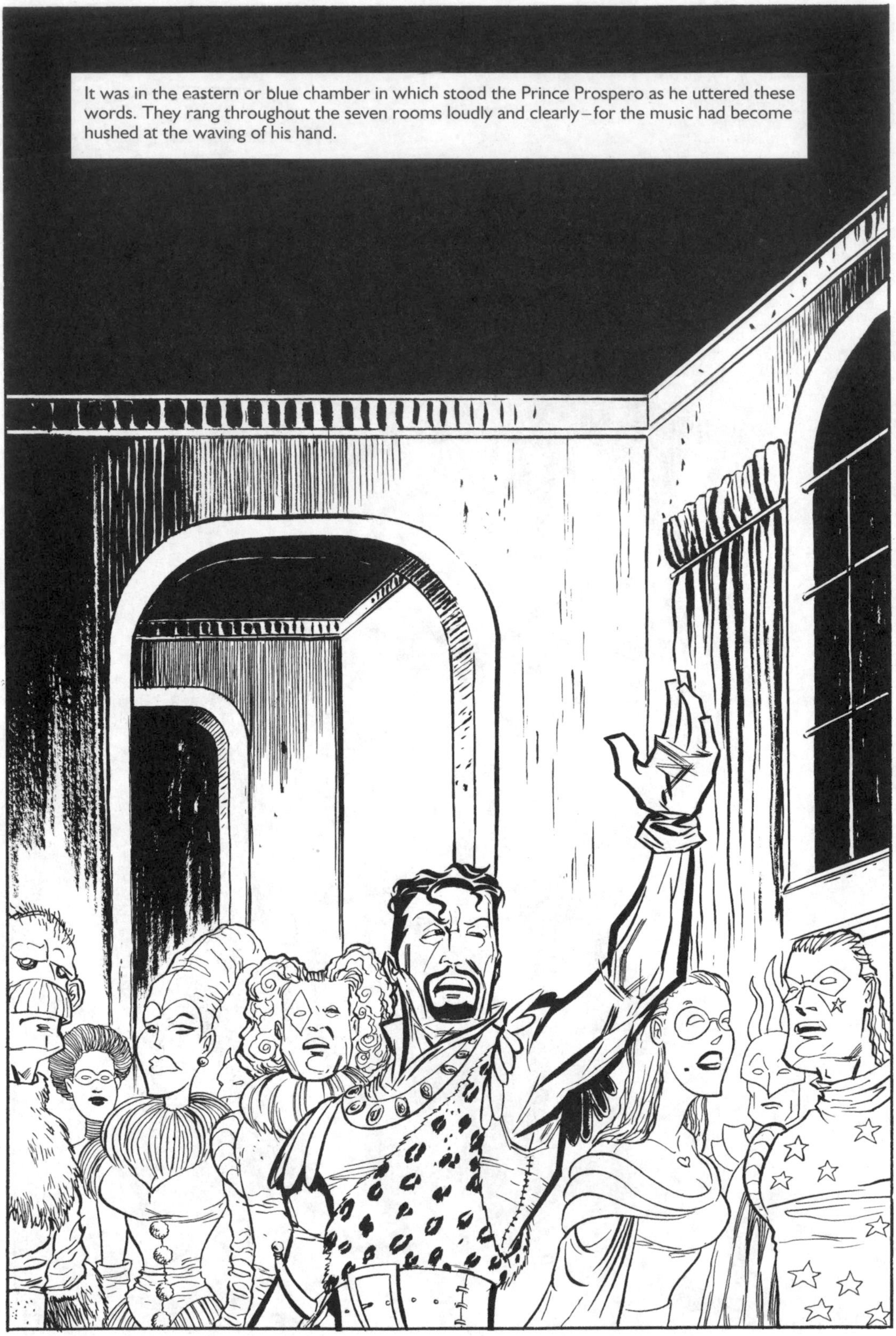
It was in the eastern or blue chamber in which stood the Prince Prospero as he uttered these words. They rang throughout the seven rooms loudly and clearly–for the music had become hushed at the waving of his hand.

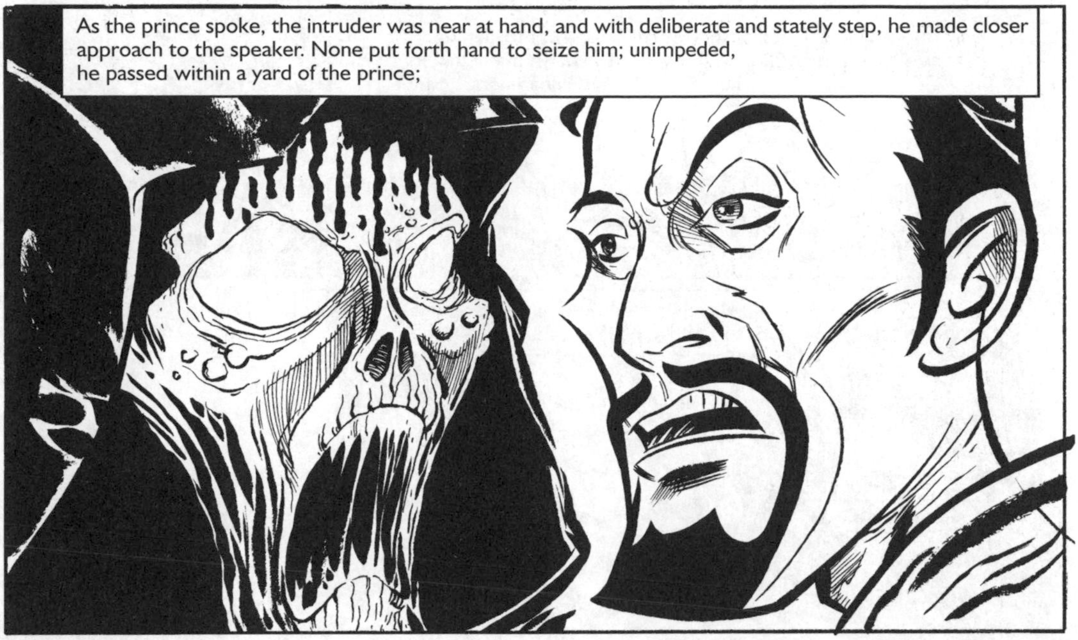
As the prince spoke, the intruder was near at hand, and with deliberate and stately step, he made closer approach to the speaker. None put forth hand to seize him; unimpeded, he passed within a yard of the prince;

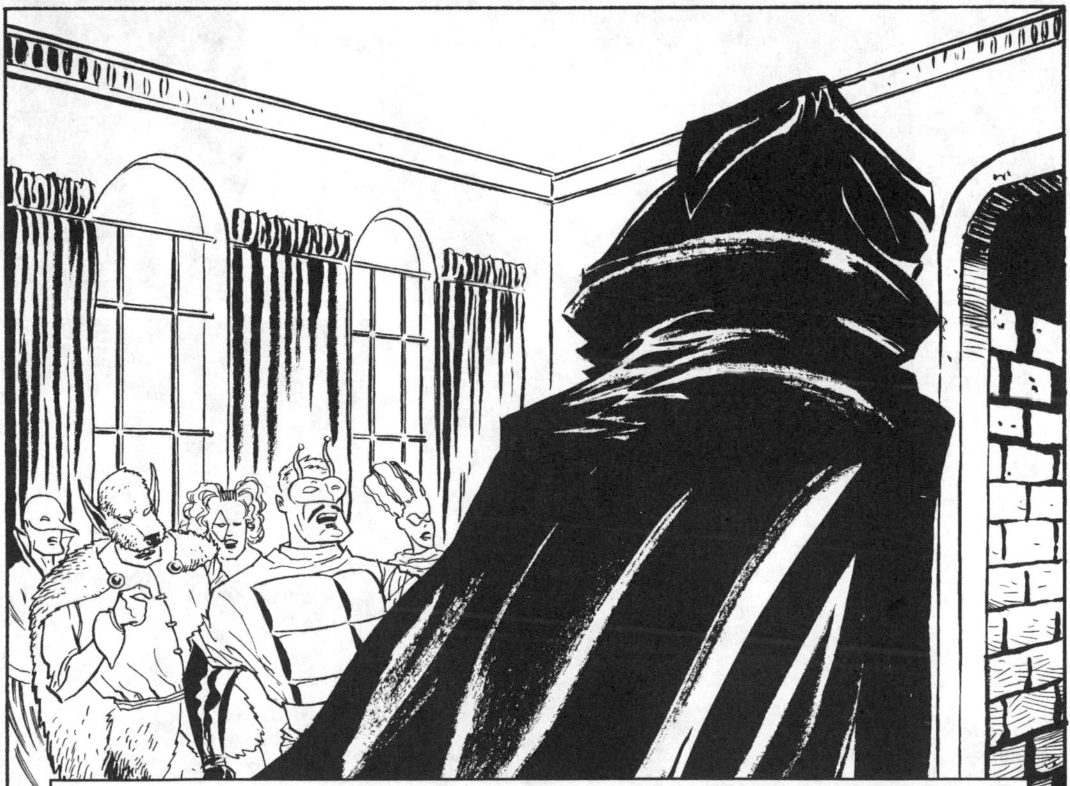
and, while the vast assembly shrank away, he made his way with the same solemn and measured step which had distinguished him from the first, through the blue chamber to the purple–to the green–to the orange–through this again to the white–and even thence to the violet, ere a movement had been made to arrest him.

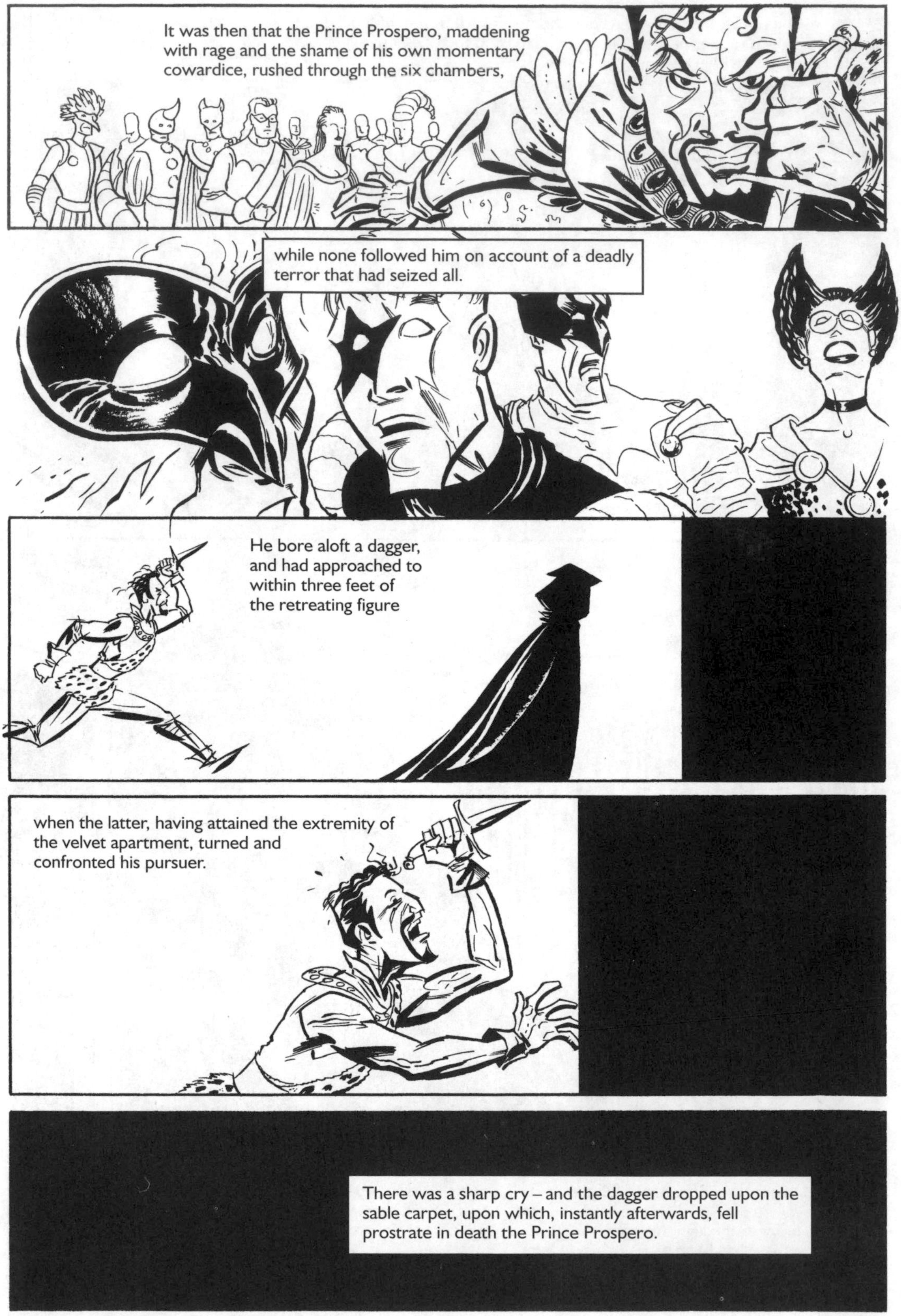
It was then that the Prince Prospero, maddening with rage and the shame of his own momentary cowardice, rushed through the six chambers,
while none followed him on account of a deadly terror that had seized all.
He bore aloft a dagger, and had approached to within three feet of the retreating figure
when the latter, having attained the extremity of the velvet apartment, turned and confronted his pursuer.
There was a sharp cry – and the dagger dropped upon the sable carpet, upon which, instantly afterwards, fell prostrate in death the Prince Prospero.

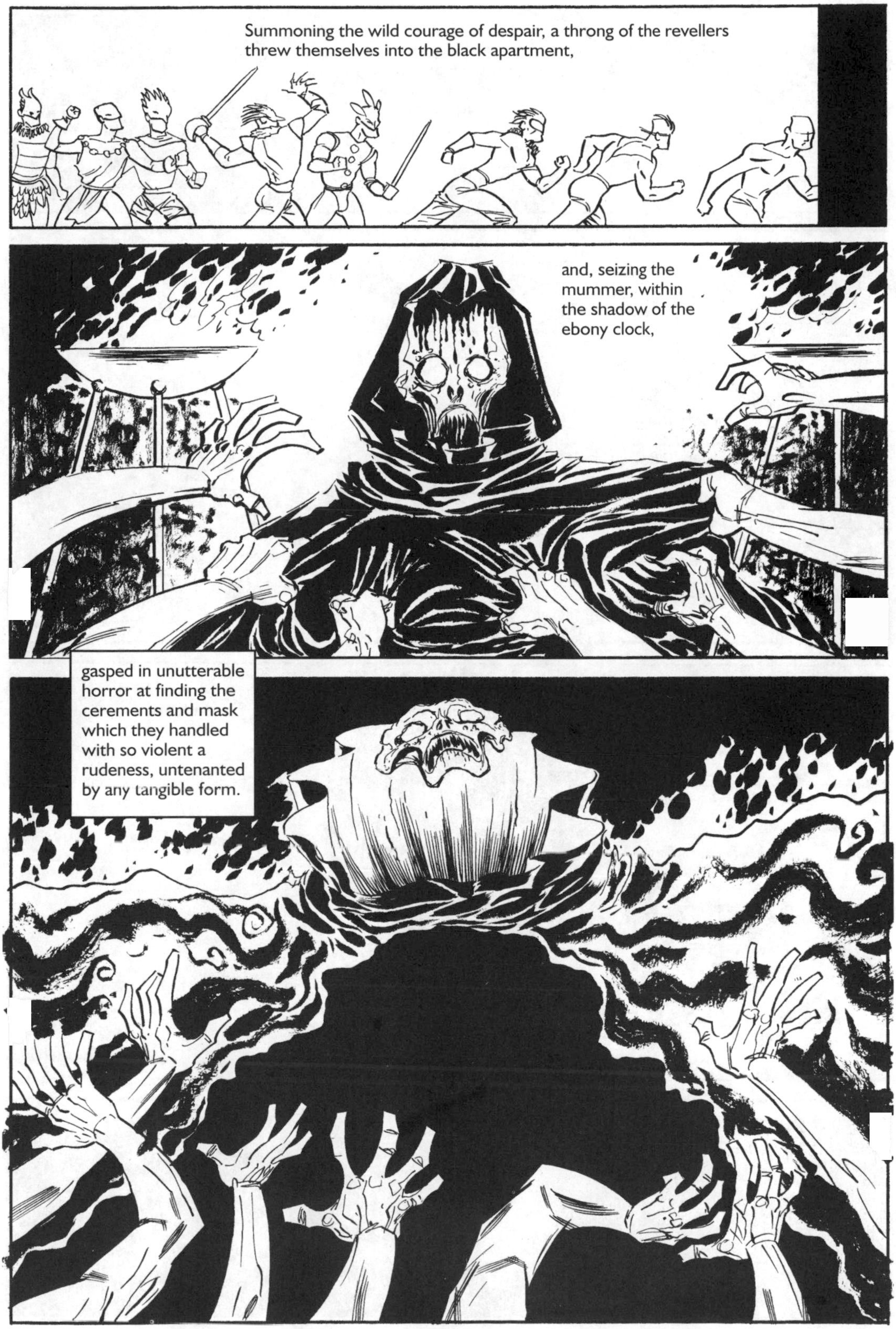
Summoning the wild courage of despair, a throng of the revellers threw themselves into the black apartment,
and, seizing the mummer, within the shadow of the ebony clock,
gasped in unutterable horror at finding the cerements and mask which they handled with so violent a rudeness, untenanted by any tangible form.

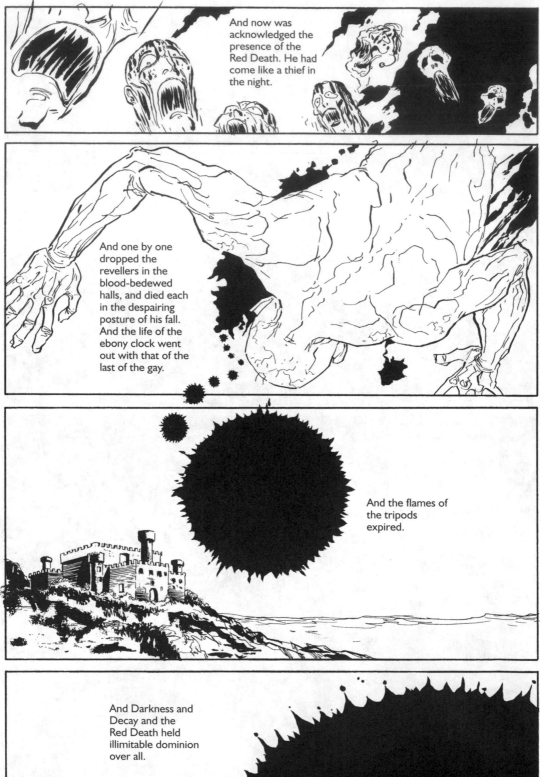

And now was acknowledged the presence of the Red Death. He had come like a thief in the night.

And one by one dropped the revellers in the blood-bedewed halls, and died each in the despairing posture of his fall. And the life of the ebony clock went out with that of the last of the gay.

And the flames of the tripods expired.

And Darkness and Decay and the Red Death held illimitable dominion over all.

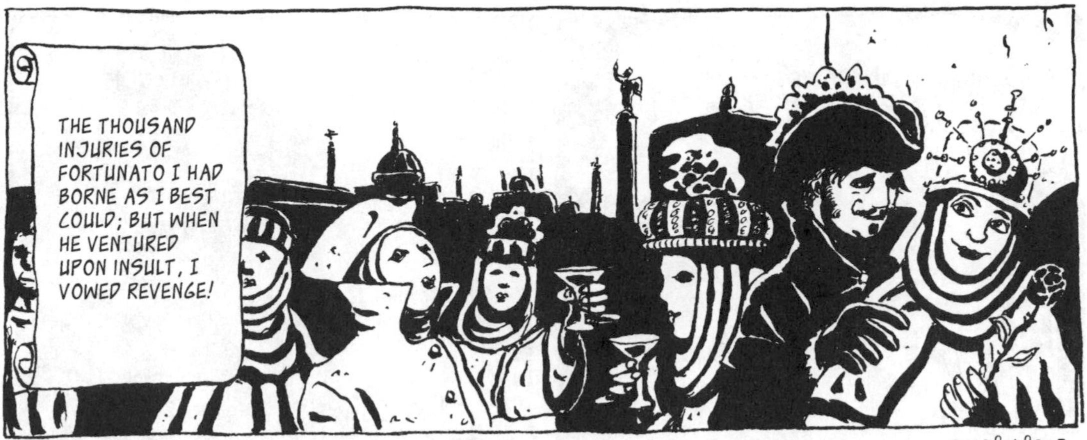
THE THOUSAND INJURIES OF FORTUNATO I HAD BORNE AS I BEST COULD; BUT WHEN HE VENTURED UPON INSULT, I VOWED REVENGE!

EDGAR ALLAN POE

PEDRO LOPEZ

The Cask of Amontillado

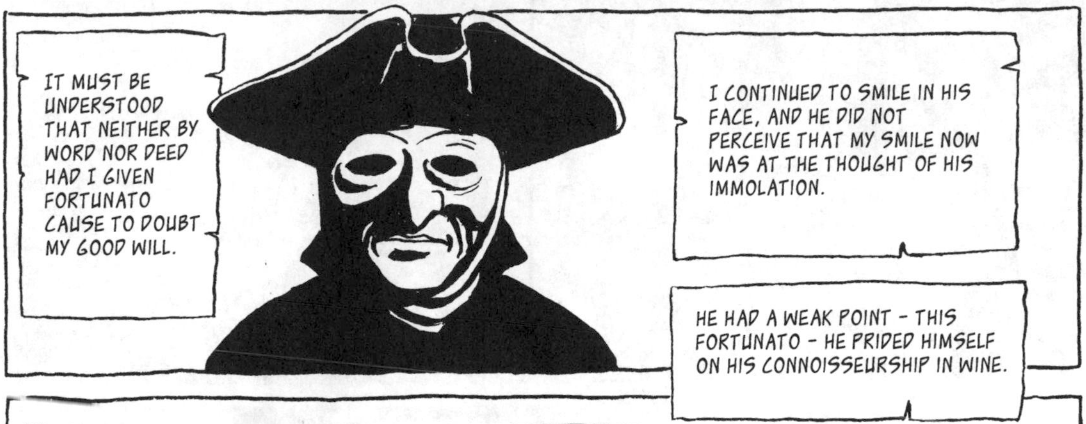
IT MUST BE UNDERSTOOD THAT NEITHER BY WORD NOR DEED HAD I GIVEN FORTUNATO CAUSE TO DOUBT MY GOOD WILL.
I CONTINUED TO SMILE IN HIS FACE, AND HE DID NOT PERCEIVE THAT MY SMILE NOW WAS AT THE THOUGHT OF HIS IMMOLATION.
HE HAD A WEAK POINT - THIS FORTUNATO - HE PRIDED HIMSELF ON HIS CONNOISSEURSHIP IN WINE.

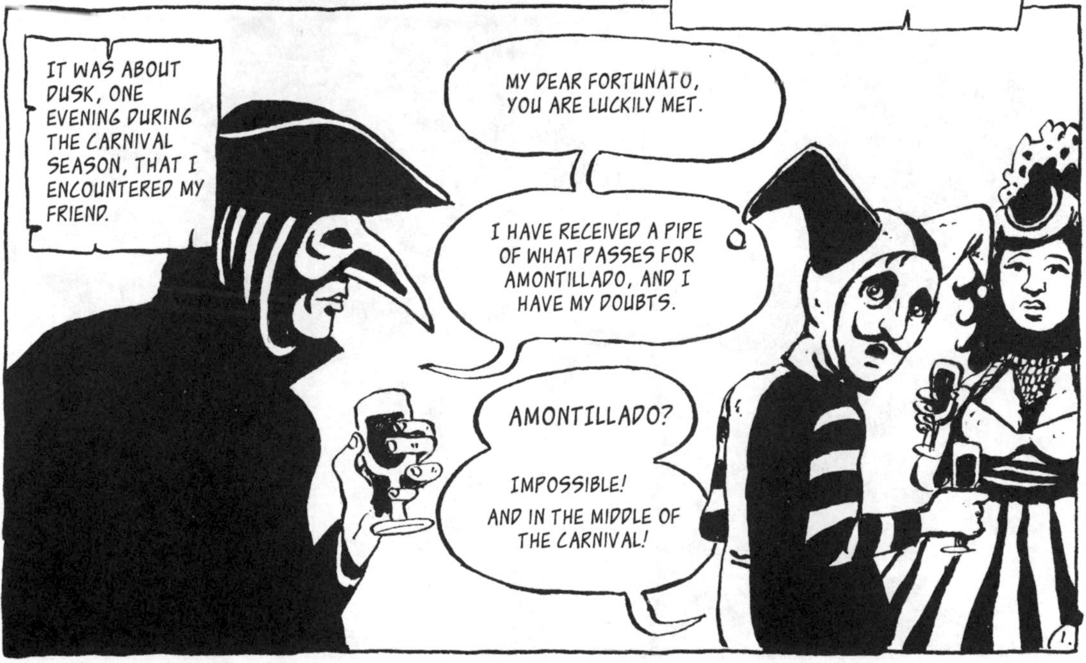
IT WAS ABOUT DUSK, ONE EVENING DURING THE CARNIVAL SEASON, THAT I ENCOUNTERED MY FRIEND.
MY DEAR FORTUNATO, YOU ARE LUCKILY MET.
I HAVE RECEIVED A PIPE OF WHAT PASSES FOR AMONTILLADO, AND I HAVE MY DOUBTS.
AMONTILLADO?
IMPOSSIBLE!
AND IN THE MIDDLE OF THE CARNIVAL!
1.

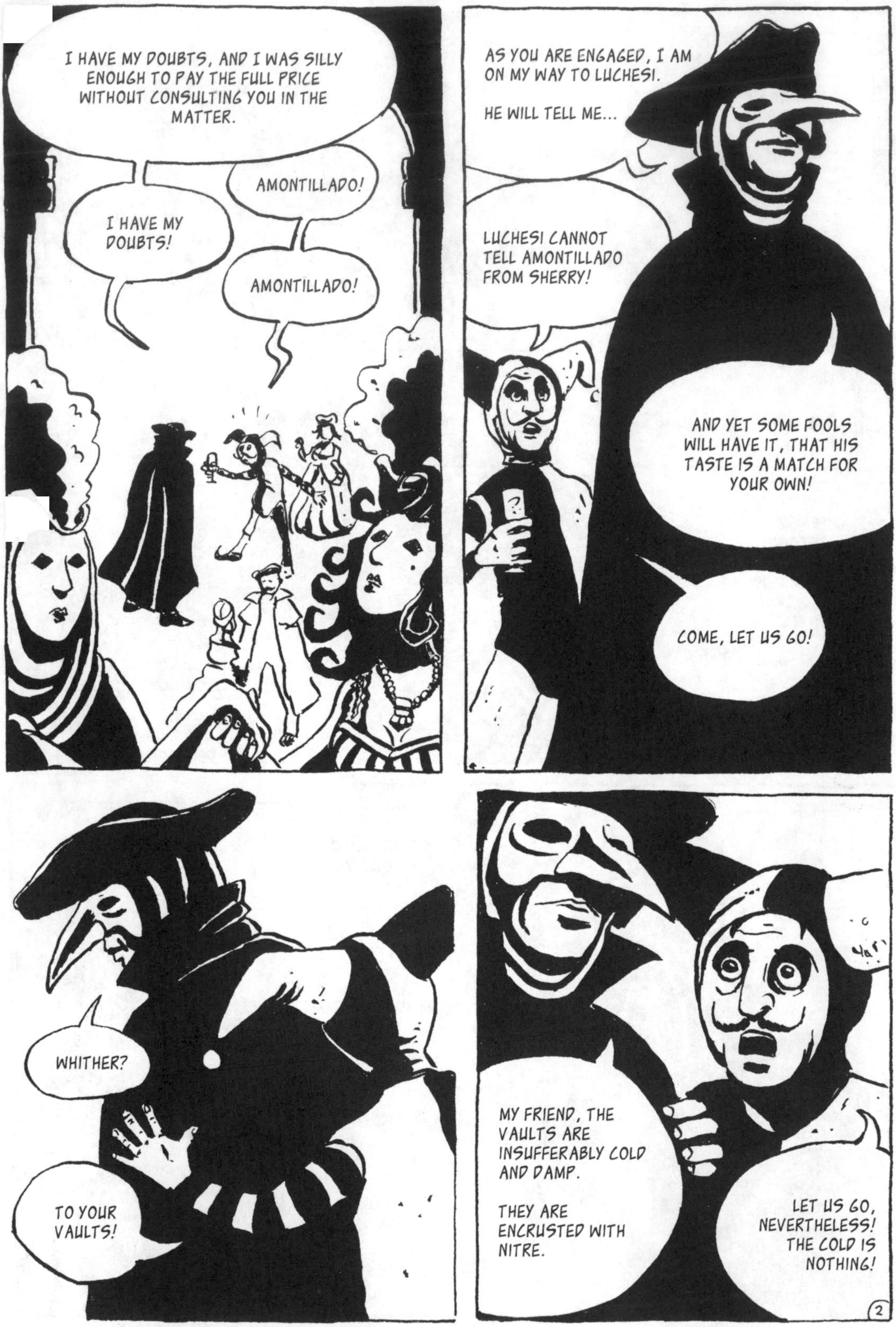
I HAVE MY DOUBTS, AND I WAS SILLY ENOUGH TO PAY THE FULL PRICE WITHOUT CONSULTING YOU IN THE MATTER.
AMONTILLADO!
I HAVE MY DOUBTS!
AMONTILLADO!
AS YOU ARE ENGAGED, I AM ON MY WAY TO LUCHESI.
HE WILL TELL ME...
LUCHESI CANNOT TELL AMONTILLADO FROM SHERRY!
AND YET SOME FOOLS WILL HAVE IT, THAT HIS TASTE IS A MATCH FOR YOUR OWN!
COME, LET US GO!
WHITHER?
TO YOUR VAULTS!
MY FRIEND, THE VAULTS ARE INSUFFERABLY COLD AND DAMP.
THEY ARE ENCRUSTED WITH NITRE.
LET US GO, NEVERTHELESS! THE COLD IS NOTHING!
2

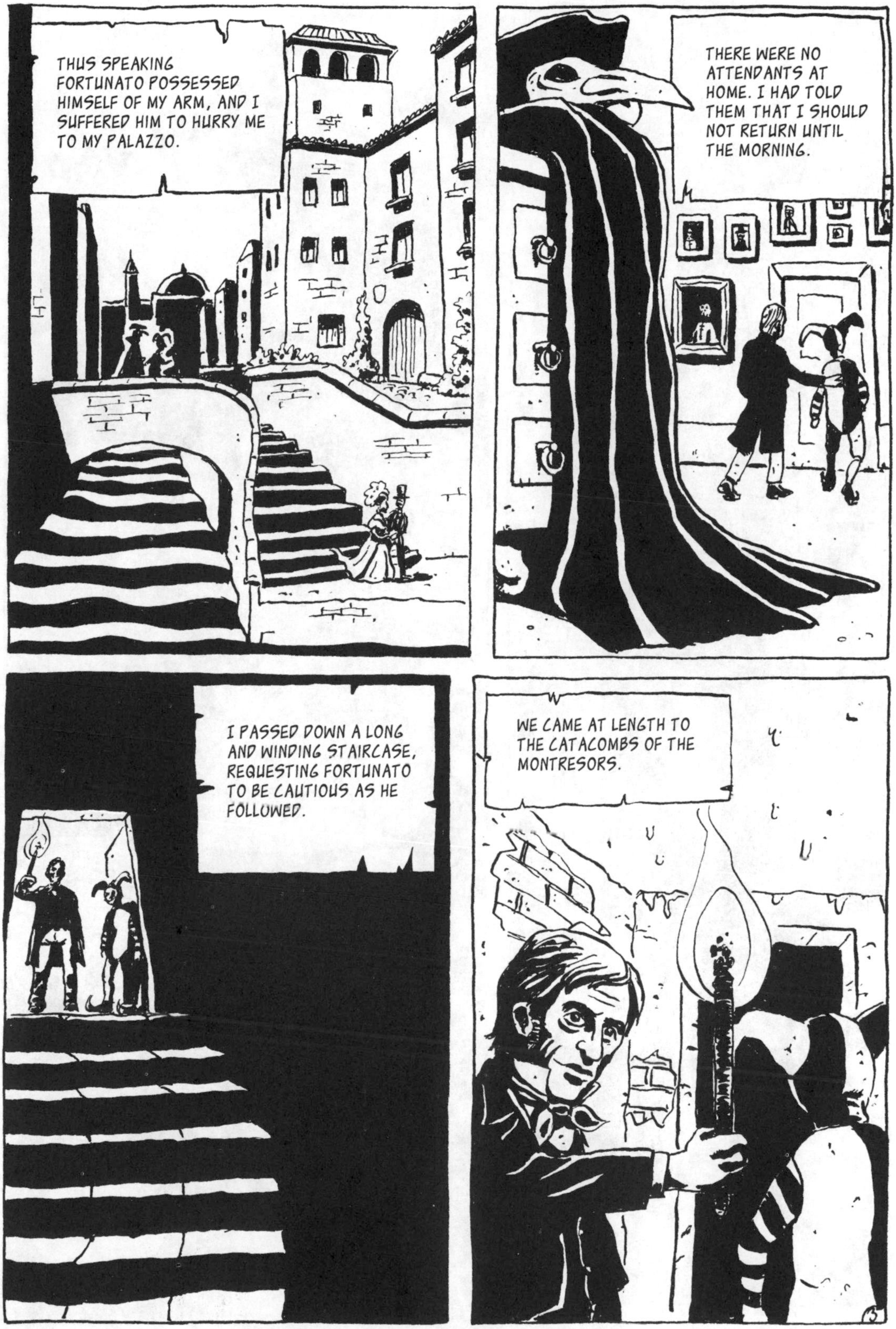
THUS SPEAKING FORTUNATO POSSESSED HIMSELF OF MY ARM, AND I SUFFERED HIM TO HURRY ME TO MY PALAZZO.
THERE WERE NO ATTENDANTS AT HOME. I HAD TOLD THEM THAT I SHOULD NOT RETURN UNTIL THE MORNING.
I PASSED DOWN A LONG AND WINDING STAIRCASE, REQUESTING FORTUNATO TO BE CAUTIOUS AS HE FOLLOWED.
WE CAME AT LENGTH TO THE CATACOMBS OF THE MONTRESORS.

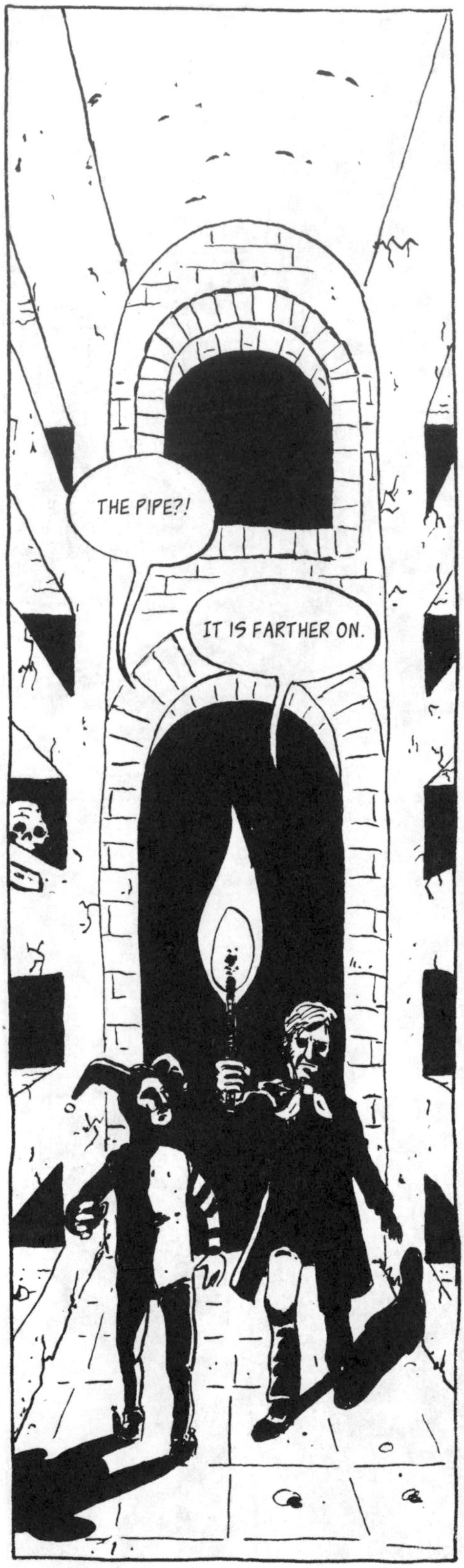
THE PIPE?!
IT IS FARTHER ON.

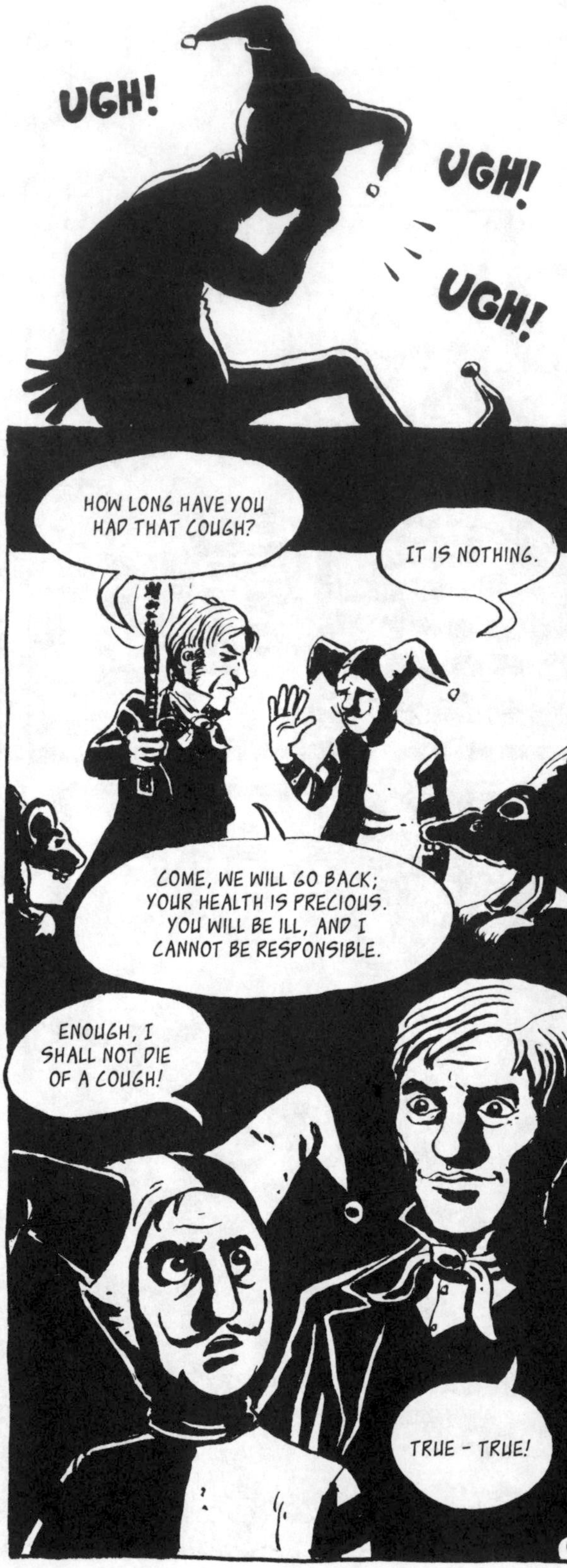
UGH!
UGH!
UGH!
HOW LONG HAVE YOU HAD THAT COUGH?
IT IS NOTHING.
COME, WE WILL GO BACK; YOUR HEALTH IS PRECIOUS. YOU WILL BE ILL, AND I CANNOT BE RESPONSIBLE.
ENOUGH, I SHALL NOT DIE OF A COUGH!
TRUE - TRUE!
4

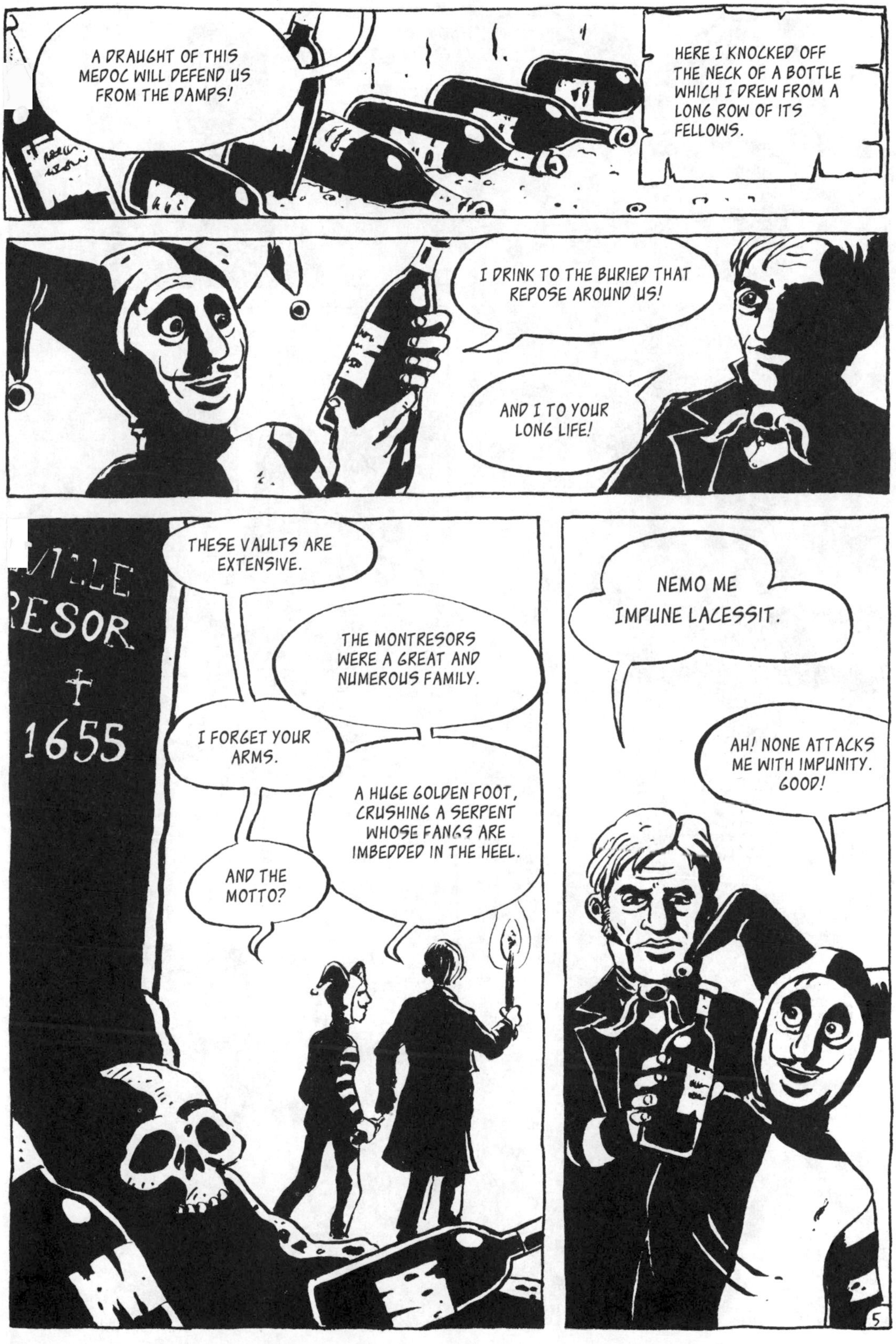
A DRAUGHT OF THIS MEDOC WILL DEFEND US FROM THE DAMPS!
HERE I KNOCKED OFF THE NECK OF A BOTTLE WHICH I DREW FROM A LONG ROW OF ITS FELLOWS.
I DRINK TO THE BURIED THAT REPOSE AROUND US!
AND I TO YOUR LONG LIFE!
RESOR
1655
THESE VAULTS ARE EXTENSIVE.
THE MONTRESORS WERE A GREAT AND NUMEROUS FAMILY.
I FORGET YOUR ARMS.
A HUGE GOLDEN FOOT, CRUSHING A SERPENT WHOSE FANGS ARE IMBEDDED IN THE HEEL.
AND THE MOTTO?
NEMO ME IMPUNE LACESSIT.
AH! NONE ATTACKS ME WITH IMPUNITY. GOOD!
5

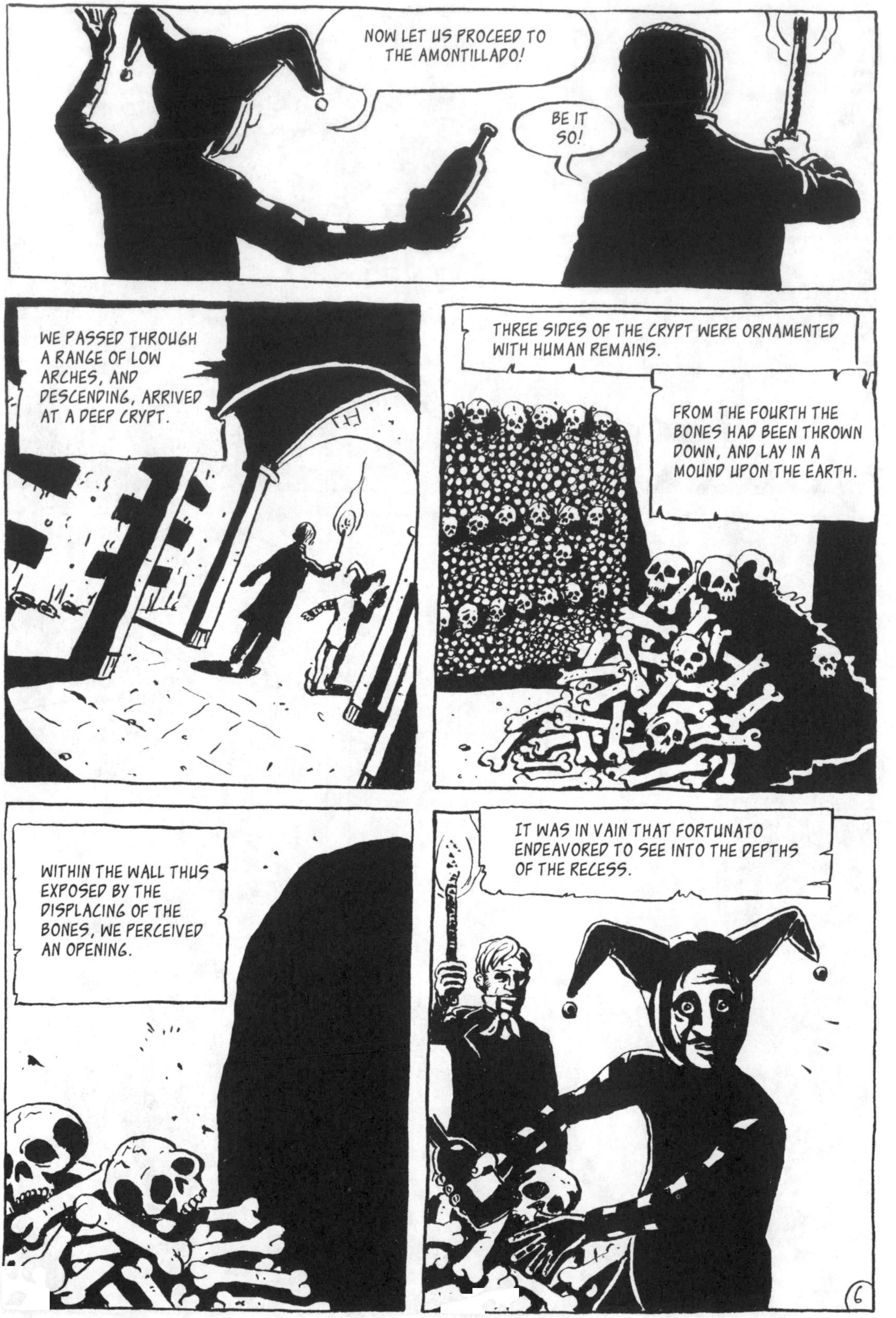
NOW LET US PROCEED TO THE AMONTILLADO!
BE IT SO!
WE PASSED THROUGH A RANGE OF LOW ARCHES, AND DESCENDING, ARRIVED AT A DEEP CRYPT.
THREE SIDES OF THE CRYPT WERE ORNAMENTED WITH HUMAN REMAINS.
FROM THE FOURTH THE BONES HAD BEEN THROWN DOWN, AND LAY IN A MOUND UPON THE EARTH.
WITHIN THE WALL THUS EXPOSED BY THE DISPLACING OF THE BONES, WE PERCEIVED AN OPENING.
IT WAS IN VAIN THAT FORTUNATO ENDEAVORED TO SEE INTO THE DEPTHS OF THE RECESS.
6

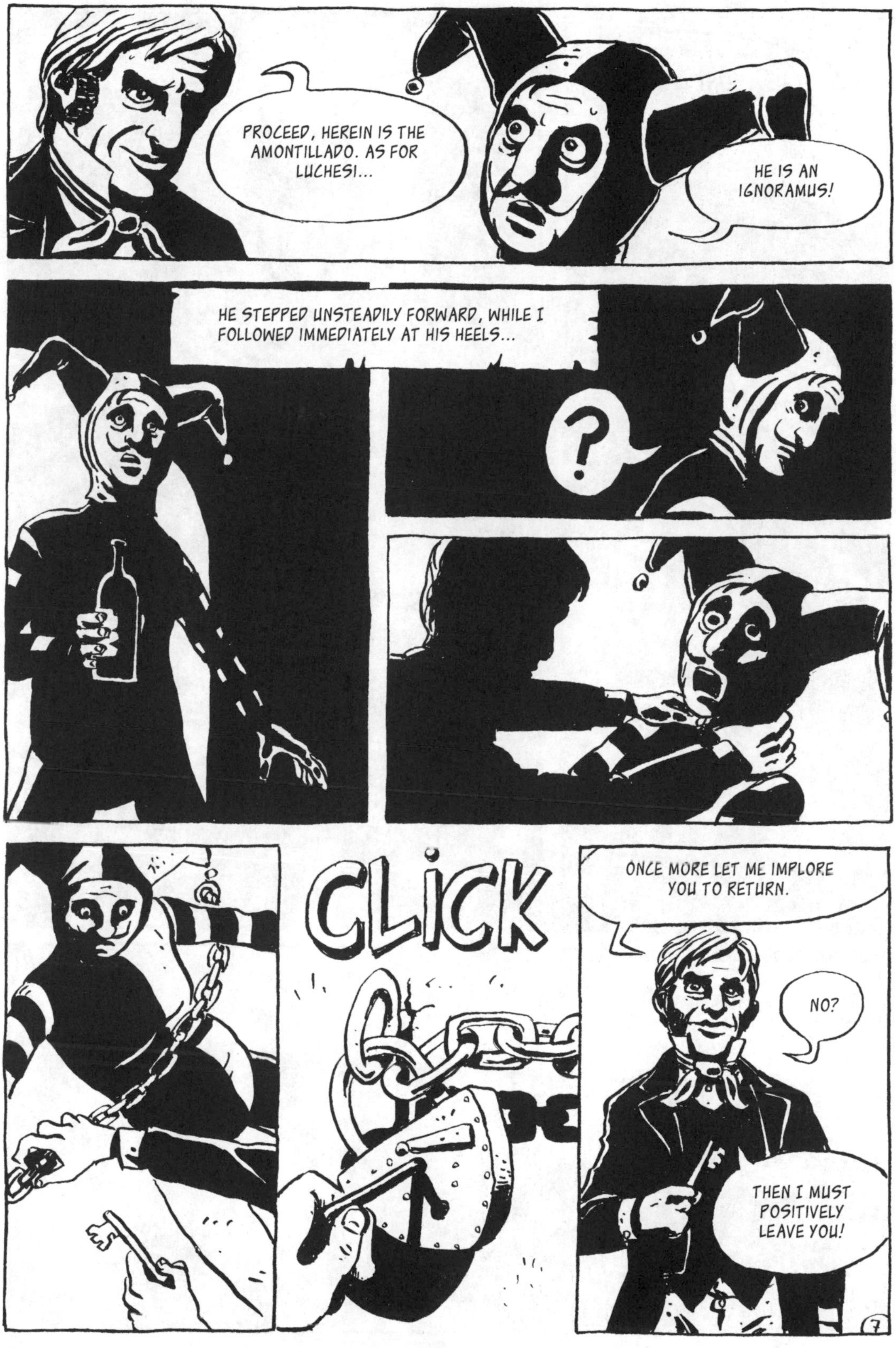
PROCEED, HEREIN IS THE AMONTILLADO. AS FOR LUCHESI...
HE IS AN IGNORAMUS!
HE STEPPED UNSTEADILY FORWARD, WHILE I FOLLOWED IMMEDIATELY AT HIS HEELS...
?
CLICK
ONCE MORE LET ME IMPLORE YOU TO RETURN.
NO?
THEN I MUST POSITIVELY LEAVE YOU!

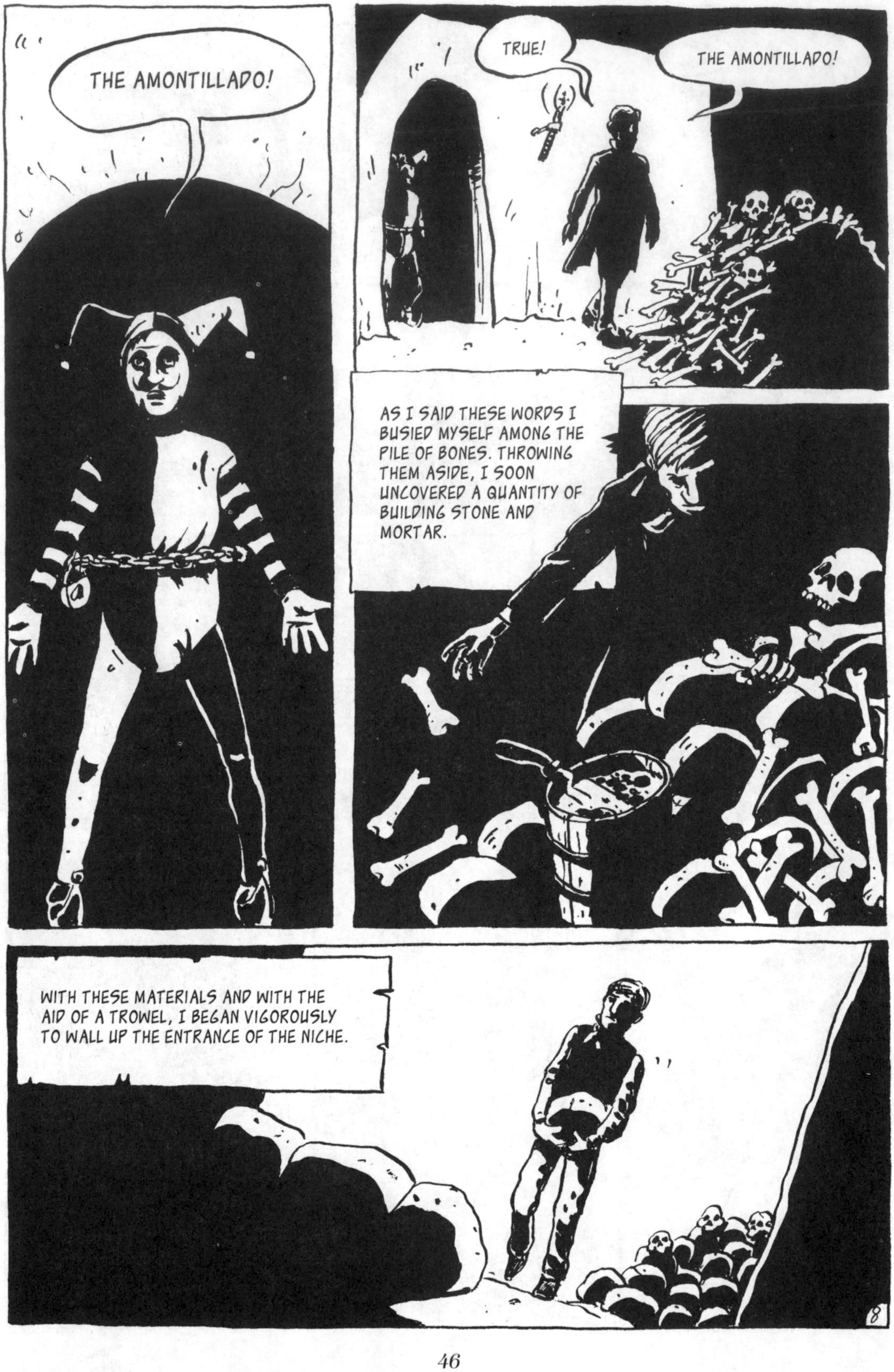
THE AMONTILLADO!
TRUE!
THE AMONTILLADO!
AS I SAID THESE WORDS I BUSIED MYSELF AMONG THE PILE OF BONES. THROWING THEM ASIDE, I SOON UNCOVERED A QUANTITY OF BUILDING STONE AND MORTAR.
WITH THESE MATERIALS AND WITH THE AID OF A TROWEL, I BEGAN VIGOROUSLY TO WALL UP THE ENTRANCE OF THE NICHE.
8

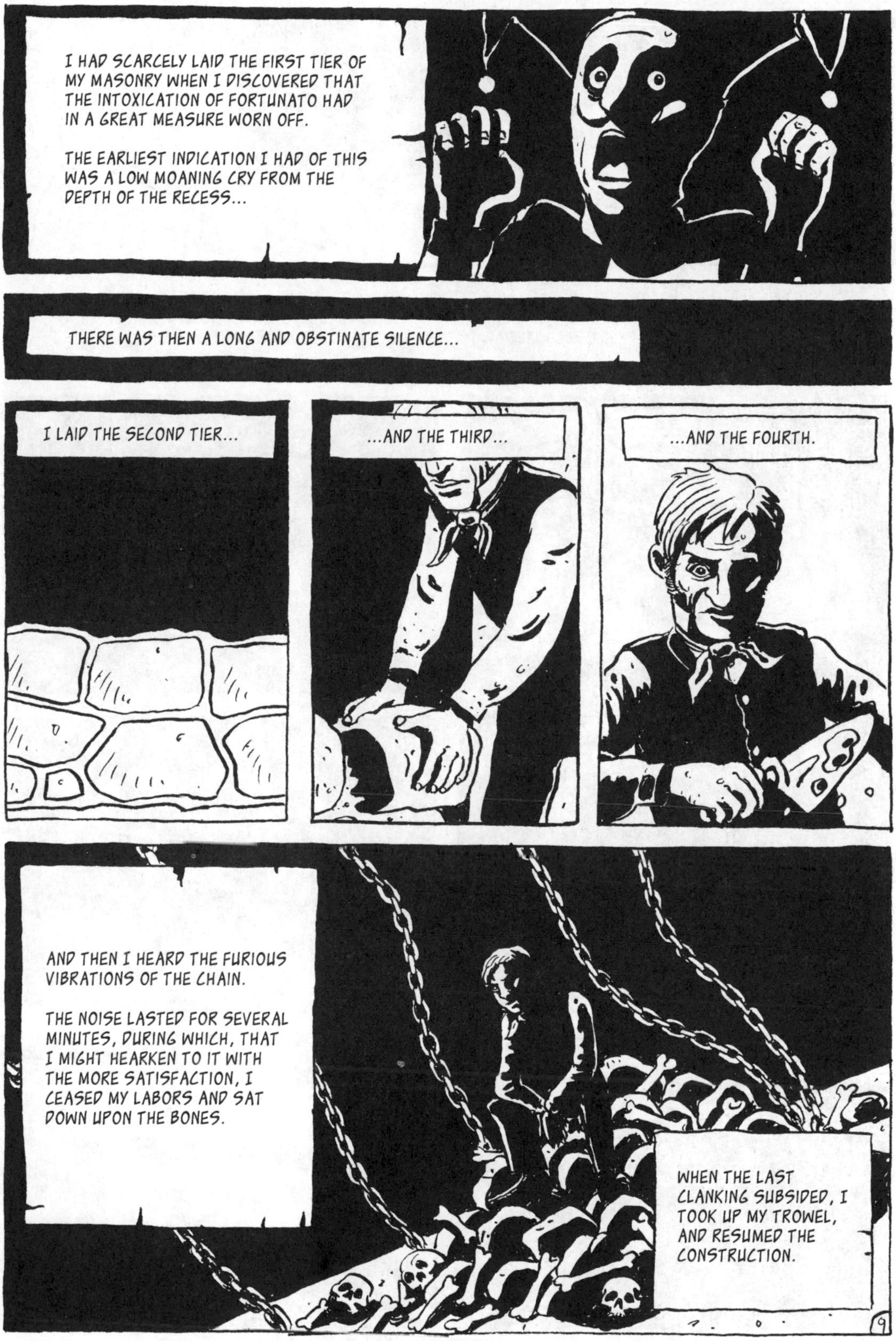
I HAD SCARCELY LAID THE FIRST TIER OF MY MASONRY WHEN I DISCOVERED THAT THE INTOXICATION OF FORTUNATO HAD IN A GREAT MEASURE WORN OFF.
THE EARLIEST INDICATION I HAD OF THIS WAS A LOW MOANING CRY FROM THE DEPTH OF THE RECESS...
THERE WAS THEN A LONG AND OBSTINATE SILENCE...
I LAID THE SECOND TIER...
...AND THE THIRD...
...AND THE FOURTH.
AND THEN I HEARD THE FURIOUS VIBRATIONS OF THE CHAIN.
THE NOISE LASTED FOR SEVERAL MINUTES, DURING WHICH, THAT I MIGHT HEARKEN TO IT WITH THE MORE SATISFACTION, I CEASED MY LABORS AND SAT DOWN UPON THE BONES.
WHEN THE LAST CLANKING SUBSIDED, I TOOK UP MY TROWEL, AND RESUMED THE CONSTRUCTION.
9

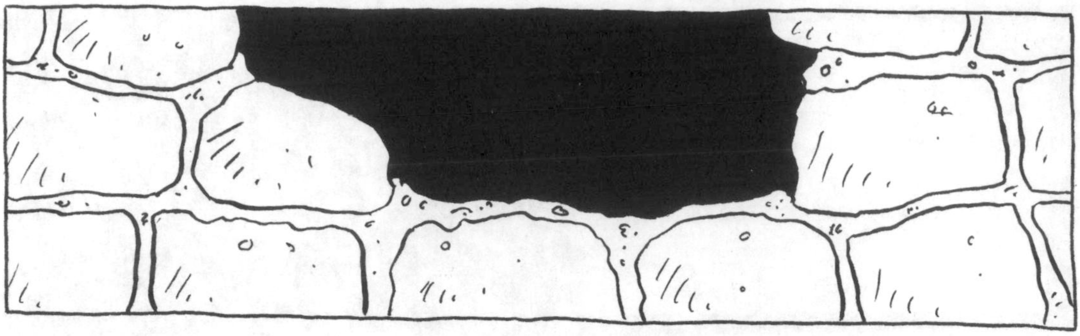

IT WAS NOW MIDNIGHT, AND MY TASK WAS DRAWING TO A CLOSE. I HAD COMPLETED THE TENTH TIER, AND I HAD FINISHED A PORTION OF THE LAST; THERE REMAINED BUT A SINGLE STONE TO BE FITTED AND PLASTERED IN. I STRUGGLED WITH ITS WEIGHT; I PLACED IT PARTIALLY IN ITS DESTINED POSITION.

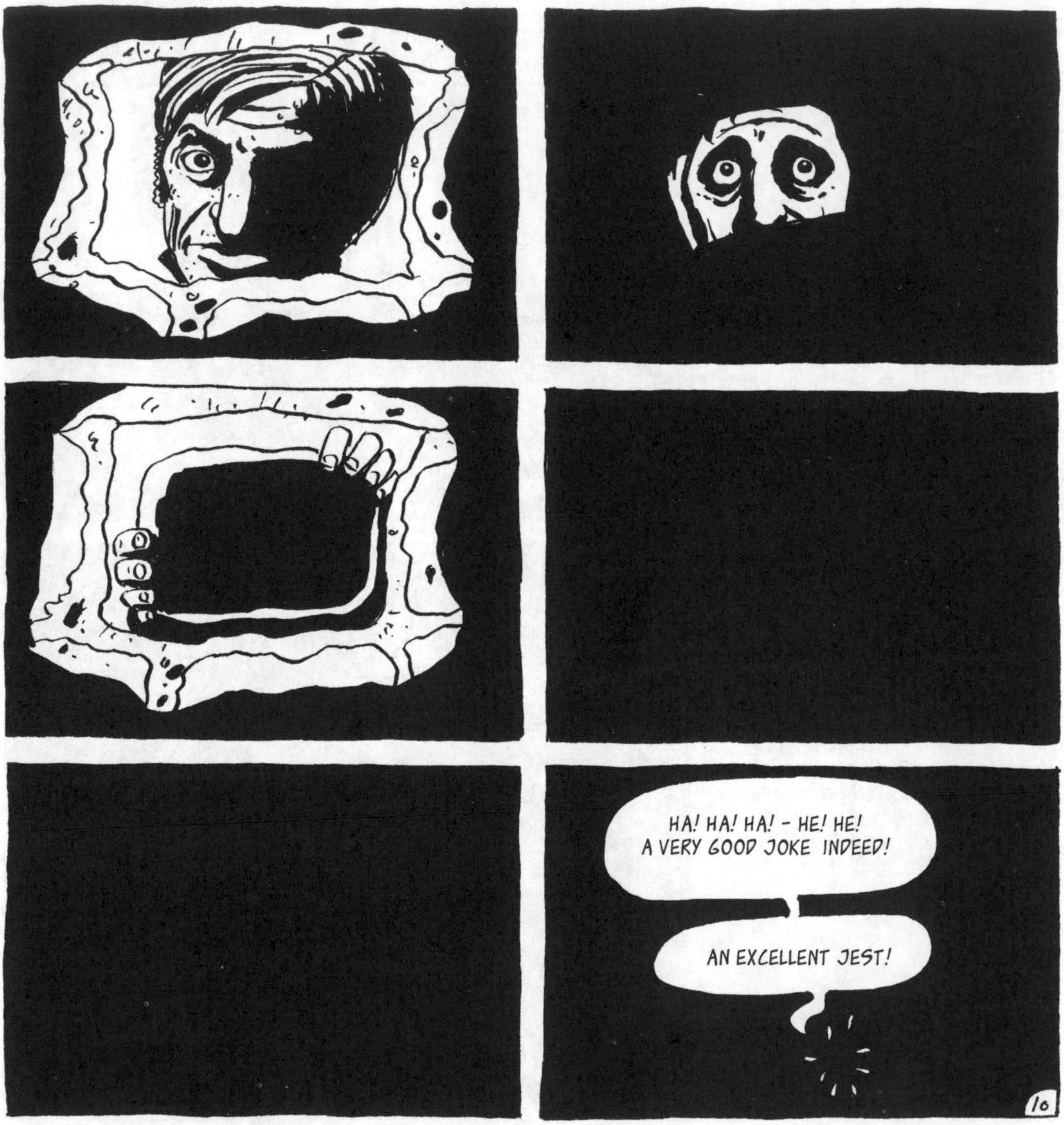
HA! HA! HA! - HE! HE!
A VERY GOOD JOKE INDEED!
AN EXCELLENT JEST!
10

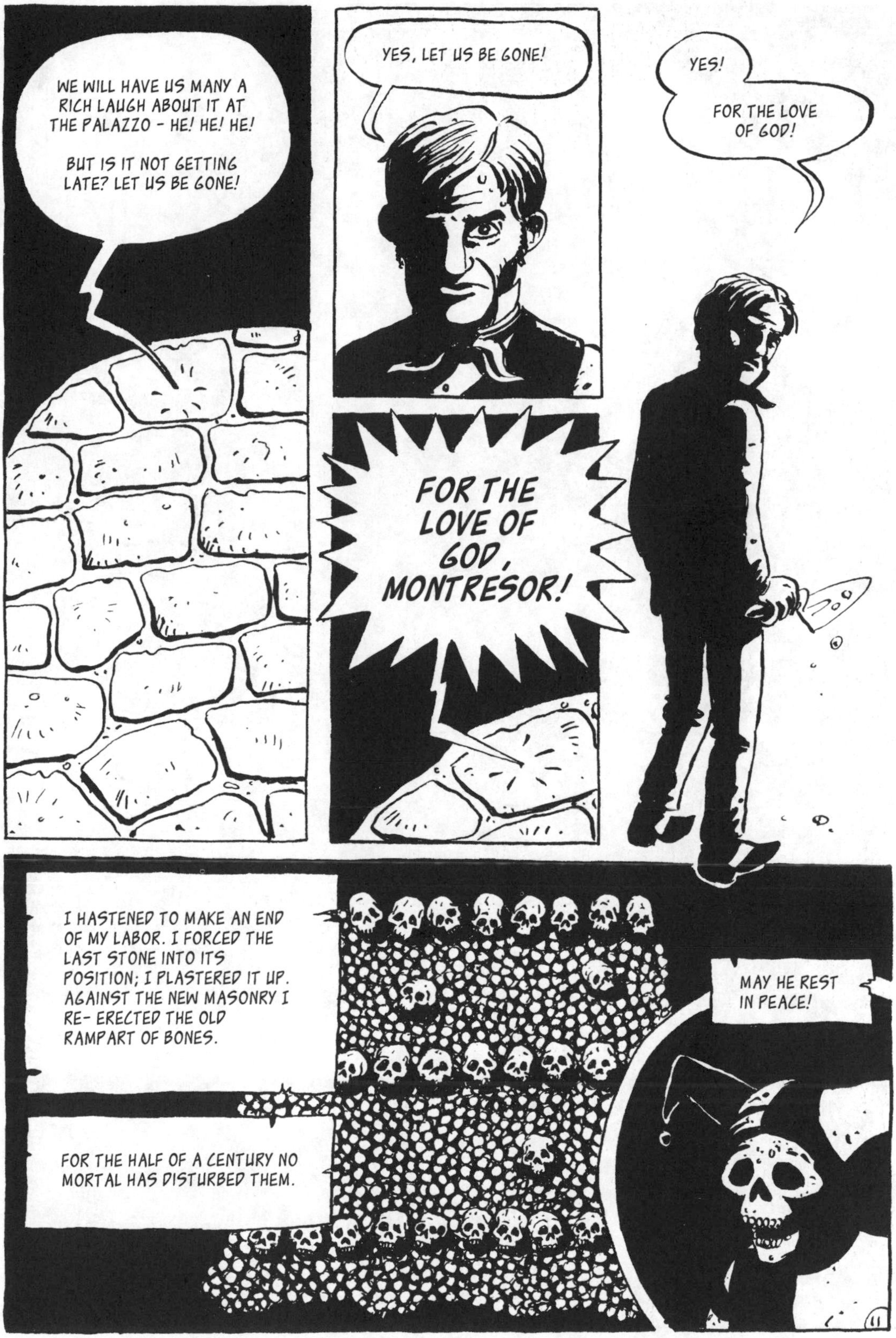
WE WILL HAVE US MANY A RICH LAUGH ABOUT IT AT THE PALAZZO - HE! HE! HE!
BUT IS IT NOT GETTING LATE? LET US BE GONE!
YES, LET US BE GONE!
FOR THE LOVE OF GOD, MONTRESOR!
YES!
FOR THE LOVE OF GOD!
I HASTENED TO MAKE AN END OF MY LABOR. I FORCED THE LAST STONE INTO ITS POSITION; I PLASTERED IT UP. AGAINST THE NEW MASONRY I RE- ERECTED THE OLD RAMPART OF BONES.
FOR THE HALF OF A CENTURY NO MORTAL HAS DISTURBED THEM.
MAY HE REST IN PEACE!

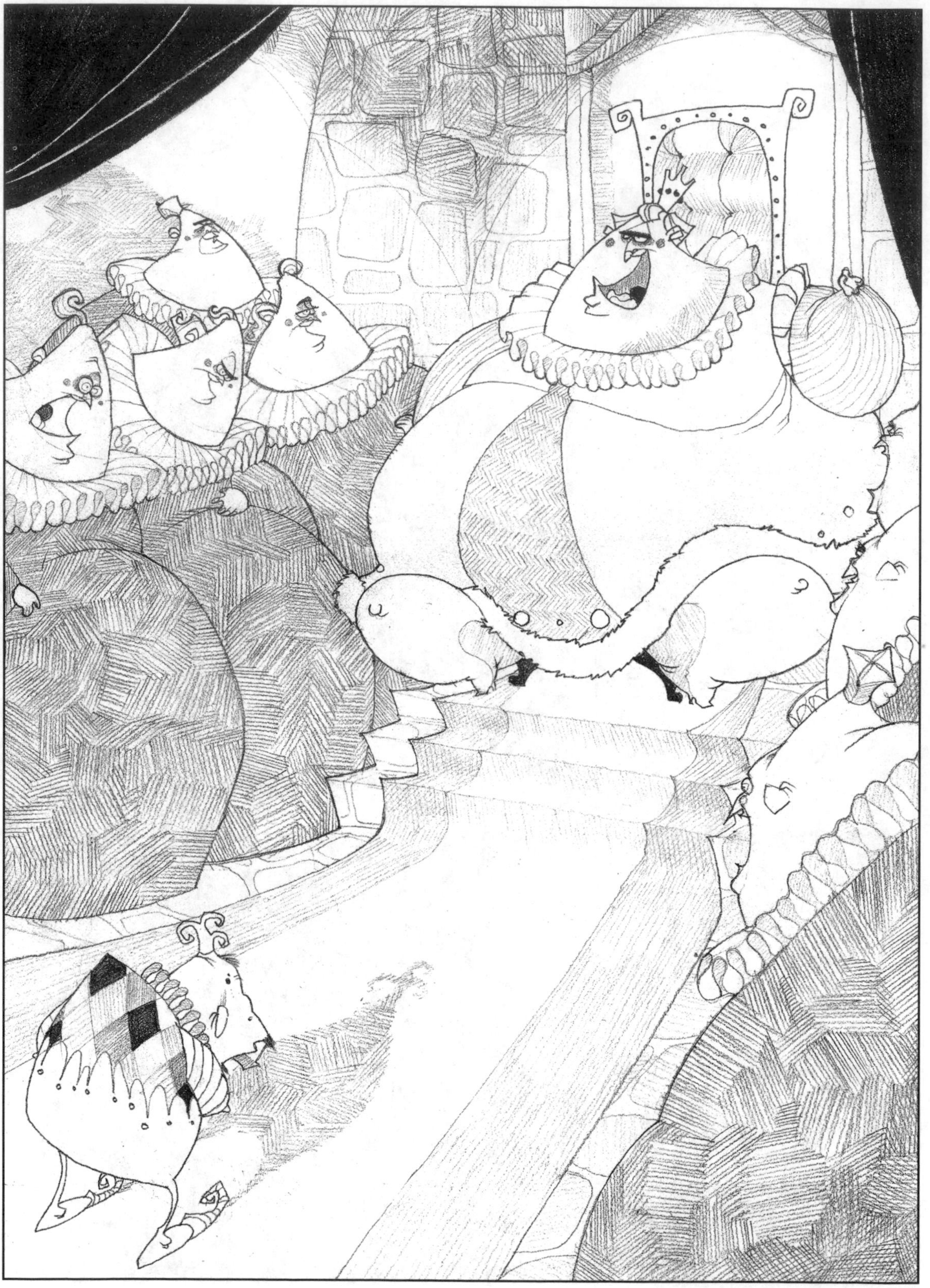

Hop-Frog

story by **EDGAR ALLAN POE**
illustrated by **LISA K. WEBER**

I never knew anyone so keenly alive to a joke as the king was. He seemed to live only for joking. To tell a good story of the joke kind, and to tell it well, was the surest road to his favor. Thus it happened that his seven ministers were all noted for their accomplishments as jokers. They all took after the king, too, in being large, corpulent, oily men, as well as inimitable jokers. Whether people grow fat by joking, or whether there is something in fat itself which predisposes to a joke, I have never been quite able to determine; but certain it is that a lean joker is a *rara avis in terris.*

About the refinements, or, as he called them, the "ghosts" of wit, the king troubled himself very little. He had an especial admiration for *breadth* in a jest, and would often put up with *length,* for the sake of it. Over-niceties wearied him. He would have preferred Rabelais' *Gargantua* to the *Zadig* of Voltaire: and, upon the whole, practical jokes suited his taste far better than verbal ones.

At the date of my narrative, professing jesters had not altogether gone out of fashion at court. Several of the great continental "powers" still retain their "fools," who wore motley, with caps and bells, and who were expected to be always ready with sharp witticisms, at a moment's notice, in consideration of the crumbs that fell from the royal table.

Our king, as a matter of course, retained his "fool." The fact is, he *required* something in the way of folly — if only to counterbalance the heavy wisdom of the seven wise men who were his ministers — not to mention himself.

His fool, or professional jester, was not *only* a fool, however. His value was trebled in the eyes of the king, by the fact of his being also a dwarf and a cripple. Dwarfs were as common at court, in those days, as fools; and many monarchs would have found it difficult to get through their days (days are rather longer at court than elsewhere) without both a jester to laugh *with,* and a dwarf to laugh *at.* But, as I have already

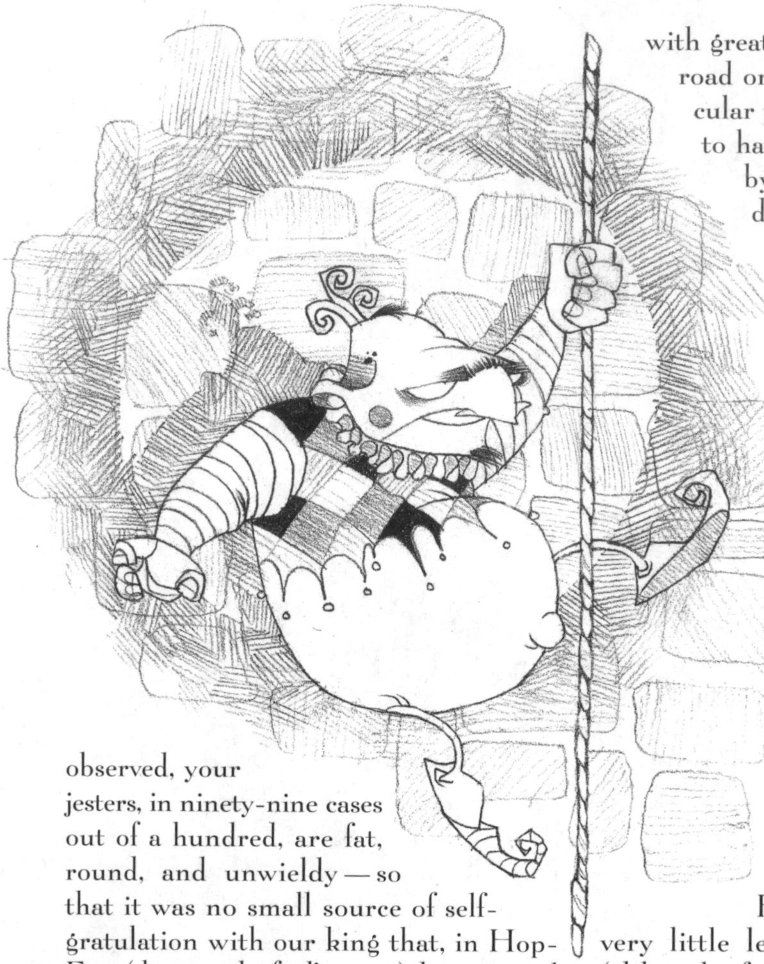

observed, your jesters, in ninety-nine cases out of a hundred, are fat, round, and unwieldy — so that it was no small source of self-gratulation with our king that, in Hop-Frog (this was the fool's name), he possessed a triplicate treasure in one person.

I believe the name "Hop-Frog" was *not* that given to the dwarf by his sponsors at baptism, but it was conferred upon him, by general consent of the several ministers, on account of his inability to walk as other men do. In fact, Hop-Frog could only get along by a sort of interjectional gait — something between a leap and a wriggle — a movement that afforded illimitable amusement, and of course consolation, to the king, for (notwithstanding the protuberance of his stomach and a constitutional swelling of the head) the king, by his whole court, was accounted a capital figure.

But although Hop-Frog, through the distortion of his legs, could move only with great pain and difficulty along a road or floor, the prodigious muscular power which nature seemed to have bestowed upon his arms, by way of compensation for deficiency in the lower limbs, enabled him to perform many feats of wonderful dexterity, where trees or ropes were in question, or any thing else to climb. At such exercises he certainly much more resembled a squirrel, or a small monkey, than a frog.

I am not able to say, with precision, from what country Hop-Frog originally came. It was from some barbarous region, however, that no person ever heard of — a vast distance from the court of our king. Hop-Frog, and a young girl very little less dwarfish than himself (although of exquisite proportions, and a marvellous dancer), had been forcibly carried off from their respective homes in adjoining provinces, and sent as presents to the king, by one of his ever-victorious generals.

Under these circumstances, it is not to be wondered at that a close intimacy arose between the two little captives. Indeed, they soon became sworn friends. Hop-Frog, who, although he made a great deal of sport, was by no means popular, had it not in his power to render Trippetta many services; but *she,* on account of her grace and exquisite beauty (although a dwarf), was universally admired and petted; so she possessed much influence; and never failed to use it, whenever she could, for the benefit of Hop-Frog.

On some grand state occasion — I forgot what — the king determined to have a masquerade, and whenever a masquerade or any thing of that kind occurred at our court, then the talents both of Hop-Frog and Trippetta were sure to be called into play. Hop-Frog, in especial, was so inventive in the way of getting up pageants, suggesting novel characters, and arranging costumes for masked balls, that nothing could be done, it seems, without his assistance.

The night appointed for the *fête* had arrived. A gorgeous hall had been fitted up, under Trippetta's eye, with every kind of device which could possibly give *éclat* to a masquerade. The whole court was in a fever of expectation. As for costumes and characters, it might well be supposed that everybody had come to a decision on such points. Many had made up their minds (as to what *rôles* they should assume) a week, or even a month, in advance; and, in fact, there was not a particle of indecision anywhere — except in the case of the king and his seven minsters. Why *they* hesitated I never could tell, unless they did it by way of a joke. More probably, they found it difficult, on account of being so fat, to make up their minds. At all events, time flew; and, as a last resort they sent for Trippetta and Hop-Frog.

When the two little friends obeyed the summons of the king they found him sitting at his wine with the seven members of his cabinet council; but the monarch appeared to be in a very ill humor. He knew that Hop-Frog was not fond of wine, for it excited the poor cripple almost to madness; and madness is no comfortable feeling. But the king loved his practical jokes, and took pleasure in forcing Hop-Frog to drink and (as the king called it) "to be merry."

"Come here, Hop-Frog," said he, as the jester and his friend entered the room;

"swallow this bumper to the health of your absent friends [here Hop-Frog sighed] and then let us have the benefit of your invention. We want characters — *characters*, man — something novel — out of the way. We are wearied with this everlasting sameness. Come, drink! the wine will brighten your wits."

Hop-Frog endeavored, as usual, to get up a jest in reply to these advances from the king; but the effort was too much. It happened to be the poor dwarf's birthday, and the command to drink to his "absent friends" forced the tears to his eyes. Many large, bitter drops fell into the goblet as he took it, humbly, from the hand of the tyrant.

"Ah! ha! ha!" roared the latter, as the dwarf reluctantly drained the beaker — "See what a glass of good wine can do! Why, your eyes are shining already!"

Poor fellow! his large eyes *gleamed,* rather than shone; for the effect of wine on his excitable brain was not more powerful than instantaneous. He placed the goblet nervously on the table, and looked round upon the company with a half-insane stare. They all seemed highly amused at the success of the king's *"joke."*

"And now to business," said the prime minister, a *very* fat man.

"Yes," said the King; "come lend us your assistance. Characters, my fine fellow; we stand in need of characters — all of us — ha! ha! ha!" and as this was seriously meant for a joke, his laugh was chorused by the seven.

Hop-Frog also laughed although feebly and somewhat vacantly.

"Come, come," said the king, impatiently, "have you nothing to suggest?"

"I am endeavoring to think of something *novel,*" replied the dwarf, abstractedly, for he was quite bewildered by the wine.

"Endeavoring!" cried the tyrant, fiercely; "what do you mean by *that?* Ah, I perceive. You are sulky, and want more wine. Here, drink this!" and he poured out another goblet full and offered it to the cripple, who merely gazed at it, gasping for breath.

"Drink, I say!" shouted the monster, "or by the fiends —"

The dwarf hesitated. The king grew purple with rage. The courtiers smirked. Trippetta, pale as a corpse, advanced to the monarch's seat, and, falling on her knees before him, implored him to spare her friend.

The tyrant regarded her, for some moments, in evident wonder at her audacity. He seemed quite at a loss what to do or say — how most becomingly to express his indignation. At last, without uttering a syllable, he pushed her violently from him, and threw the contents of the brimming goblet in her face.

The poor girl got up the best she could, and, not daring even to sigh, resumed her position at the foot of the table.

There was a dead silence for about half a minute, during which the falling of a leaf, or of a feather, might have been heard. It was interrupted by a low, but harsh and protracted *grating* sound which seemed to come at once from every corner of the room.

"What — what — *what* are you making that noise for?" demanded the king, turning furiously to the dwarf.

The latter seemed to have recovered, in great measure, from his intoxication, and looking fixedly but quietly into the tyrant's face, merely ejaculated:

"I — I? How could it have been me?"

"The sound appeared to come from without," observed one of the courtiers. "I fancy it was the parrot at the window, whetting his bill upon his cage-wires."

"True," replied the monarch, as if much relieved by the suggestion; "but, on the honor of a knight, I could have sworn that it was the gritting of this vagabond's teeth."

Hereupon the dwarf laughed (the king was too confirmed a joker to object to any one's laughing), and displayed a set of large, powerful, and very repulsive teeth. Moreover, he avowed his perfect willingness to swallow as much wine as desired. The monarch was pacified; and having drained another bumper with no very perceptible ill effect, Hop-Frog entered at once, and with spirit, into the plans for the masquerade.

"I cannot tell what was the association of idea," observed he, very tranquilly, and as if he had never tasted wine in his life, "but *just after* your majesty had struck the girl and thrown the wine in her face — *just after* your majesty had done this, and while the parrot was making that odd noise outside the window, there came into my mind a capital diversion — one of my own country frolics — often enacted among us, at our masquerades: but here it will be new altogether. Unfortunately, however, it requires a company of eight persons and —"

"Here we *are!*" cried the king, laughing at his acute discovery of the coincidence; "eight to a fraction — I and my seven ministers. Come! what is the diversion?"

"We call it," replied the cripple, "the Eight Chained Ourang-Outangs, and it really is excellent sport if well enacted."

"*We* will enact it," remarked the king, drawing himself up, and lowering his eyelids.

"The beauty of the game," continued Hop-Frog, "lies in the fright it occasions among the women."

"Capital!" roared in chorus the monarch and his ministry.

"I will equip you as ourang-outangs," proceeded the dwarf; "leave all that to me. The resemblance shall be so striking, that the company of masqueraders will take you for real beasts — and of course, they will be as much terrified as astonished."

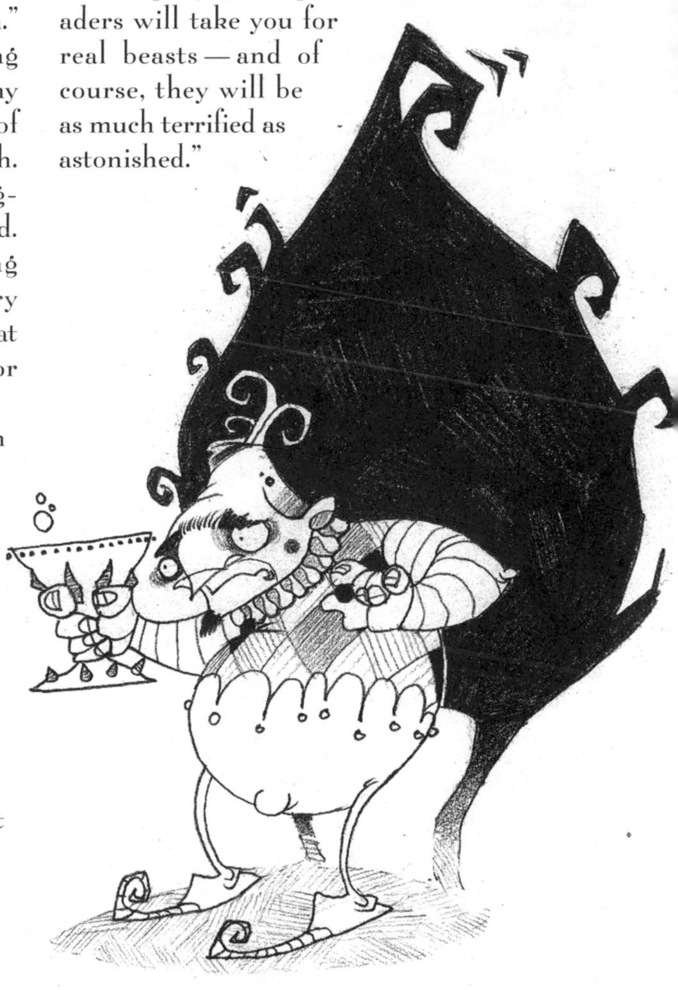

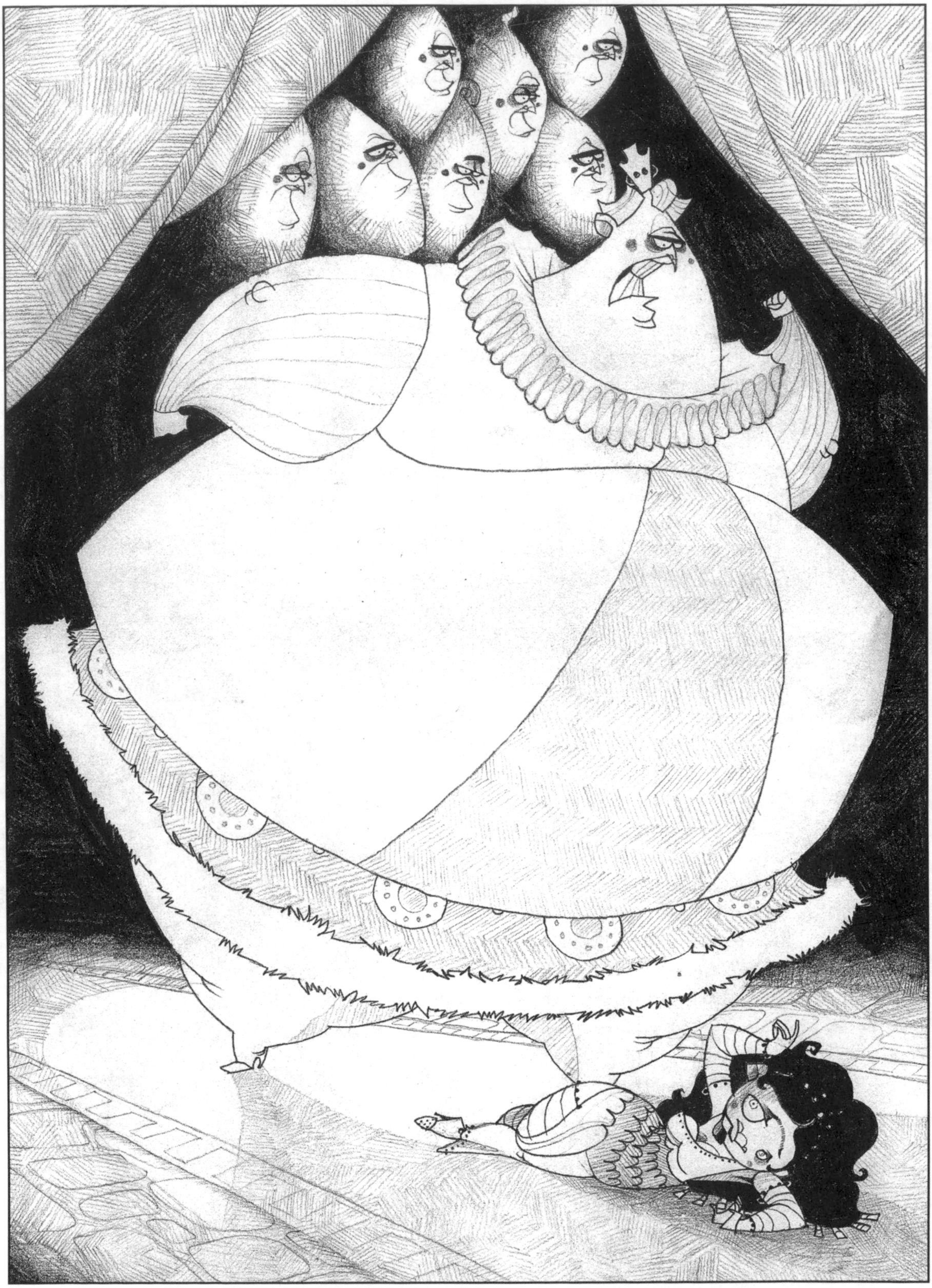

"Oh, this is exquisite!" exclaimed the king. "Hop-Frog! I will make a man of you."

"The chains are for the purpose of increasing the confusion by their jangling. You are supposed to have escaped, *en masse,* from your keepers. Your majesty cannot conceive the *effect* produced, at a masquerade, by eight chained ourang-outangs, imagined to be real ones by most of the company; and rushing in with savage cries, among the crowd of delicately and gorgeously habited men and women. The *contrast* is inimitable!"

"It *must* be," said the king: and the council arose hurriedly (as it was growing late), to put in execution the scheme of Hop-Frog.

His mode of equipping the party as ourang-outangs was very simple, but effective enough for his purposes. The animals in question had, at the epoch of my story, very rarely been seen in any part of the civilized world; and as the imitations made by the dwarf were sufficiently beast-like and more than sufficiently hideous, their truthfulness to nature was thus thought to be secured.

The king and his ministers were first encased in tight-fitting stockinet shirts and drawers. They were then saturated with tar. At this stage of the process, some one of the party suggested feathers; but the suggestion was at once overruled by the dwarf, who soon convinced the eight, by ocular demonstration, that the hair of such a brute as the ourang-outang was much more efficiently represented by *flax.* A thick coating of the latter was accordingly plastered upon the coating of tar. A long chain was now procured. First, it was passed about the waist of the king, *and tied,* then about another of the party, and also tied; then about all successively, in the same manner. When this chaining arrangement was complete, and the party stood as far apart from each other as possible, they formed a circle; and to make all things appear natural, Hop-Frog passed the residue of the chain in two diameters, at right angles, across the circle, after the fashion adopted, at the present day, by those who capture Chimpanzees, or other large apes, in Borneo.

The grand saloon in which the masquerade was to take place was a circular room, very lofty, and receiving the light of the sun only through a single window at top. At night

(the season for which the apartment was especially designed) it was illuminated principally by a large chandelier, depending by a chain from the centre of the sky-light, and lowered, or elevated, by means of a counter-balance as usual; but (in order not to look unsightly) this latter passed outside the cupola and over the roof.

The arrangements of the room had been left to Trippetta's superintendence; but, in some particulars, it seems, she had been guided by the calmer judgment of her friend the dwarf. At his suggestion it was that, on this occasion, the chandelier was removed. Its waxen drippings (which, in weather so warm, it was quite impossible to prevent) would have been seriously detrimental to the rich dresses of the guests, who, on account of the crowded state of the saloon, could not *all* be expected to keep from out its center — that is to say, from under the chandelier. Additional sconces were set in various parts of the hall, out of the way, and a flambeau, emitting sweet odor, was placed in the right hand of each of the caryatides that stood against the wall — some fifty or sixty altogether.

The eight ourang-outangs, taking Hop-Frog's advice, waited patiently until midnight (when the room was thoroughly filled with masqueraders) before making their appearance. No sooner had the clock ceased striking, however, than they rushed, or rather rolled in, all together — for the impediments of their chains caused most of the party to fall, and all to stumble as they entered.

The excitement among the masqueraders was prodigious, and filled the heart of the king with glee. As had been anticipated, there were not a few of the guests who supposed the ferocious-looking creatures to be beasts of *some* kind in reality, if not precisely ourang-outangs. Many of the women swooned with affright; and had not the king taken the precaution to exclude all weapons from the saloon, his party might soon have expiated their frolic in their blood. As it was, a general rush was made for the doors; but the king had ordered them to be locked immediately upon his entrance; and, at the dwarf's suggestion, the keys had been deposited with *him*.

While the tumult was at its height, and each masquerader attentive only to his own safety (for, in fact, there was much real danger from the pressure of the excited crowd), the chain by which the chandelier ordinarily hung, and which had been drawn up on its removal, might have been seen very gradually to descend, until its hooked extremity came within three feet of the floor.

Soon after this, the king and his seven friends having reeled about the hall in all directions, found themselves, at length, in its centre, and, of course, in immediate contact with the chain. While they were thus situated, the dwarf, who had followed noiselessly at their heels, inciting them to keep up the commotion, took hold of their own chain at the intersection of the two portions which crossed the circle diametrically and at right angles. Here, with the rapidity of thought, he inserted the hook from which the chandelier had been wont to depend; and, in an instant, by some unseen agency, the chandelier-chain was drawn so far upward as to take the hook out of reach, and, as an inevitable consequence, to drag the ourang-outangs together in close connection, and face to face.

The masqueraders, by this time, had recovered, in some measure, from their alarm; and, beginning to regard the whole matter as a well-contrived pleasantry, set up a loud shout of laughter at the predicament of the apes.

"Leave them to *me!*" now screamed Hop-Frog, his shrill voice making itself easily heard through all the din. "Leave them to *me*. I fancy *I* know them. If I can only get a good look at them, *I* can soon tell who they are."

Here, scrambling over the heads of the crowd, he managed to get to the wall; when, seizing a flambeau from one of the caryatides, he returned, as he went, to the center of the room—leaping, with the agility of a monkey, upon the king's head, and thence clambered a few feet up the chain; holding down the torch to examine the group of ourang-outangs, and still screaming: "I shall soon find out who they are!"

And now, while the whole assembly (the apes included) were convulsed with

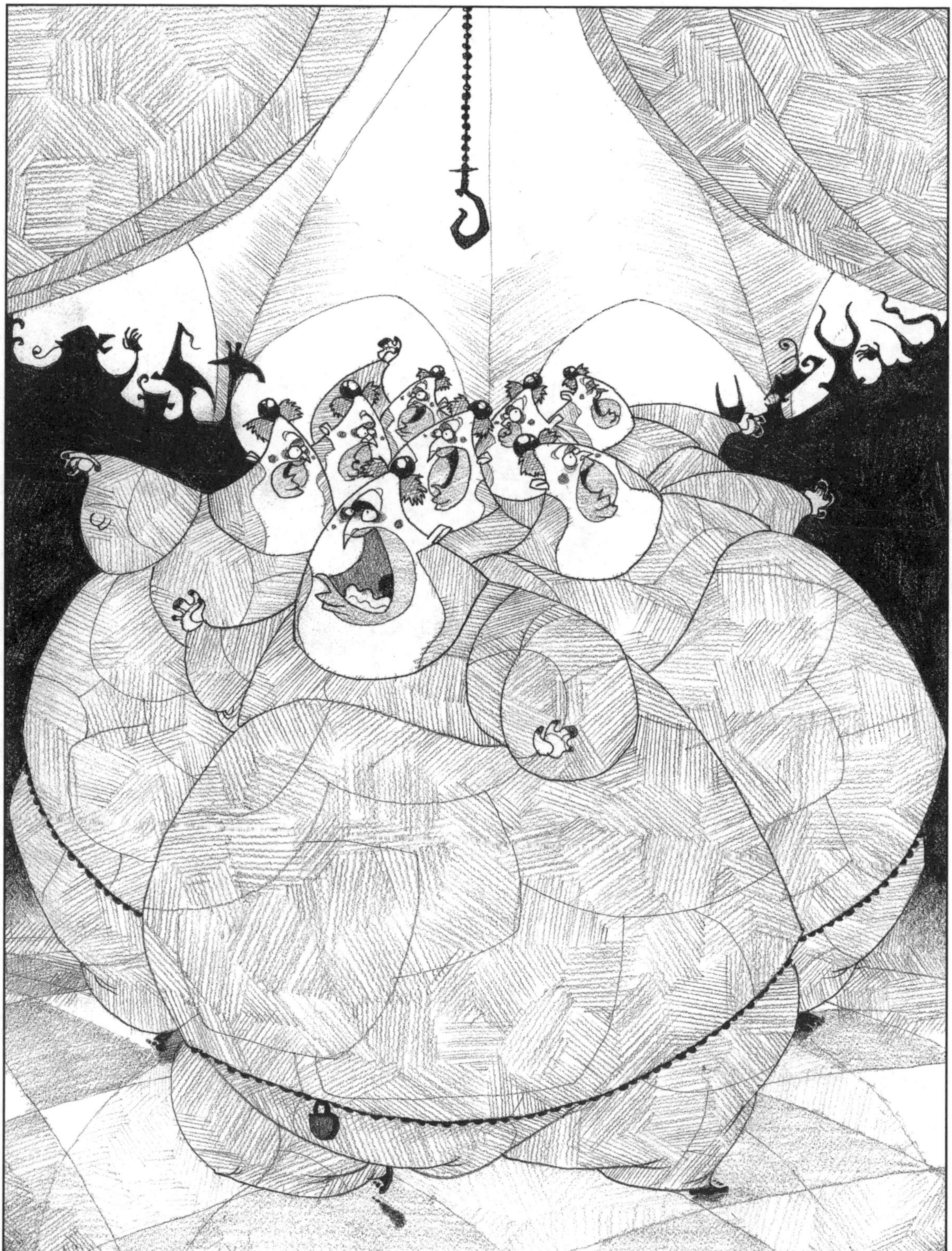

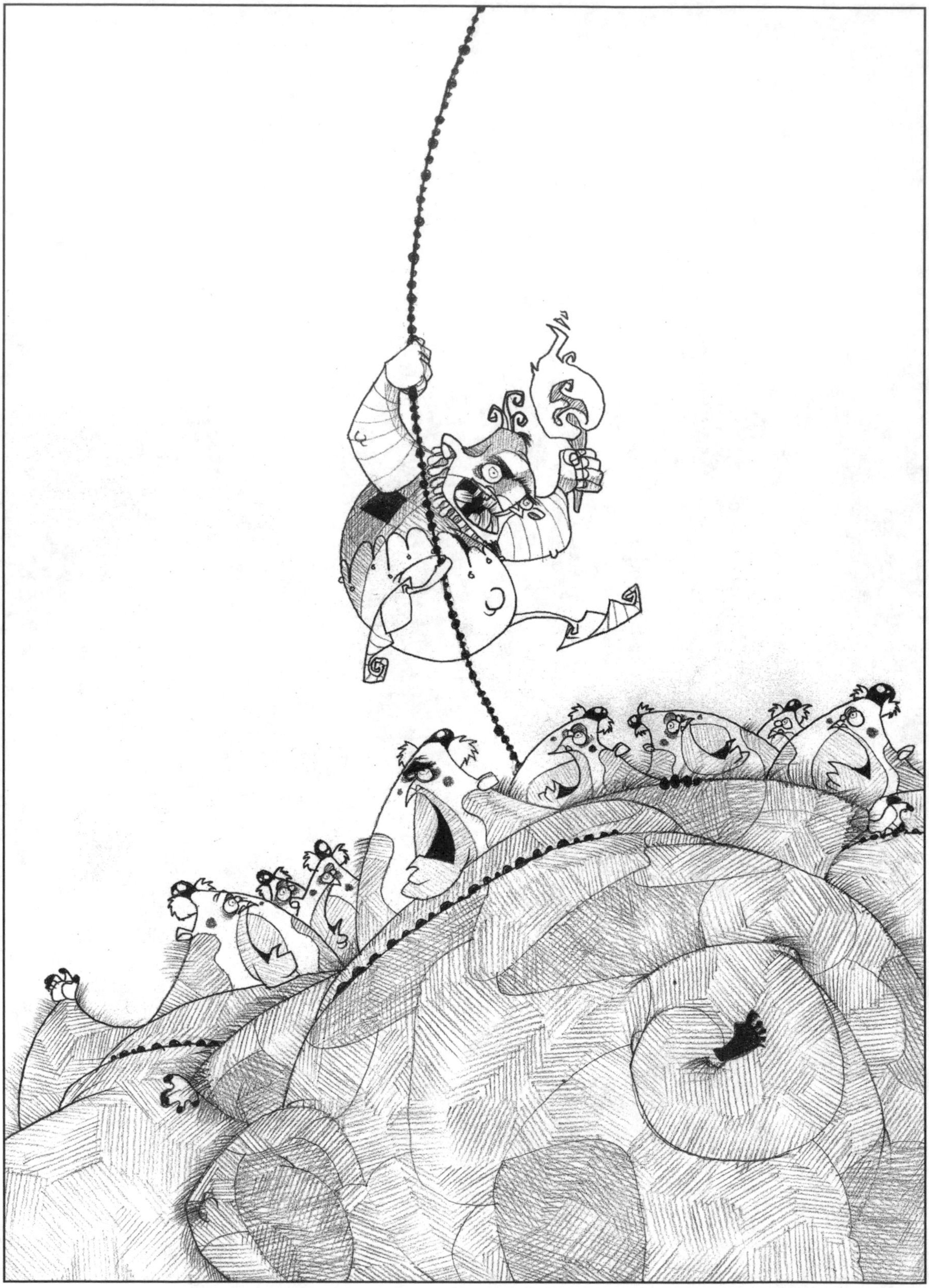

laughter, the jester suddenly uttered a shrill whistle; when the chain flew violently up for about thirty feet — dragging with it the dismayed and struggling ourang-outangs, and leaving them suspended in mid-air between the sky-light and the floor. Hop-Frog, clinging to the chain as it rose, still maintained his relative position in respect to the eight maskers, and still (as if nothing were the matter) continued to thrust his torch down toward them, as though endeavoring to discover who they were.

So thoroughly astonished was the whole company at this ascent, that a dead silence, of about a minute's duration, ensued. It was broken by just such a low, harsh, *grating* sound, as had before attracted the attention of the king and his councillors when the former threw the wine in the face of Trippetta. But, on the present occasion, there could be no question as to *whence* the sound issued. It came from the fang-like teeth of the dwarf, who ground them and gnashed them as he foamed at the mouth, and glared, with an expression of maniacal rage, into the up-turned countenances of the king and his seven companions.

"Ah, ha!" said at length the infuriated jester. "Ah, ha! I begin to see who these people *are* now!" Here, pretending to scrutinize the king more closely, he held the flambeau to the flaxen coat which enveloped him, and which instantly burst into a sheet of vivid flame. In less than half a minute the whole eight ourang-outangs were blazing fiercely, amid the shrieks of the multitude who gazed at them from below, horror-stricken, and without the power to render them the slightest assistance.

At length the flames, suddenly increasing in virulence, forced the jester to climb higher up the chain, to be out of their reach; and, as he made this movement, the crowd again sank, for a brief instant, into silence. The dwarf seized his opportunity, and once more spoke:

"I now see *distinctly,*" he said, "what manner of people these maskers are. They are a great king and his seven privy-councillors,— a king who does not scruple to strike a defenseless girl and his seven councillors who abet him in the outrage. As for myself, I am simply Hop-Frog, the jester — *and this is my last jest.*"

Owing to the high combustibility of both the flax and the tar to which it adhered, the dwarf had scarcely made an end of his brief speech before the work of vengeance was complete. The eight corpses swung in their chains, a fetid, blackened, hideous, and indistinguishable mass. The cripple hurled his torch at them, clambered leisurely to the ceiling, and disappeared through the skylight.

It is supposed that Trippetta, stationed on the roof of the saloon, had been the accomplice of her friend in his fiery revenge, and that, together, they effected their escape to their own country; for neither was seen again.

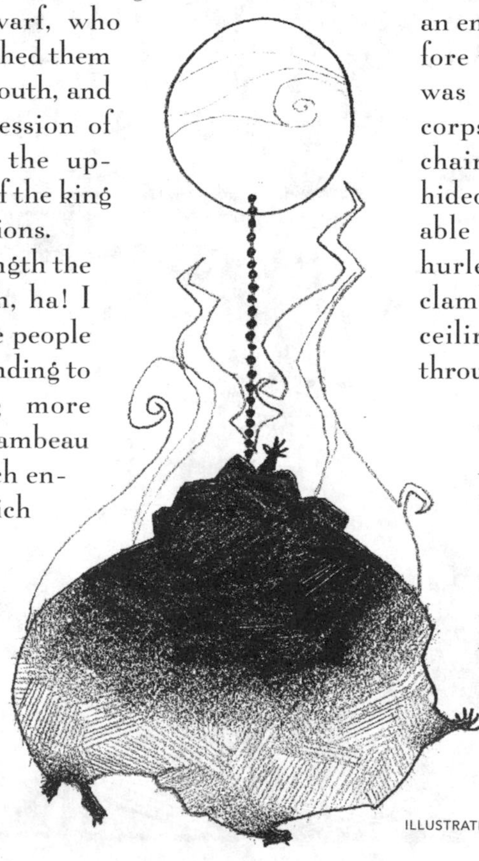

The Bells

adapted by
RAFAEL NIEVES
illustrated by
JUAN GOMEZ

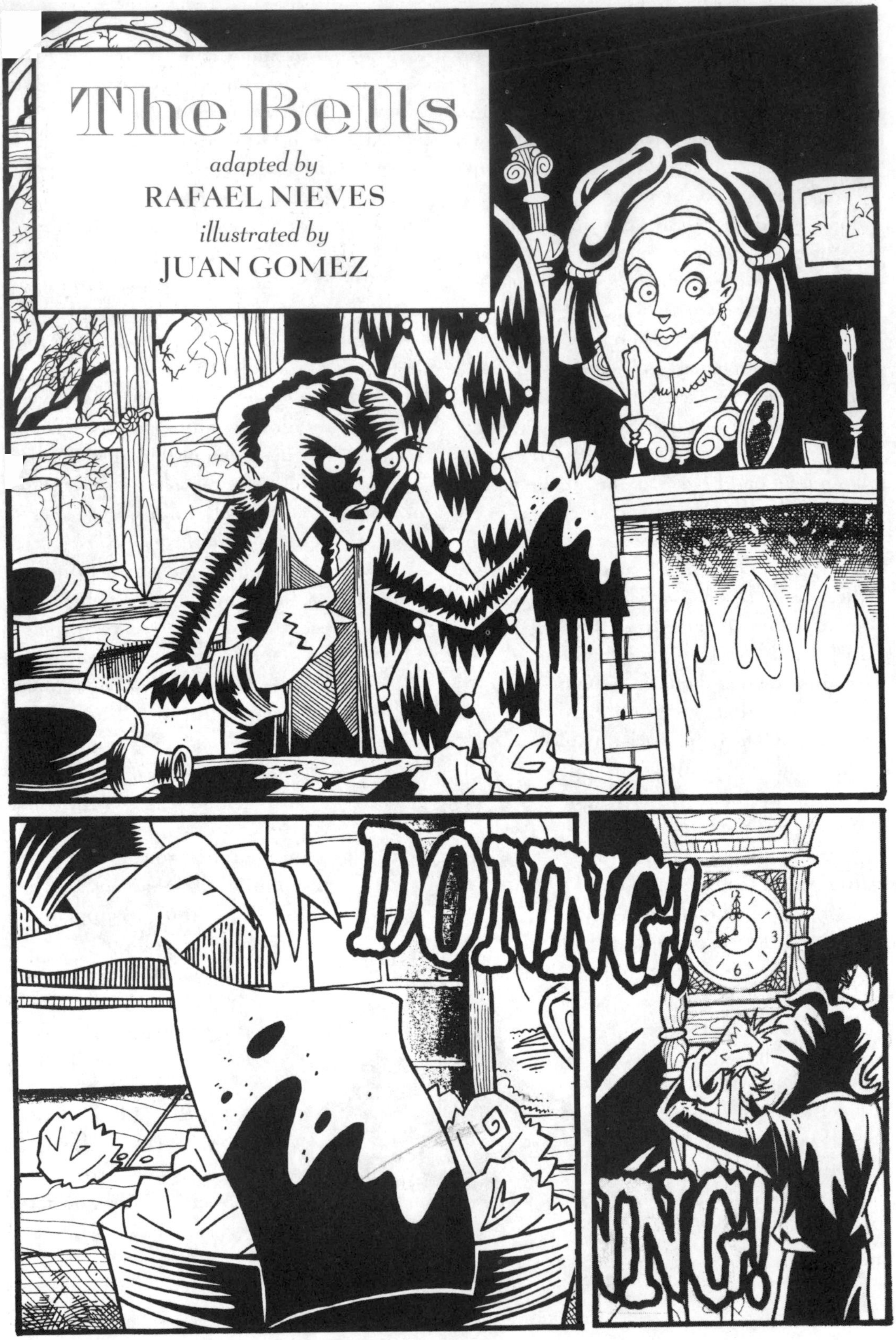
DONNG!
NG!

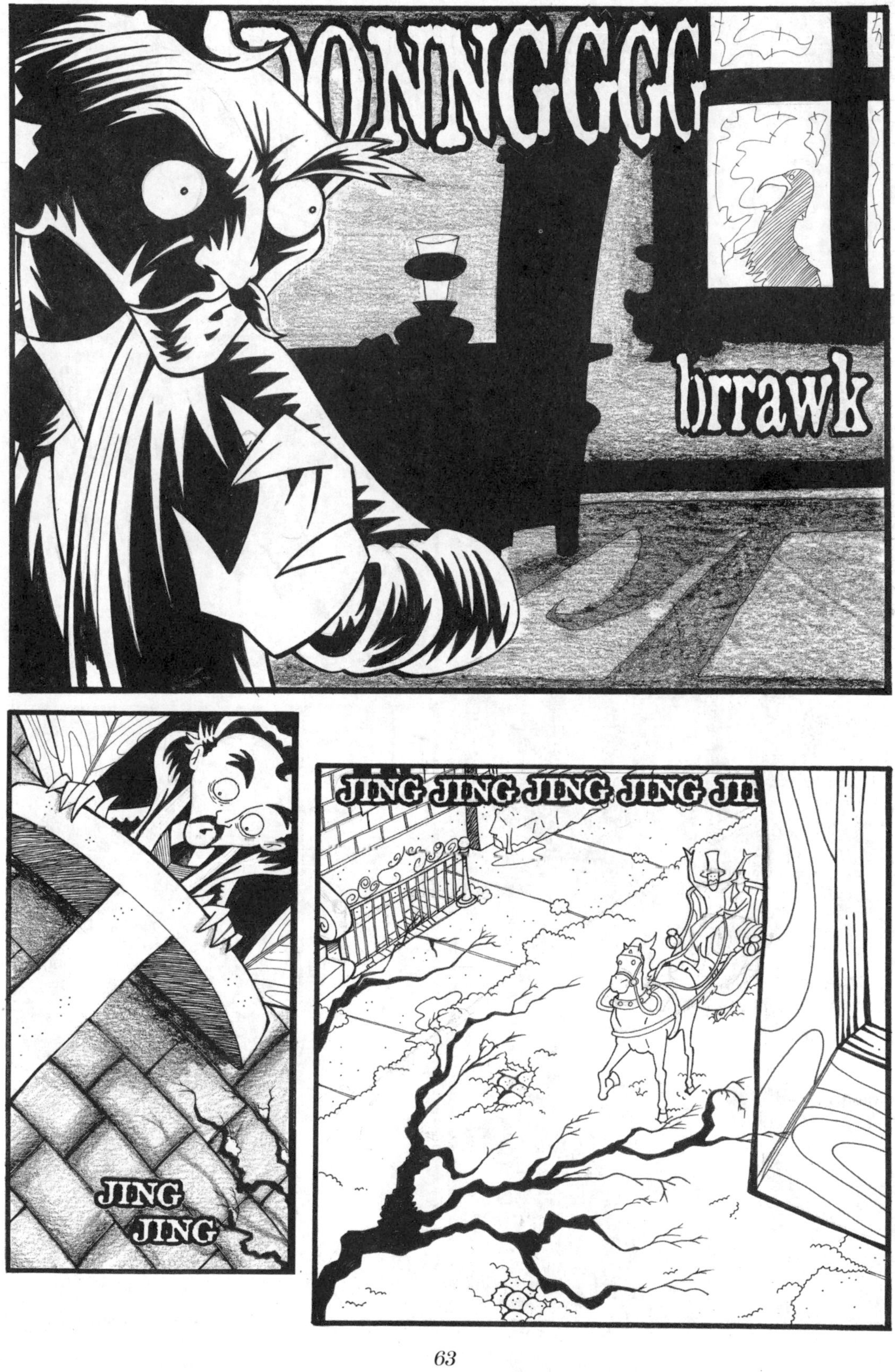
ONNGGG
brrawk
JING
JING
JING JING JING JING JI

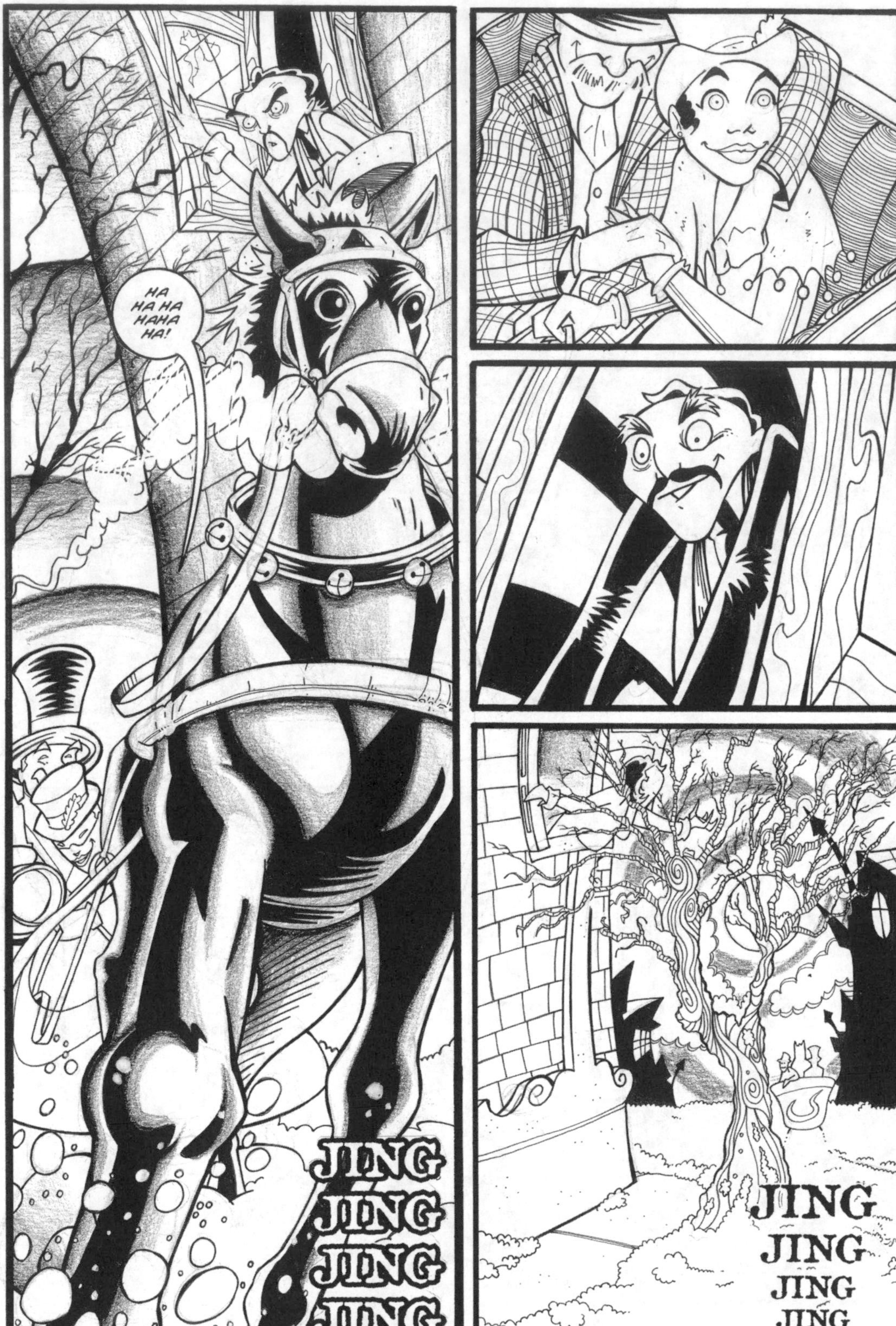
HA HA HA HAHA HA!
JING
JING
JING
JING
JING
JING
JING
JING

SCRITCH
SCRITCH
SCRITCH

"HEAR THE SLEDGES WITH THE BELLS--SILVER BELLS!

ells—
silver bells!
What a world of merri-
their melody foretells!
How they tinkle, tinkle,
tile,
In the icy air of night!
while the

"WHAT A WORLD OF MERRIMENT THEIR MELODY FORETELLS!

"HOW THEY TINKLE, TINKLE, TINKLE,
IN THE ICY AIR OF NIGHT!
WHILE THE STARS THAT OVERSPRINKLE
ALL THE HEAVENS, SEEM TO TWINKLE
WITH A CRYSTALLINE DELIGHT;

"KEEPING TIME, TIME, TIME, IN A SORT OF RUNIC RHYME,
TO THE TINTINNABULATION THAT SO MUSICALLY WELLS
FROM THE BELLS, BELLS, BELLS, BELLS, BELLS, BELLS, BELLS--

"FROM THE JINGLING AND THE TINKLING OF THE BELLS."

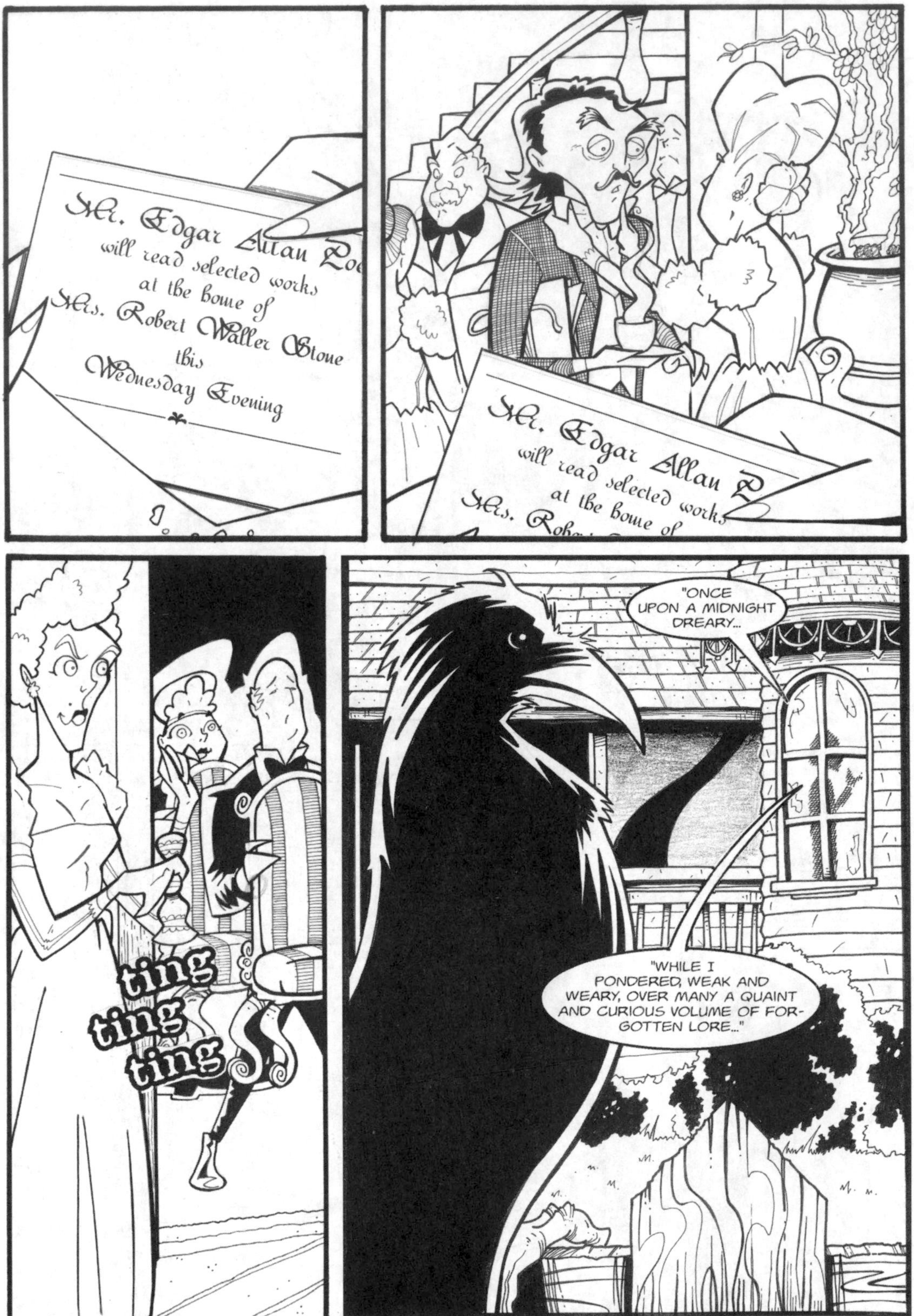
Mr. Edgar Allan Poe
will read selected works
at the home of
Mrs. Robert Waller Stone
this
Wednesday Evening
ting
ting
ting
"ONCE UPON A MIDNIGHT DREARY...
"WHILE I PONDERED, WEAK AND WEARY, OVER MANY A QUAINT AND CURIOUS VOLUME OF FORGOTTEN LORE..."

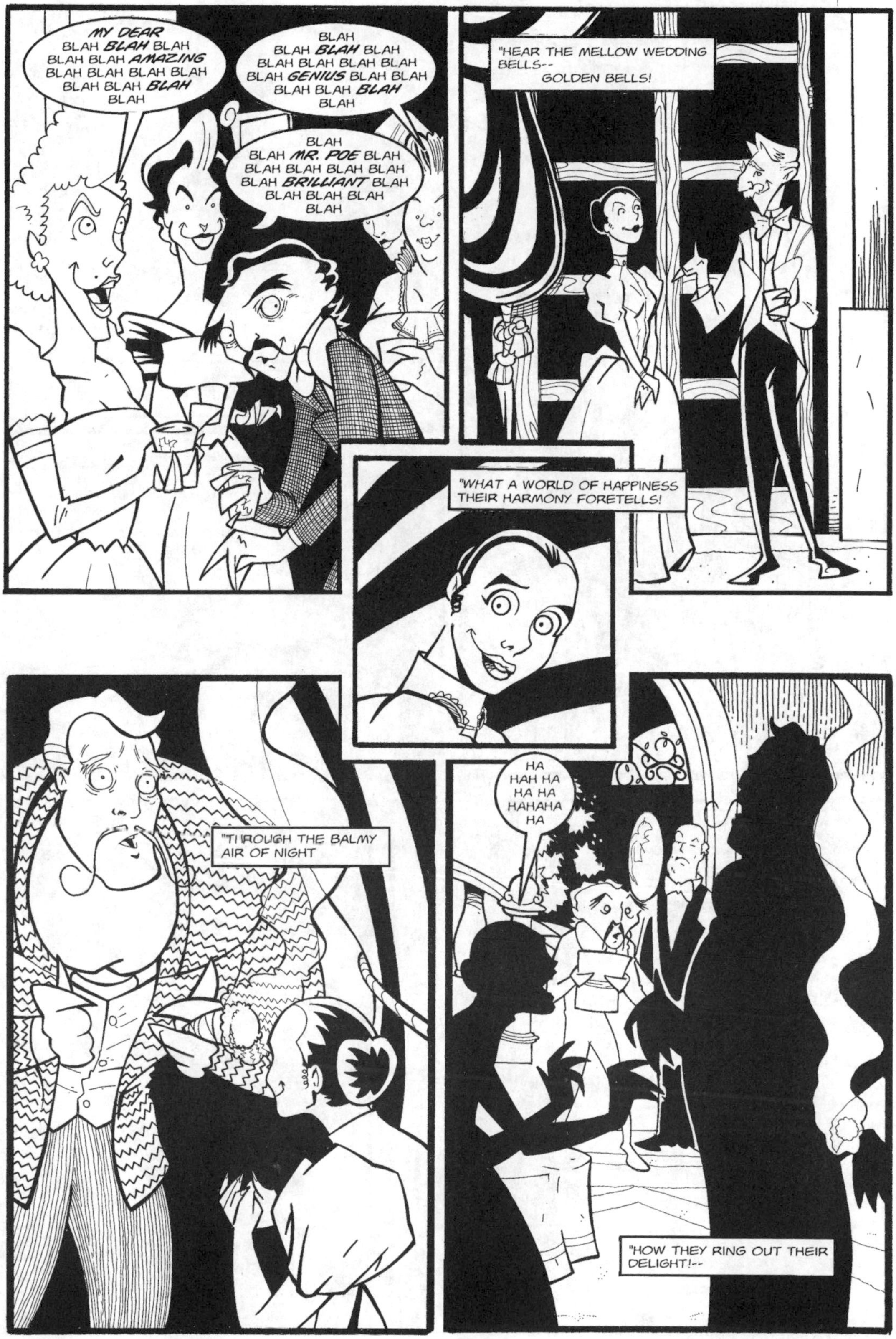
MY DEAR BLAH BLAH BLAH BLAH BLAH AMAZING BLAH BLAH BLAH BLAH BLAH BLAH BLAH BLAH
BLAH BLAH BLAH BLAH BLAH BLAH BLAH BLAH GENIUS BLAH BLAH BLAH BLAH BLAH BLAH
BLAH BLAH MR. POE BLAH BLAH BLAH BLAH BLAH BLAH BRILLIANT BLAH BLAH BLAH BLAH BLAH BLAH
"HEAR THE MELLOW WEDDING BELLS-- GOLDEN BELLS!
"WHAT A WORLD OF HAPPINESS THEIR HARMONY FORETELLS!
"THROUGH THE BALMY AIR OF NIGHT
HA HAH HA HA HA HAHAHA HA
"HOW THEY RING OUT THEIR DELIGHT!--

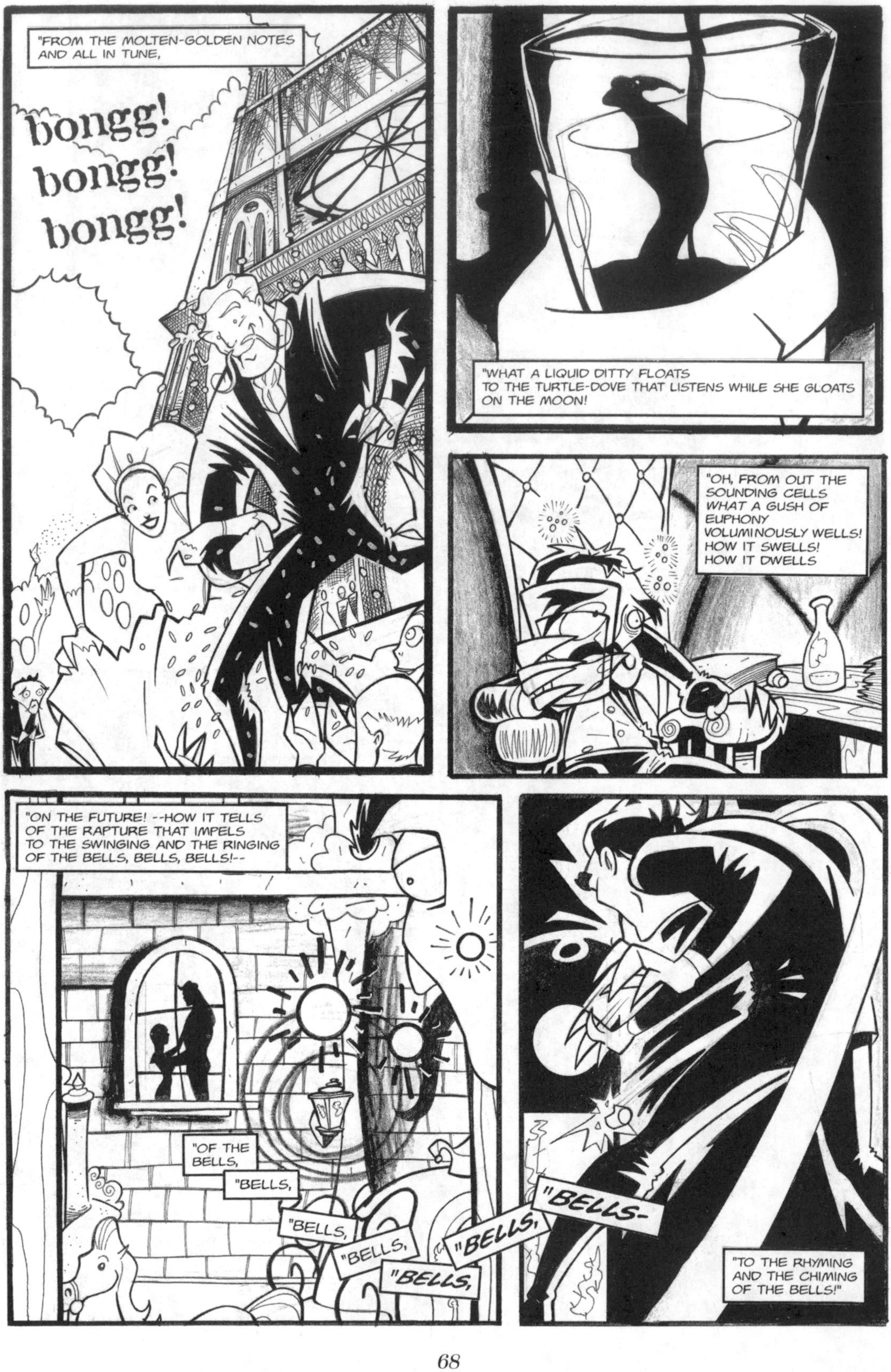
"FROM THE MOLTEN-GOLDEN NOTES AND ALL IN TUNE,
bongg! bongg! bongg!
"WHAT A LIQUID DITTY FLOATS TO THE TURTLE-DOVE THAT LISTENS WHILE SHE GLOATS ON THE MOON!
"OH, FROM OUT THE SOUNDING CELLS WHAT A GUSH OF EUPHONY VOLUMINOUSLY WELLS! HOW IT SWELLS! HOW IT DWELLS
"ON THE FUTURE! --HOW IT TELLS OF THE RAPTURE THAT IMPELS TO THE SWINGING AND THE RINGING OF THE BELLS, BELLS, BELLS!--
"OF THE BELLS,
"BELLS,
"BELLS,
"BELLS,
"BELLS,
"BELLS,
"BELLS-
"TO THE RHYMING AND THE CHIMING OF THE BELLS!"

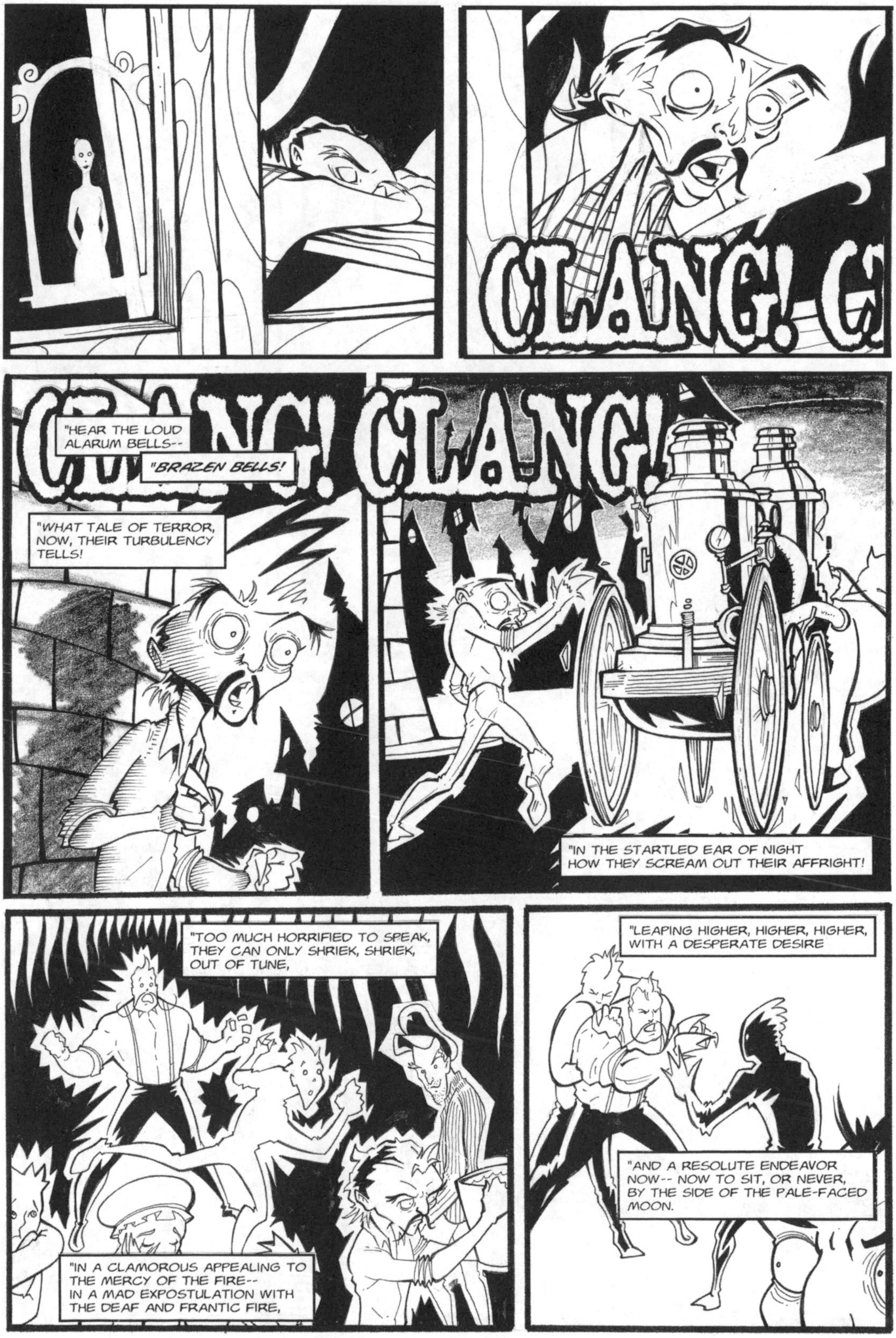

CLANG! CL
CLANG! CLANG!
"HEAR THE LOUD ALARUM BELLS--
"BRAZEN BELLS!
"WHAT TALE OF TERROR, NOW, THEIR TURBULENCY TELLS!
"IN THE STARTLED EAR OF NIGHT HOW THEY SCREAM OUT THEIR AFFRIGHT!
"TOO MUCH HORRIFIED TO SPEAK, THEY CAN ONLY SHRIEK, SHRIEK, OUT OF TUNE,
"IN A CLAMOROUS APPEALING TO THE MERCY OF THE FIRE-- IN A MAD EXPOSTULATION WITH THE DEAF AND FRANTIC FIRE,
"LEAPING HIGHER, HIGHER, HIGHER, WITH A DESPERATE DESIRE
"AND A RESOLUTE ENDEAVOR NOW-- NOW TO SIT, OR NEVER, BY THE SIDE OF THE PALE-FACED MOON.

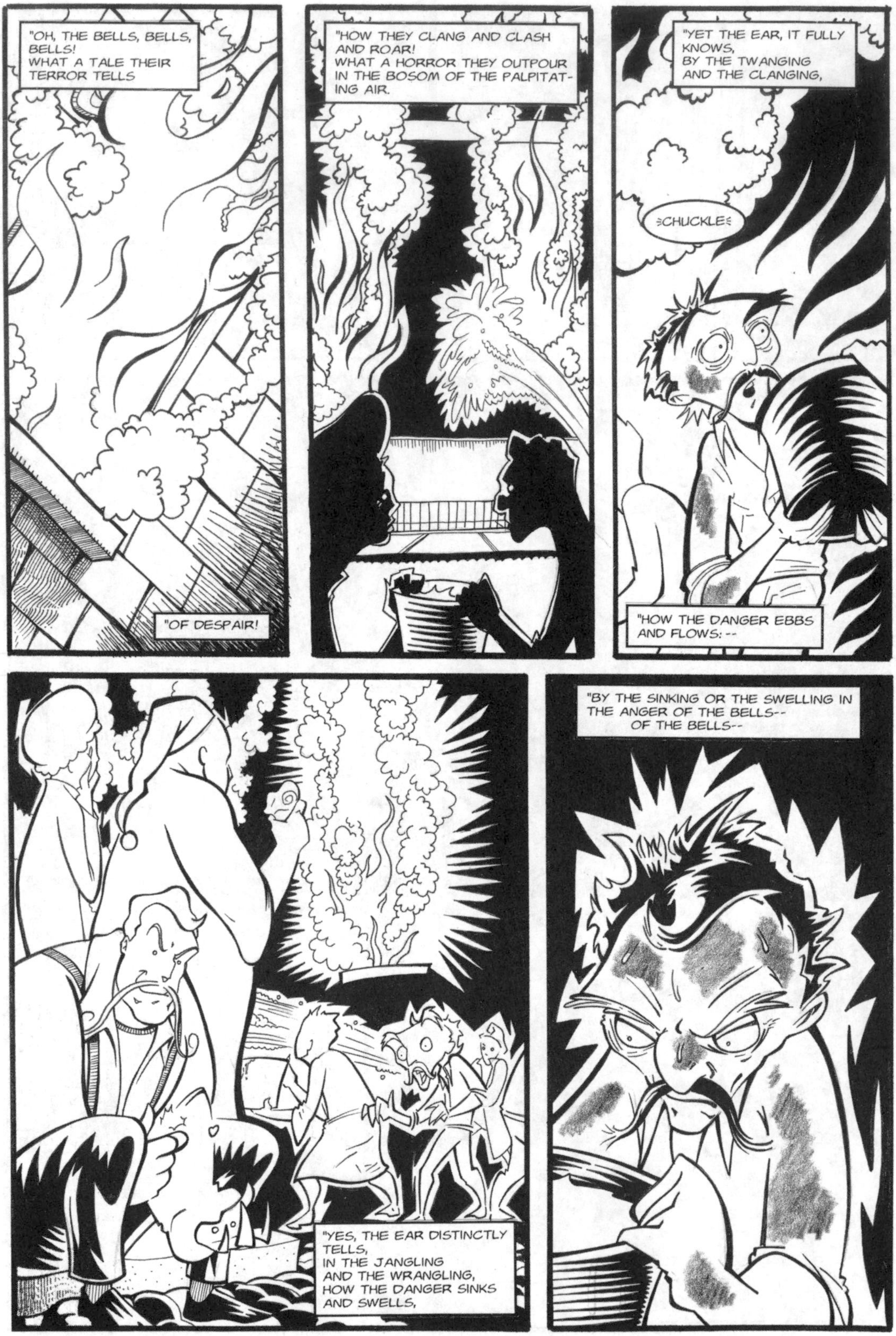
"OH, THE BELLS, BELLS, BELLS!
WHAT A TALE THEIR TERROR TELLS
"OF DESPAIR!
"HOW THEY CLANG AND CLASH AND ROAR!
WHAT A HORROR THEY OUTPOUR
IN THE BOSOM OF THE PALPITATING AIR.
"YET THE EAR, IT FULLY KNOWS,
BY THE TWANGING
AND THE CLANGING,
CHUCKLE
"HOW THE DANGER EBBS AND FLOWS: --
"YES, THE EAR DISTINCTLY TELLS,
IN THE JANGLING
AND THE WRANGLING,
HOW THE DANGER SINKS AND SWELLS,
"BY THE SINKING OR THE SWELLING IN THE ANGER OF THE BELLS--
OF THE BELLS--

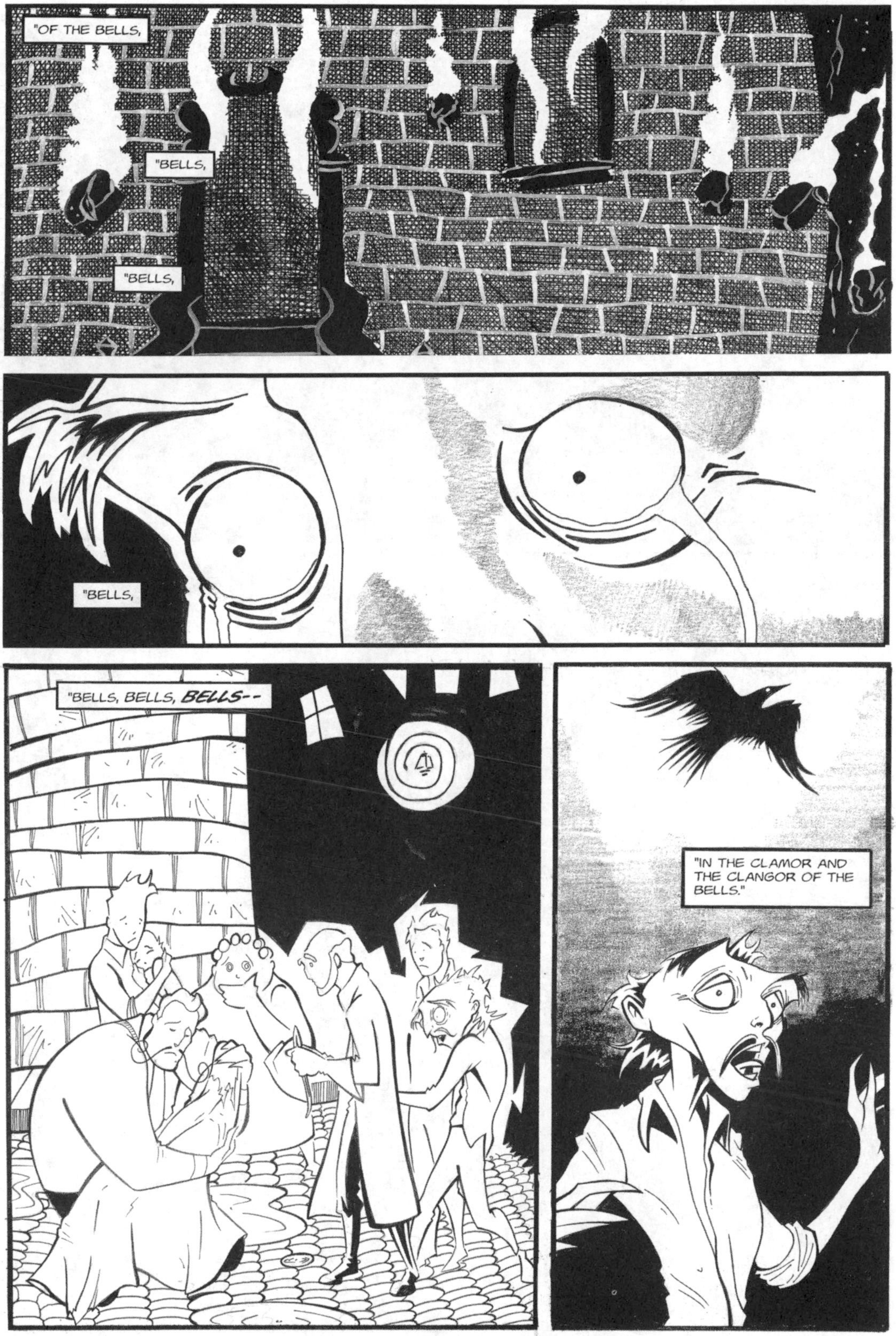
"OF THE BELLS,
"BELLS,
"BELLS,
"BELLS,
"BELLS, BELLS, BELLS--
"IN THE CLAMOR AND THE CLANGOR OF THE BELLS."

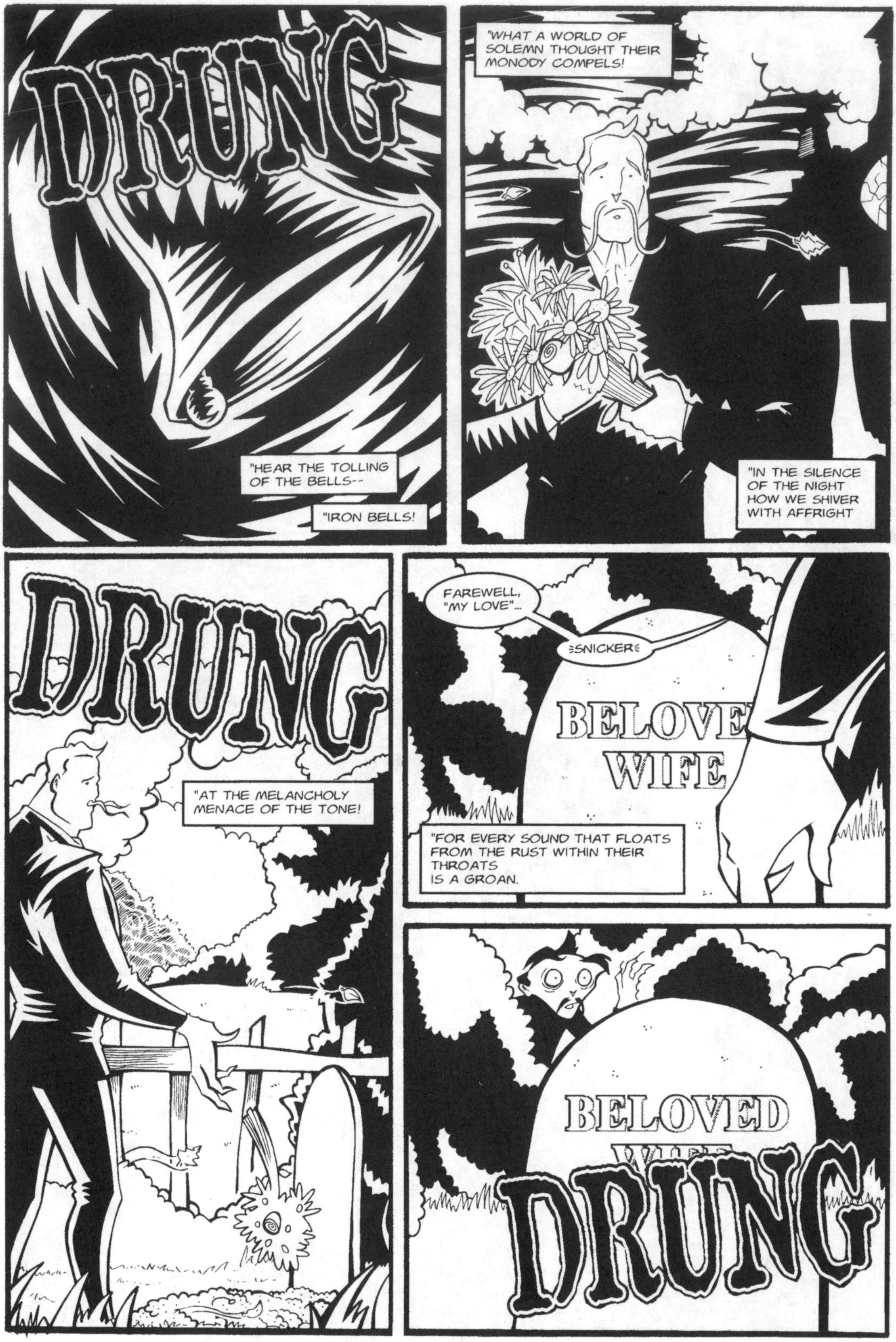
DRUNG
"HEAR THE TOLLING OF THE BELLS--
"IRON BELLS!
"WHAT A WORLD OF SOLEMN THOUGHT THEIR MONODY COMPELS!
"IN THE SILENCE OF THE NIGHT HOW WE SHIVER WITH AFFRIGHT
DRUNG
"AT THE MELANCHOLY MENACE OF THE TONE!
FAREWELL, "MY LOVE"...
SNICKER
BELOVE
WIFE
"FOR EVERY SOUND THAT FLOATS FROM THE RUST WITHIN THEIR THROATS IS A GROAN.
BELOVED
DRUNG

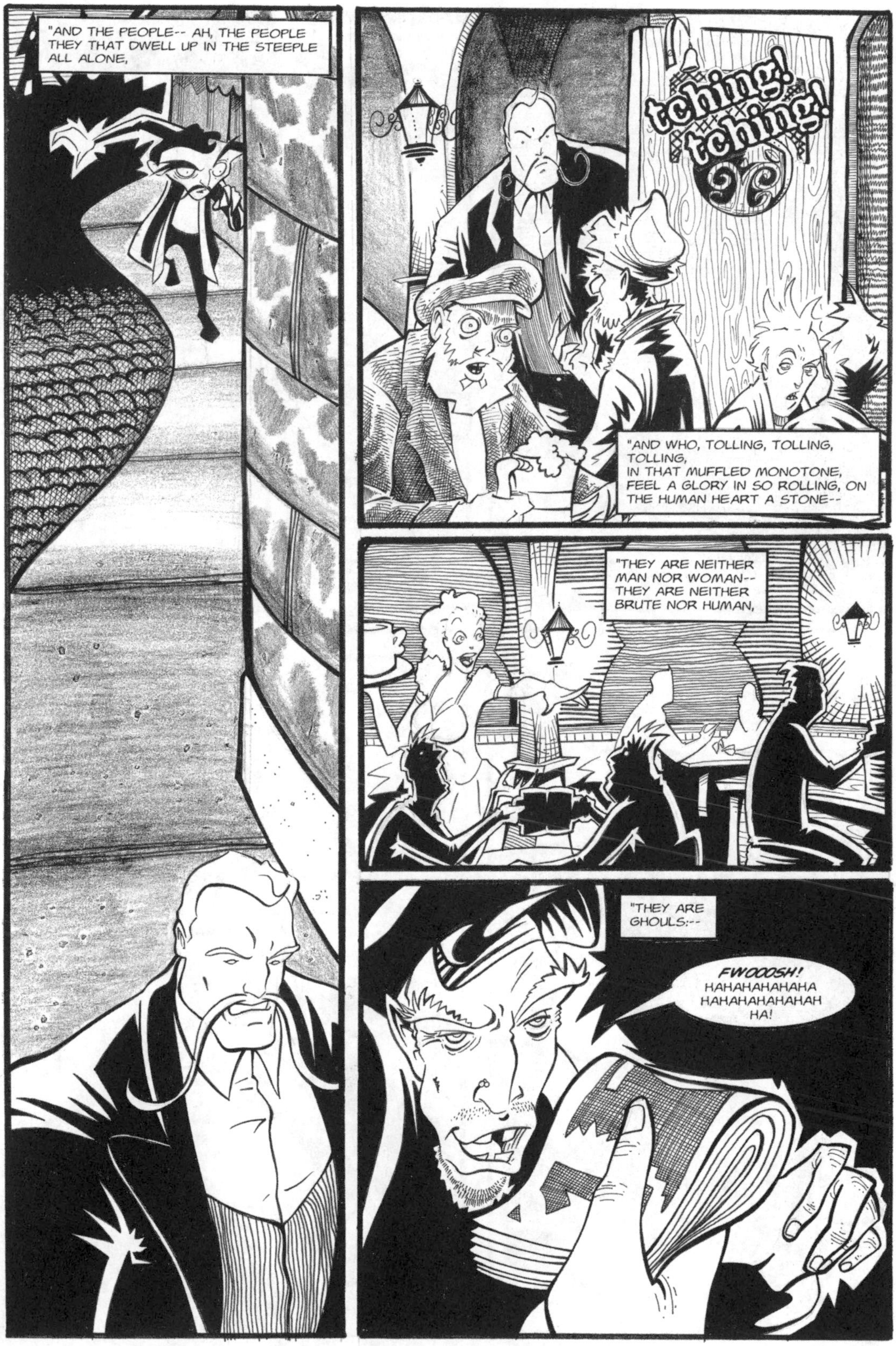
"AND THE PEOPLE-- AH, THE PEOPLE
THEY THAT DWELL UP IN THE STEEPLE
ALL ALONE,
tching! tching!
"AND WHO, TOLLING, TOLLING,
TOLLING,
IN THAT MUFFLED MONOTONE,
FEEL A GLORY IN SO ROLLING, ON
THE HUMAN HEART A STONE--
"THEY ARE NEITHER
MAN NOR WOMAN--
THEY ARE NEITHER
BRUTE NOR HUMAN,
"THEY ARE
GHOULS:--
FWOOOSH!
HAHAHAHAHAHA
HAHAHAHAHAHAH
HA!

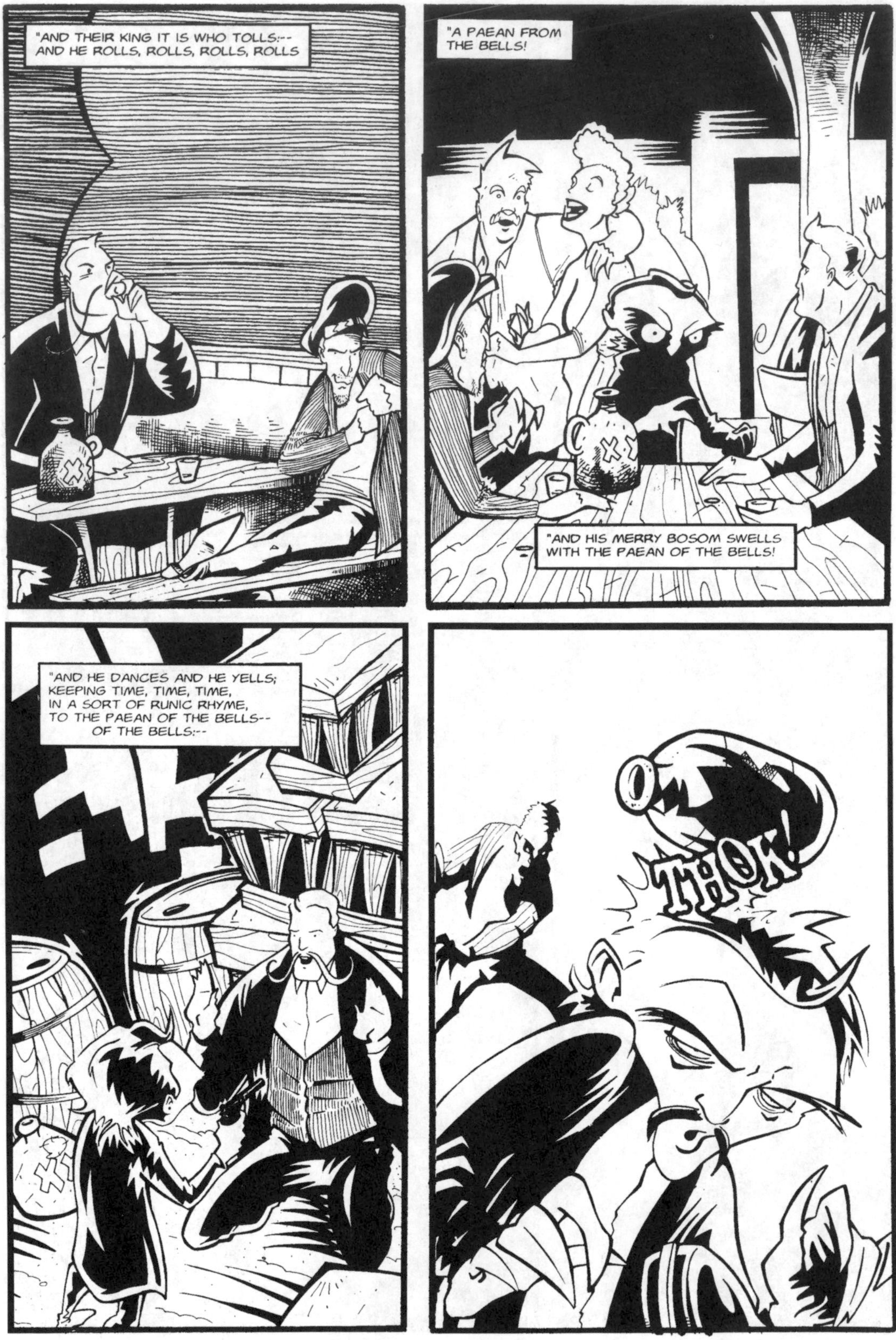
"AND THEIR KING IT IS WHO TOLLS:--
AND HE ROLLS, ROLLS, ROLLS, ROLLS
"A PAEAN FROM THE BELLS!
"AND HIS MERRY BOSOM SWELLS WITH THE PAEAN OF THE BELLS!
"AND HE DANCES AND HE YELLS; KEEPING TIME, TIME, TIME, IN A SORT OF RUNIC RHYME, TO THE PAEAN OF THE BELLS-- OF THE BELLS:--
THOK!

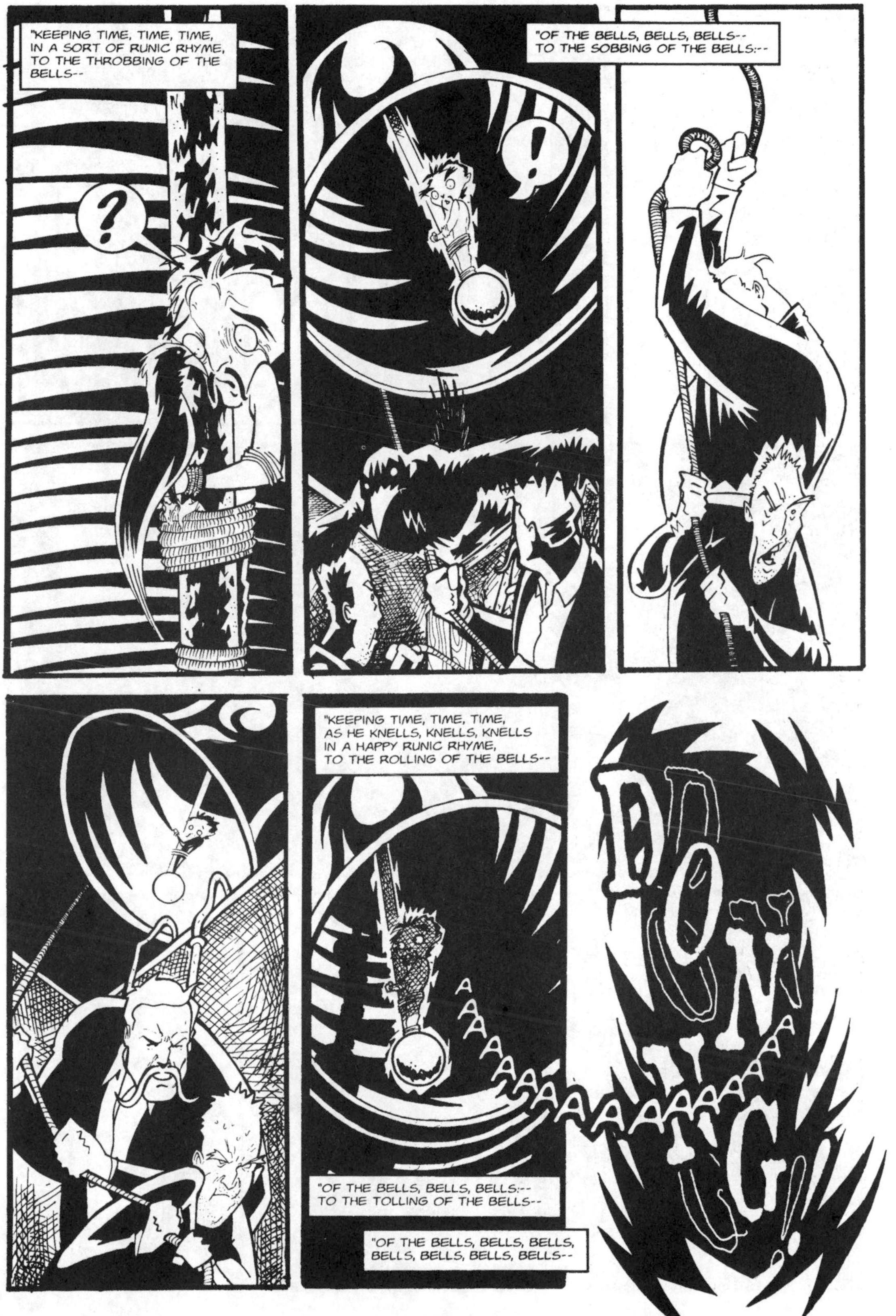
"KEEPING TIME, TIME, TIME,
IN A SORT OF RUNIC RHYME,
TO THE THROBBING OF THE BELLS--
?
!
"OF THE BELLS, BELLS, BELLS--
TO THE SOBBING OF THE BELLS:--
"KEEPING TIME, TIME, TIME,
AS HE KNELLS, KNELLS, KNELLS
IN A HAPPY RUNIC RHYME,
TO THE ROLLING OF THE BELLS--
DONG!!
AAAAAAAAAAAAAAAAAA
"OF THE BELLS, BELLS, BELLS:--
TO THE TOLLING OF THE BELLS--
"OF THE BELLS, BELLS, BELLS,
BELLS, BELLS, BELLS, BELLS--

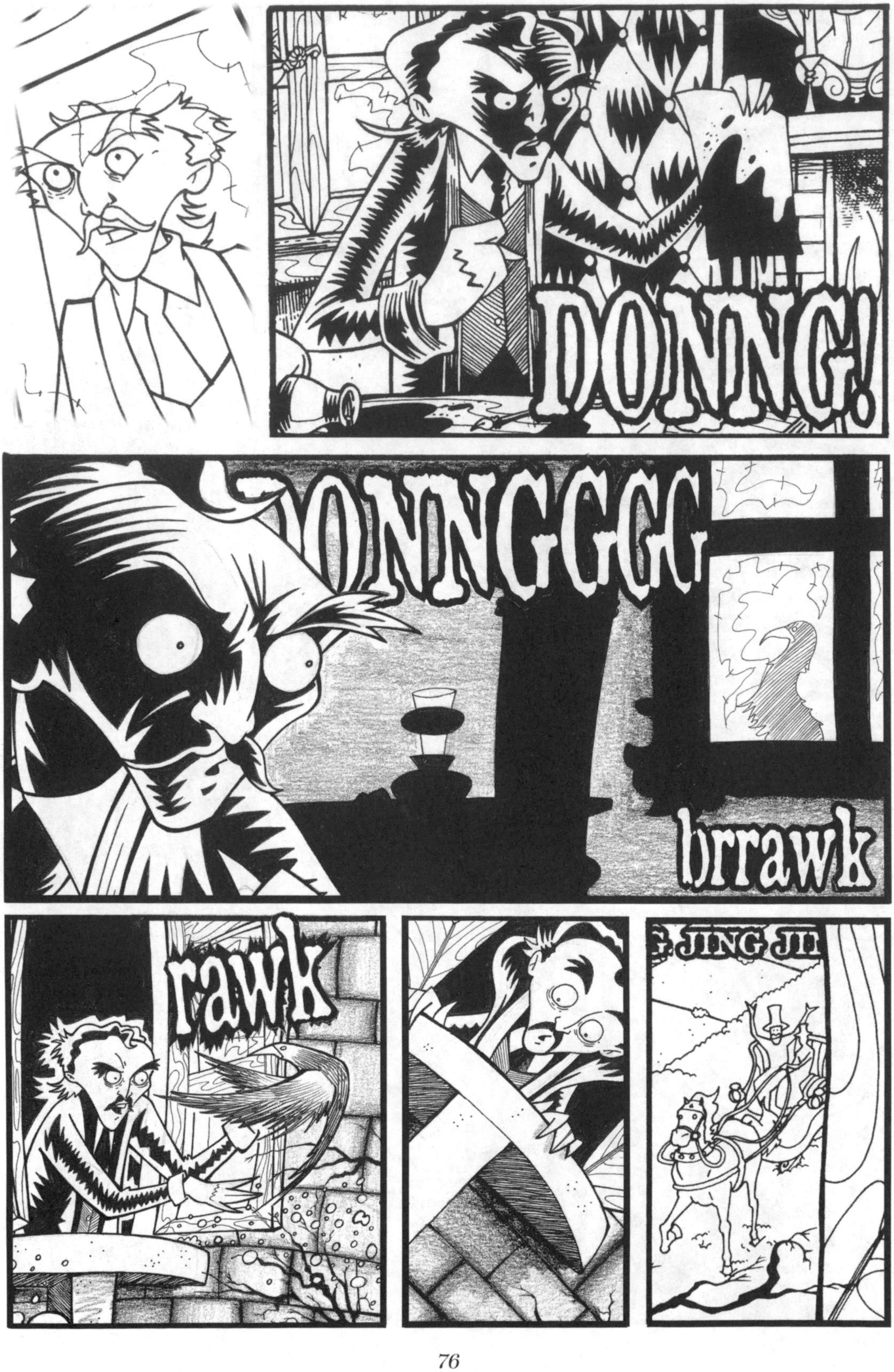
DONNG!
DONNGGG
brrawk
rawk
G JING JI

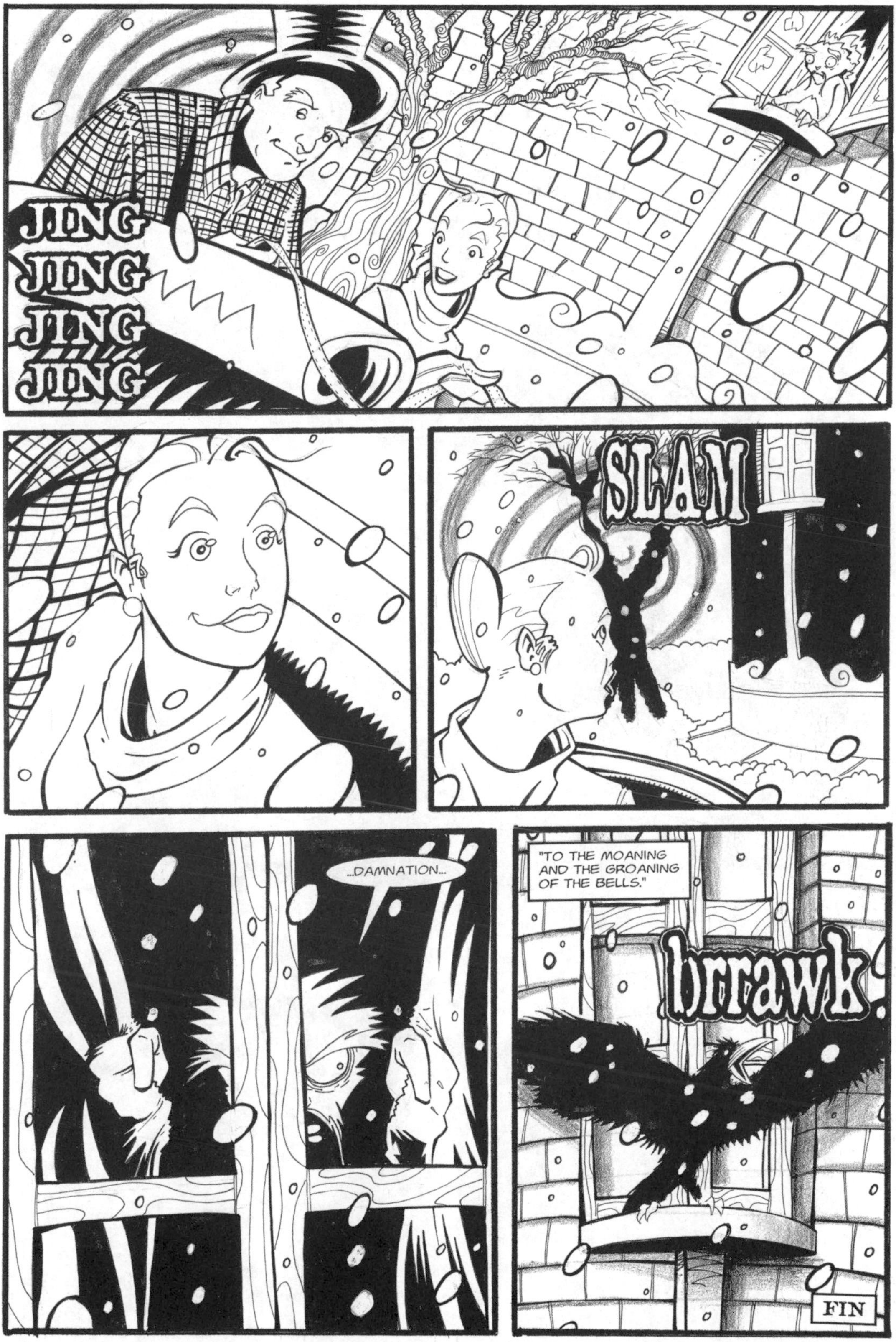
JING
JING
JING
JING
SLAM
...DAMNATION...
"TO THE MOANING AND THE GROANING OF THE BELLS."
brrawk
FIN

Spirits of the Dead

by EDGAR ALLAN POE

illustrated by ANDY EWEN

Thy soul shall find itself alone
'Mid dark thoughts of the grey tomb-stone;
Not one, of all the crowd, to pry
Into thine hour of secrecy.

Be silent in that solitude,
Which is not loneliness—for then
The spirits of the dead who stood
In life before thee are again
In death around thee, and their will
Shall then overshadow thee: be still.

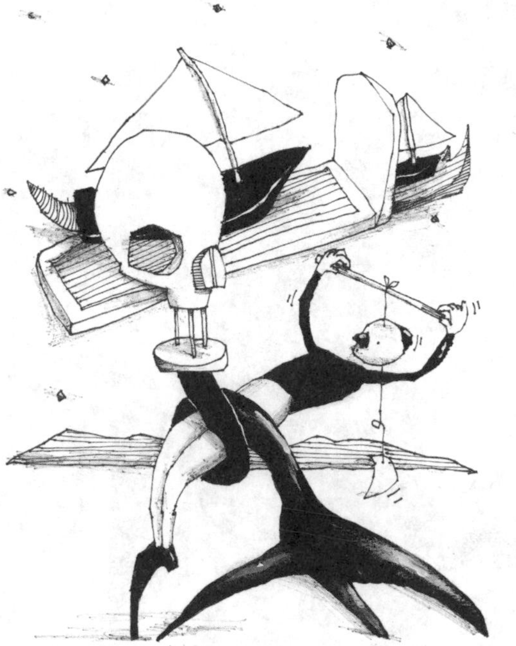

For the night, though clear, shall frown,
And the stars shall look not down
From their high thrones in the Heaven
With light like hope to mortals given,
But their red orbs, without beam,
To thy weariness shall seem
As a burning and a fever
Which would cling to thee for ever.

Now are thoughts thou shalt not banish,
Now are visions ne'er to vanish;
From thy spirit shall they pass
No more, like dew-drop from the grass.

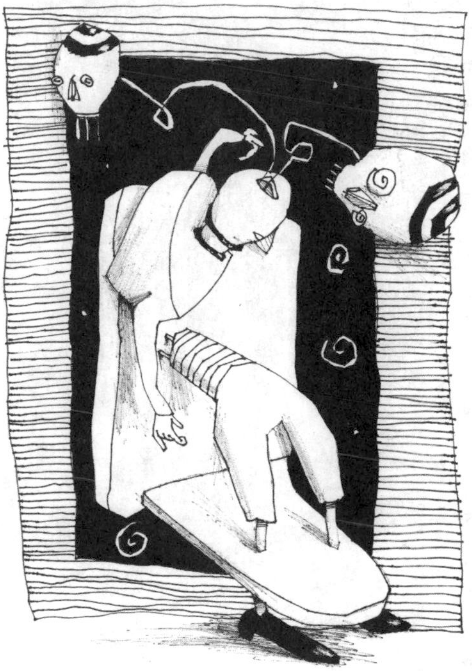

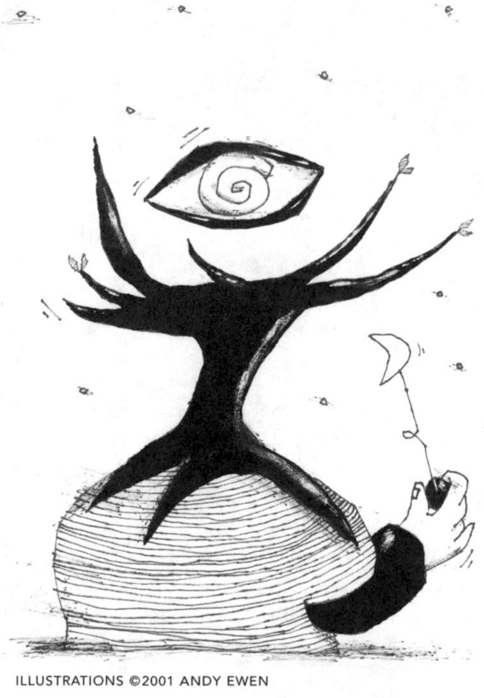

The breeze, the breath of God, is still,
And the mist upon the hill
Shadowy, shadowy, yet unbroken,
Is a symbol and a token.
How it hangs upon the trees,
A mystery of mysteries!

The haunted Palace

illustrated by John Coulthart

In the greenest of our valleys
By good angels tenanted,
Once a fair and stately palace—
Radiant palace—reared its head.
In the monarch Thought's
          dominion—
It stood there!
Never seraph spread a pinion
Over fabric half so fair!

Banners yellow, glorious, golden,
On its roof did float and flow,
(This—all this—was in the olden
          Time long ago,)
And every gentle air that dallied,
In that sweet day,
Along the ramparts plumed
          and pallid,
A wingèd odor went away.

Wanderers in that happy valley,
Through two luminous windows, saw
Spirits moving musically,
To a lute's well-tunèd law,
Round about a throne where, sitting
(Porphyrogene!)
In state his glory well-befitting,
The ruler of the realm was seen.

And all with pearl and ruby glowing
Was the fair palace-door,
Through which came flowing,
flowing, flowing,
And sparkling evermore,
A troop of Echoes, whose sweet duty
Was but to sing,
In voices of surpassing beauty,
The wit and wisdom of their king.

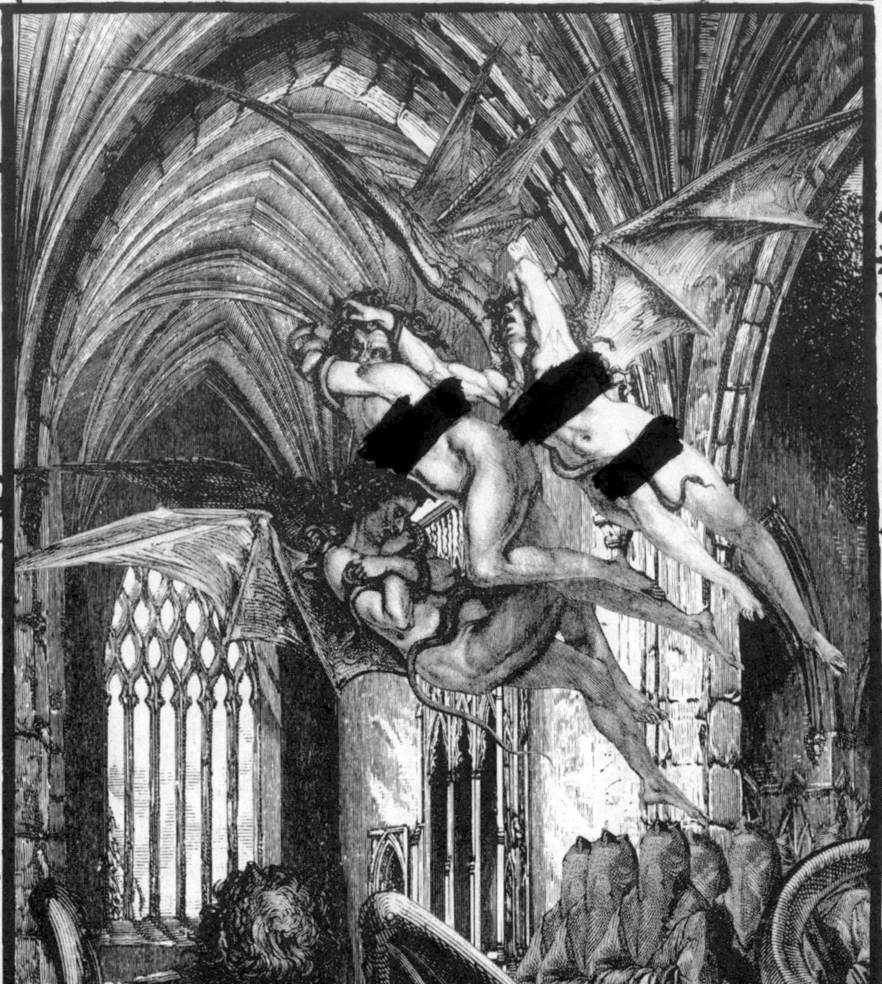

But evil things, in robes of sorrow,
Assailed the monarch's high estate.
(Ah, let us mourn!–
for never morrow
Shall dawn upon him desolate!)
And round about his home the glory
That blushed and bloomed,
Is but a dim-remembered story
Of the old time entombed.

And travellers, now,
within that valley,
Through the red-litten windows see
Vast forms, that move fantastically
To a discordant melody,
While, like a ghastly rapid river,
Through the pale door
A hideous throng rush out forever
And laugh–but smile no more.

THE FALL OF THE HOUSE OF USHER

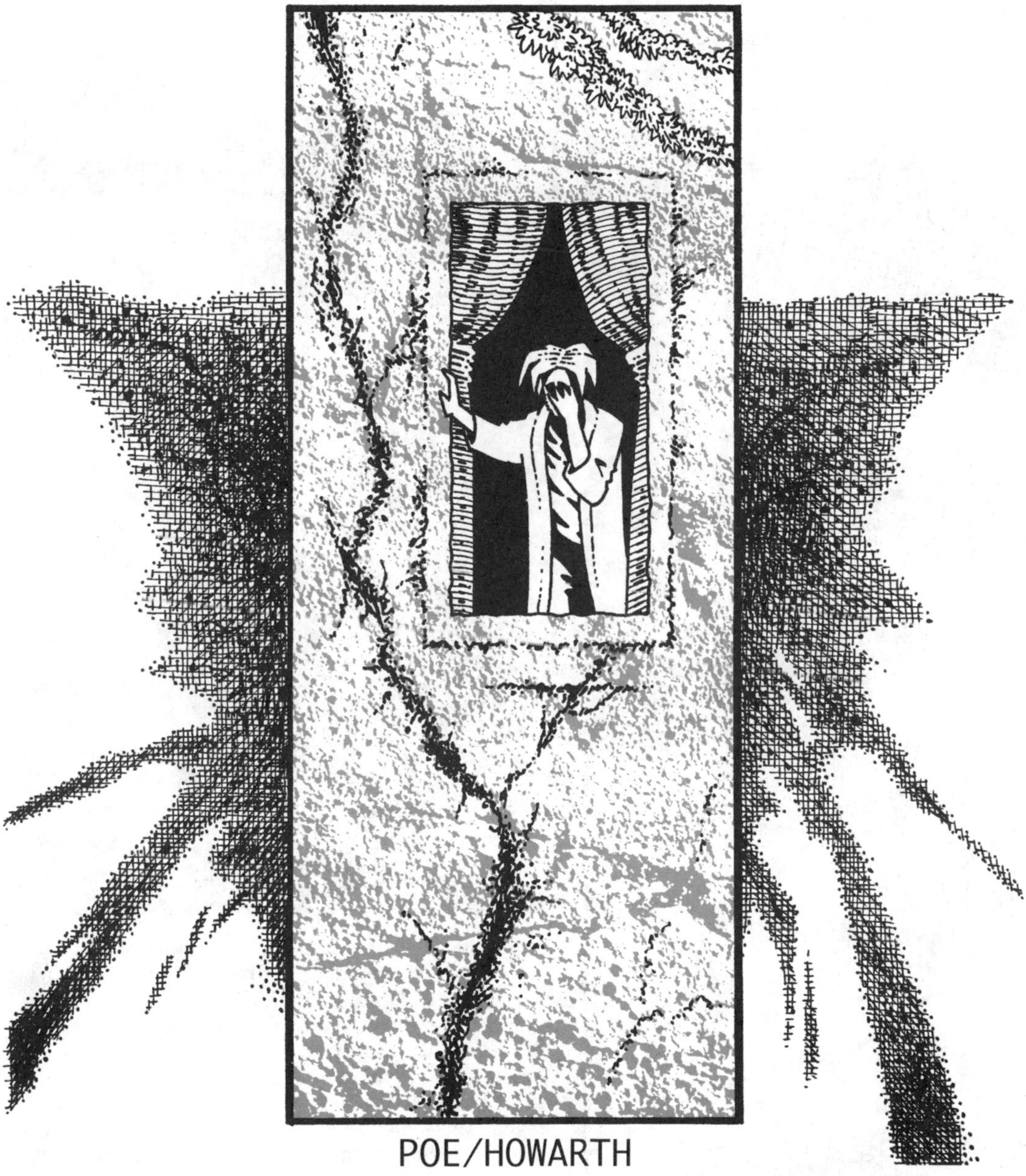

POE/HOWARTH

During the whole of a dark and soundless day in the autumn of the year, I had been passing alone, on horseback, through a singularly dreary tract of country; and at length found myself within view of the melancholy House of Usher. With the first glimpse of the building, a sense of insufferable gloom pervaded my spirit.

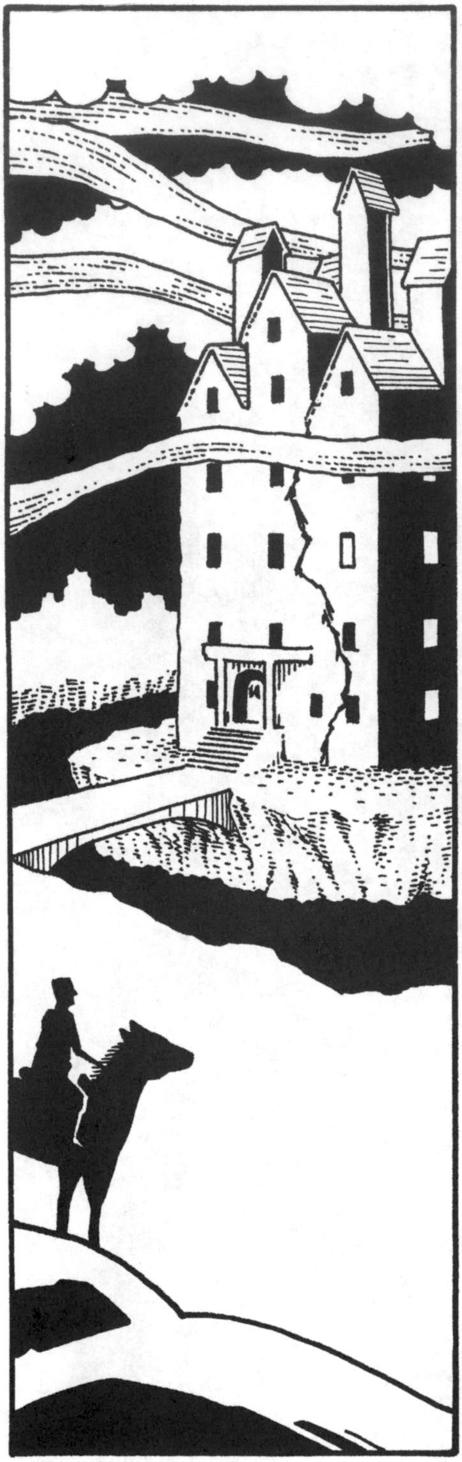

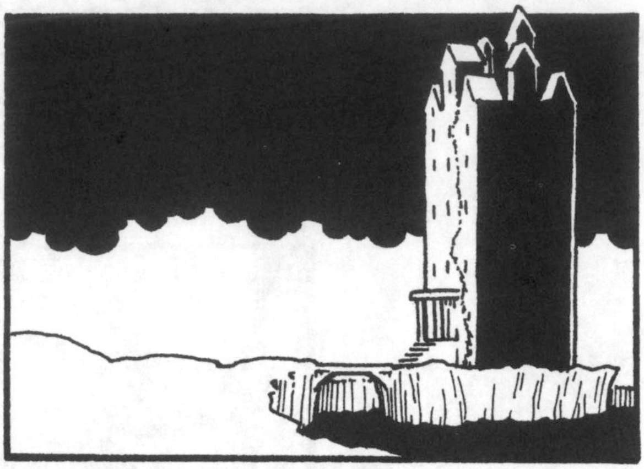

Nevertheless, in this mansion of gloom I now proposed to myself a sojourn of some weeks.

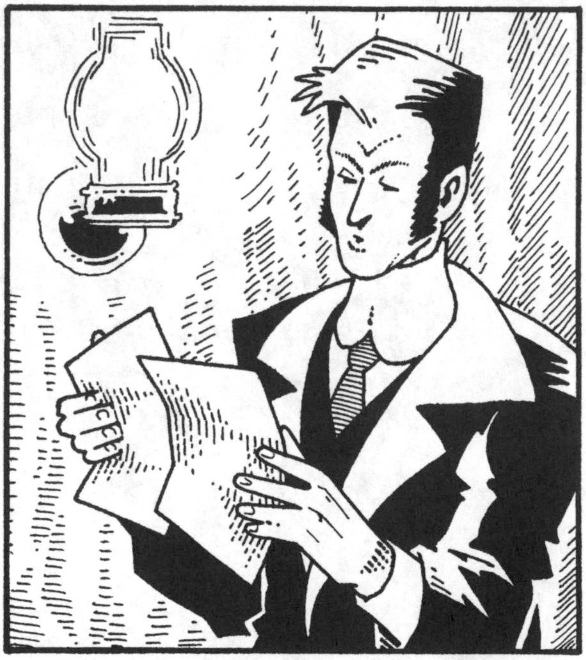

Its proprietor, Roderick Usher, had been one of my companions in boyhood; but many years had elapsed since our last meeting. A letter, however, had lately reached me which, in its wildly importunate nature, had admitted of no other than a personal reply. The writer spoke of acute bodily illness–of a mental disorder which oppressed him–and of an earnest desire to see me, as his best, and indeed his only personal friend. I accordingly obeyed forthwith what I considered a very singular summons.

Although, as boys, we had been intimate associates, I really knew little of my friend. His reserve had been always excessive and habitual.

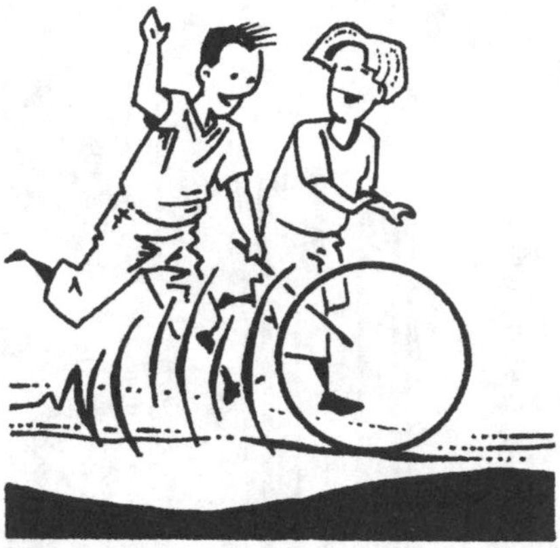

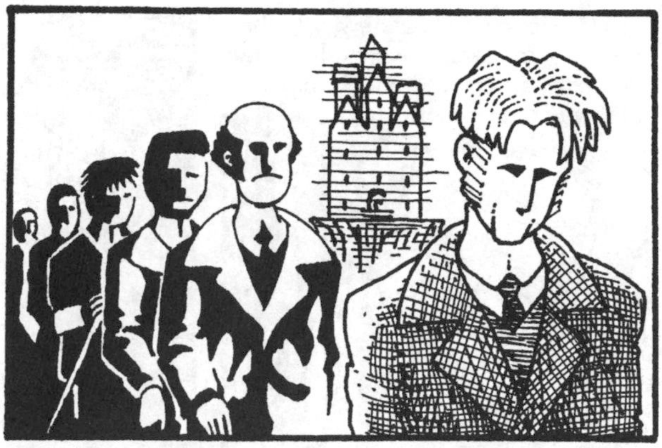

I was aware, however, of the very remarkable fact that the entire Usher family lay in the direct line of descent, and had always so lain. The undeviating transmission, from sire to son, of the patrimony with the name had, at length, merged the two in the quaint appellation of the "House of Usher"– which seemed to include both the family and the mansion.

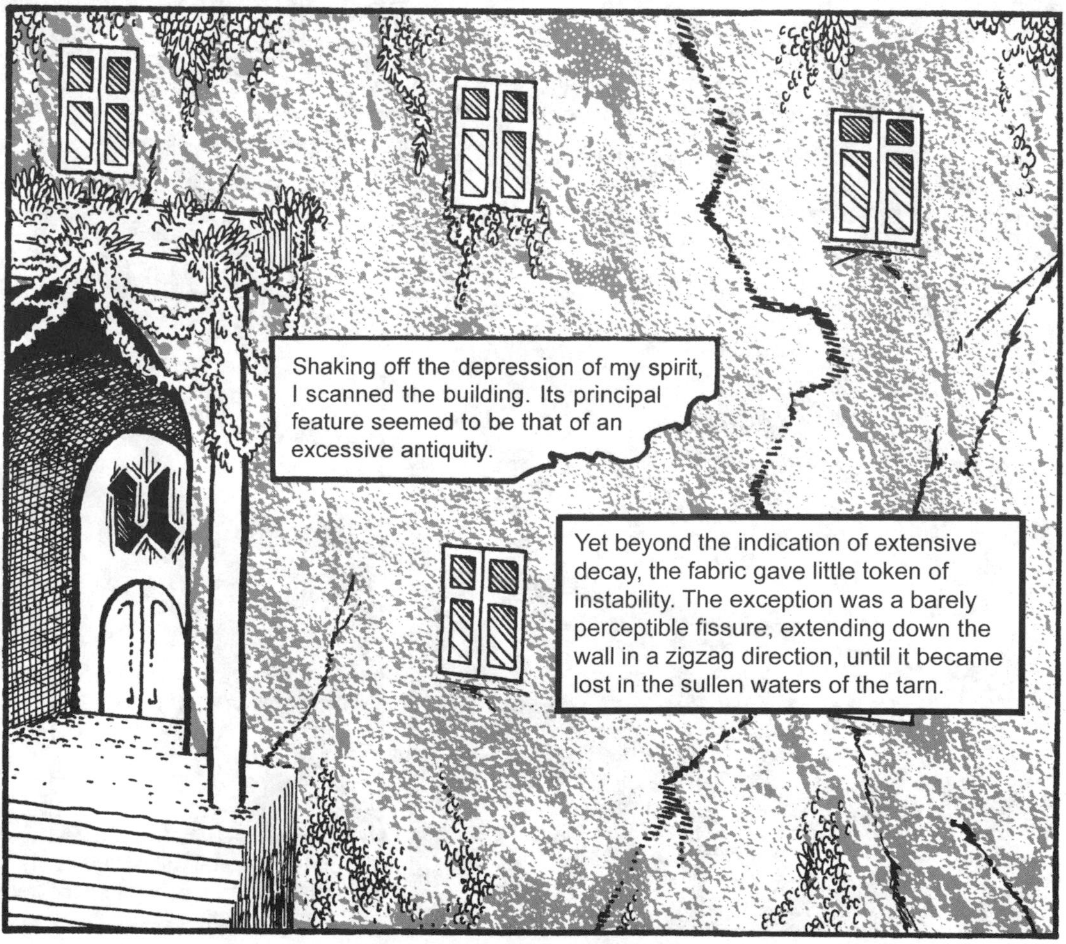
Shaking off the depression of my spirit, I scanned the building. Its principal feature seemed to be that of an excessive antiquity.
Yet beyond the indication of extensive decay, the fabric gave little token of instability. The exception was a barely perceptible fissure, extending down the wall in a zigzag direction, until it became lost in the sullen waters of the tarn.

I rode over a short causeway to the house. A servant in waiting took my horse, and I entered the Gothic archway of the hall.

A valet thence conducted me, in silence, through many dark and intricate passages to the studio of his master.

Much that I encountered on the way contributed to heighten the vague sentiments of which I have already spoken.

On one of the staircases, I met the physician of the family. He accosted me with trepidation and passed on.

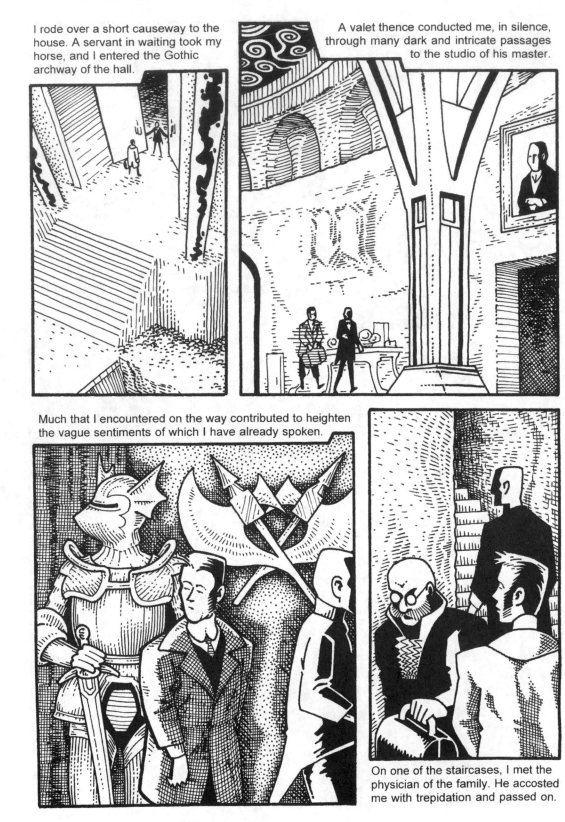

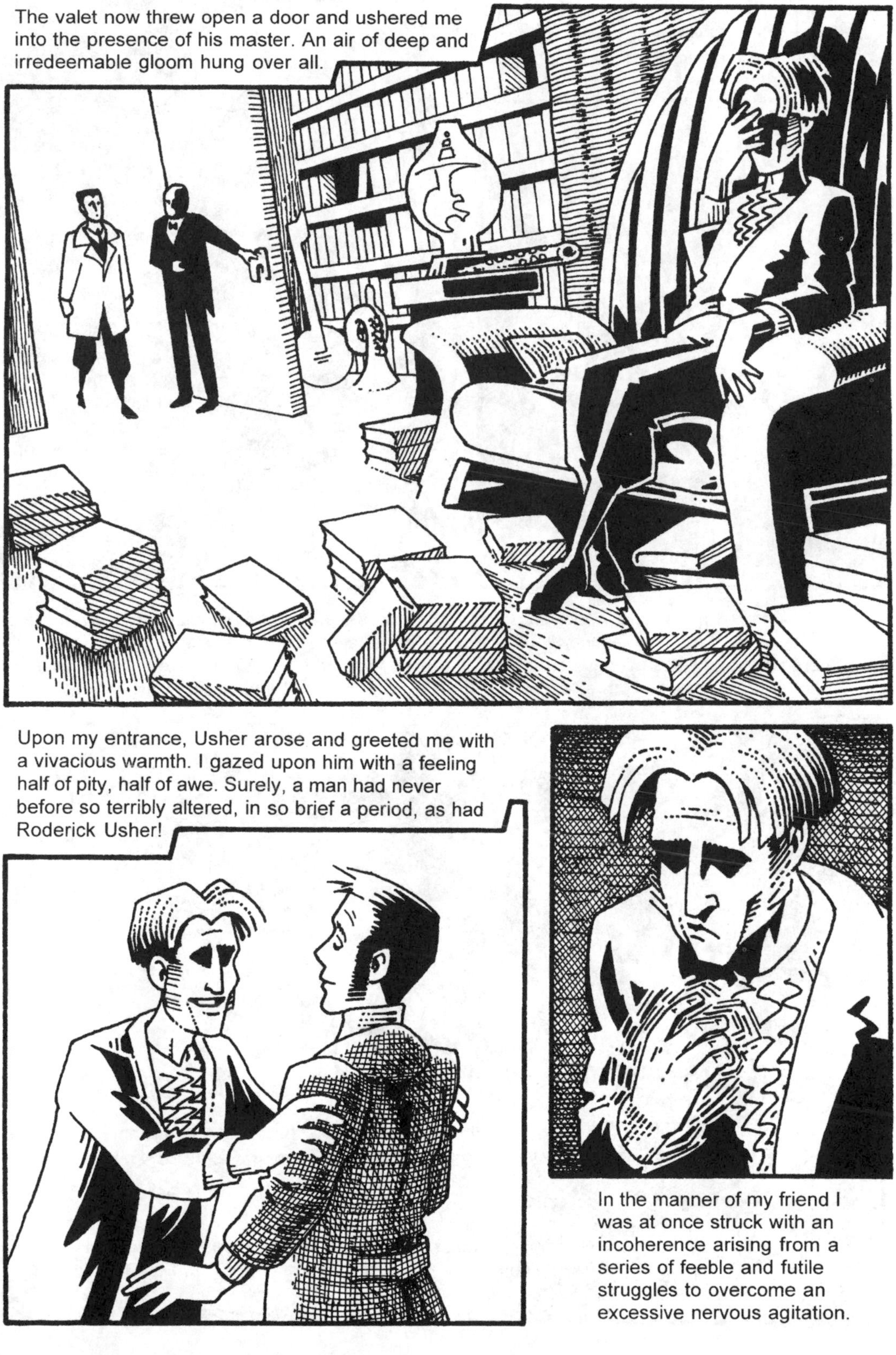
The valet now threw open a door and ushered me into the presence of his master. An air of deep and irredeemable gloom hung over all.
Upon my entrance, Usher arose and greeted me with a vivacious warmth. I gazed upon him with a feeling half of pity, half of awe. Surely, a man had never before so terribly altered, in so brief a period, as had Roderick Usher!
In the manner of my friend I was at once struck with an incoherence arising from a series of feeble and futile struggles to overcome an excessive nervous agitation.

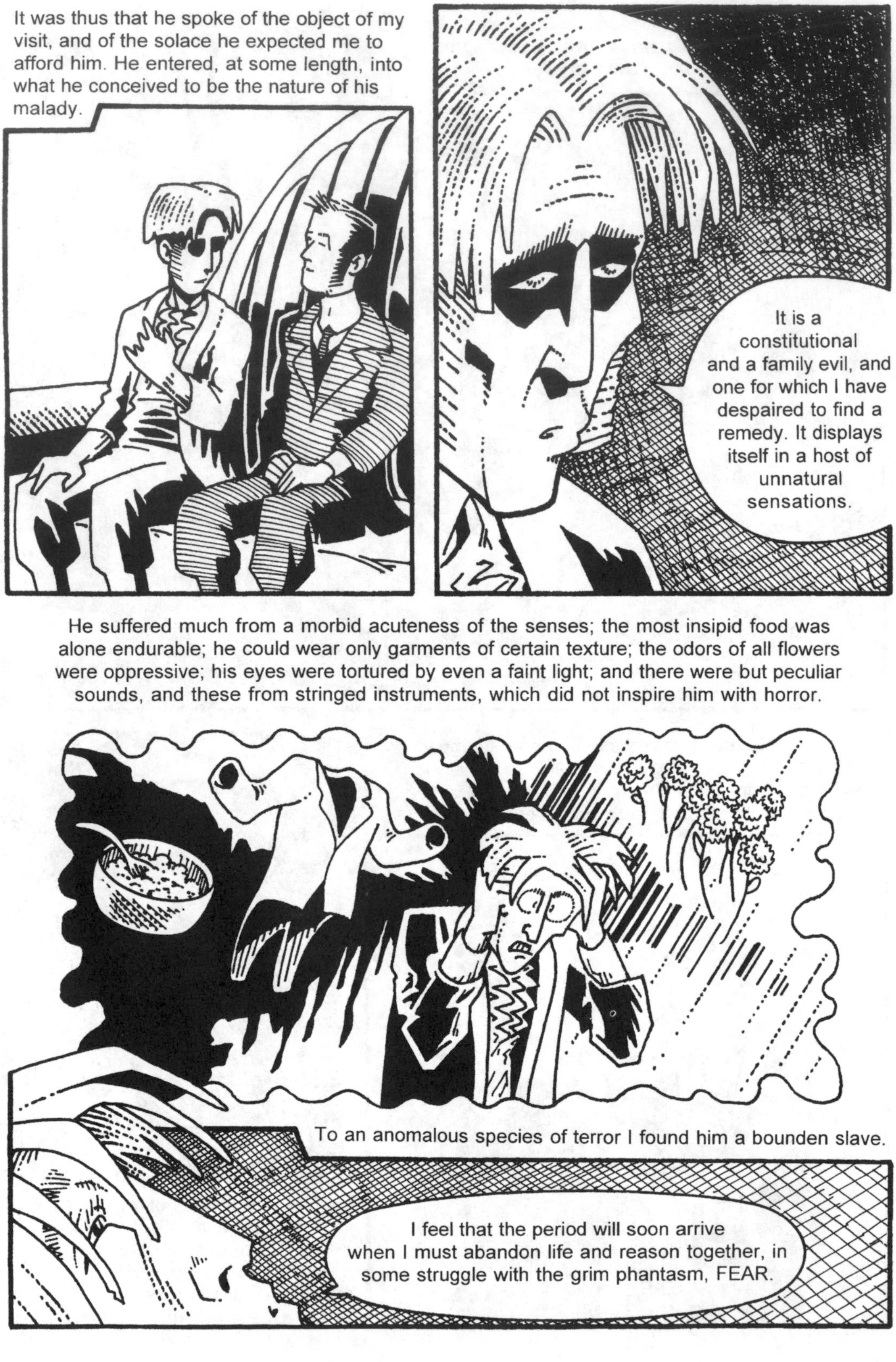
It was thus that he spoke of the object of my visit, and of the solace he expected me to afford him. He entered, at some length, into what he conceived to be the nature of his malady.
It is a constitutional and a family evil, and one for which I have despaired to find a remedy. It displays itself in a host of unnatural sensations.
He suffered much from a morbid acuteness of the senses; the most insipid food was alone endurable; he could wear only garments of certain texture; the odors of all flowers were oppressive; his eyes were tortured by even a faint light; and there were but peculiar sounds, and these from stringed instruments, which did not inspire him with horror.
To an anomalous species of terror I found him a bounden slave.
I feel that the period will soon arrive when I must abandon life and reason together, in some struggle with the grim phantasm, FEAR.

He admitted, although with hesitation, that much of the peculiar gloom which thus afflicted him could be traced to a far more palpable origin—to the severe and long-continued illness of a beloved sister—his sole companion for long years, and his last relative on earth.

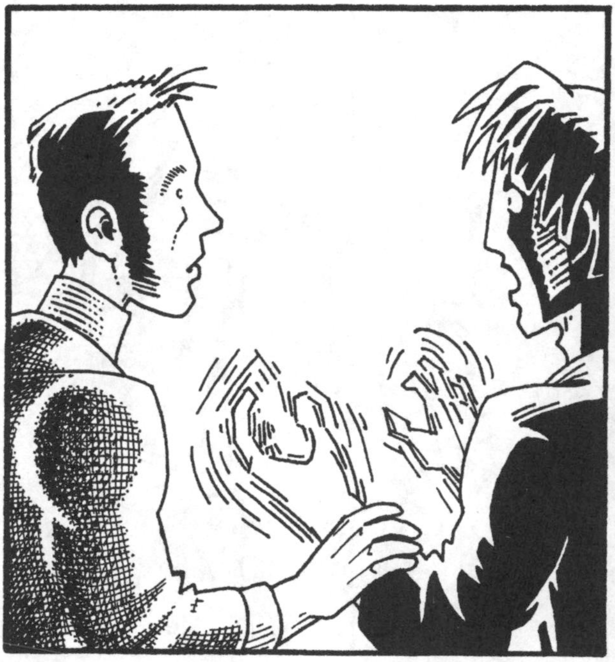

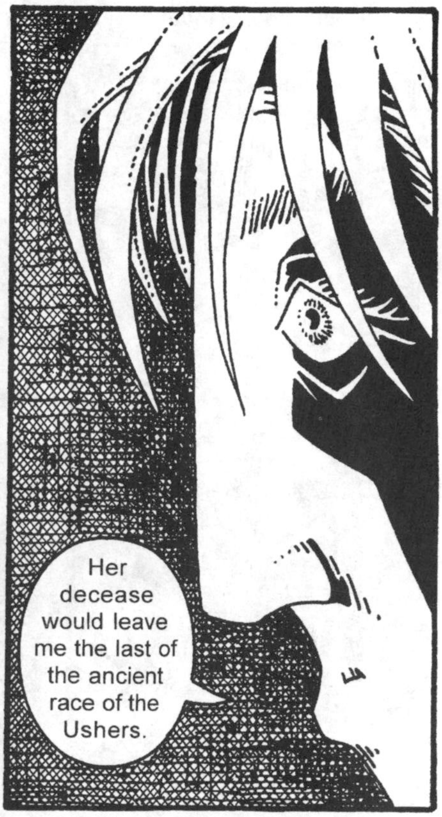
Her decease would leave me the last of the ancient race of the Ushers.

While he spoke, the lady Madeline passed slowly through the apartment.
I regarded her with an astonishment not unmingled with dread.

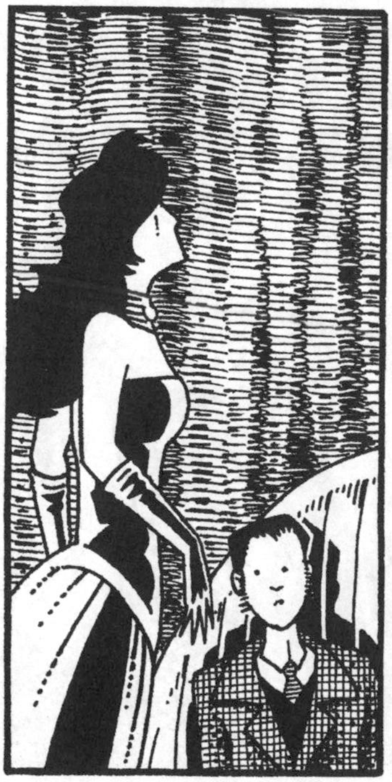

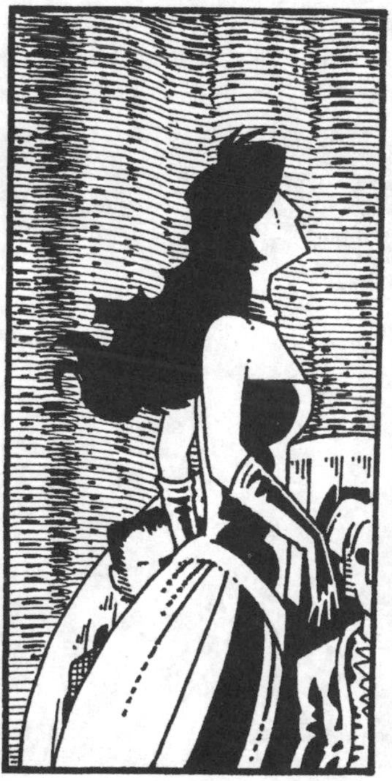

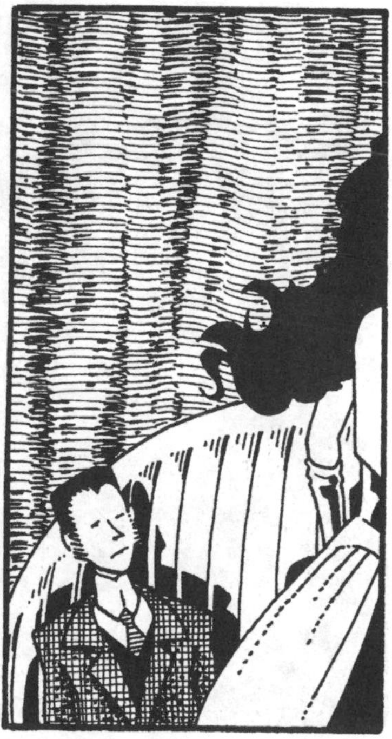

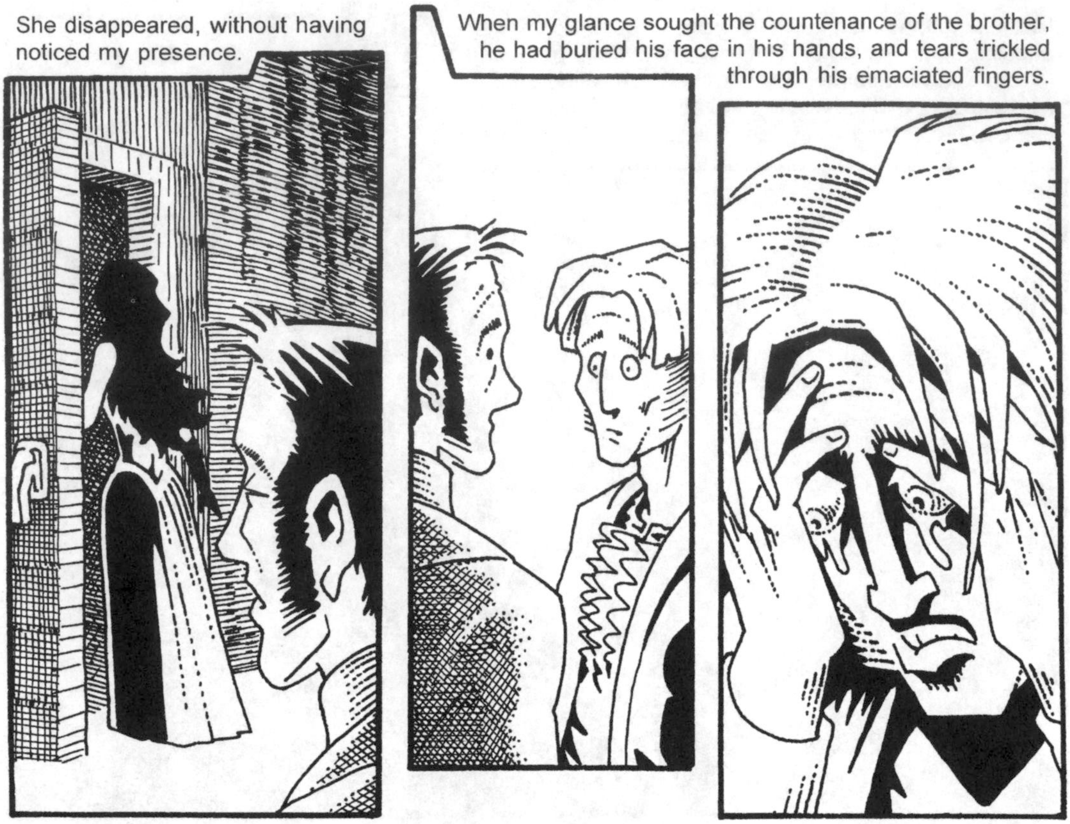
She disappeared, without having noticed my presence.
When my glance sought the countenance of the brother, he had buried his face in his hands, and tears trickled through his emaciated fingers.

The disease of the lady Madeline had long baffled the skill of her physicians. A settled apathy, a gradual wasting away of the person, and frequent although transient affections of a cataleptical character were the unusual diagnosis. Hitherto she had steadily borne up against the pressure of her malady; but, on the evening of my arrival at the house, she succumbed (as her brother told me with inexpressible agitation) to the power of the destroyer; and I learned that the glimpse I had obtained of her person would thus probably be the last I should obtain.

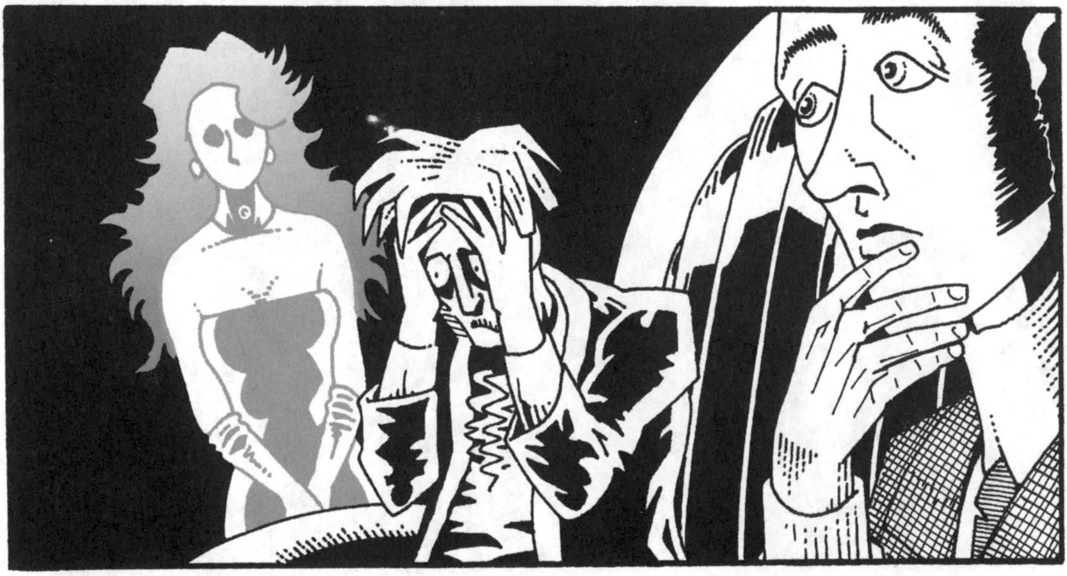

For several days ensuing, her name was unmentioned by either Usher or myself; and during this period I was busied in earnest endeavors to alleviate the melancholy of my friend.

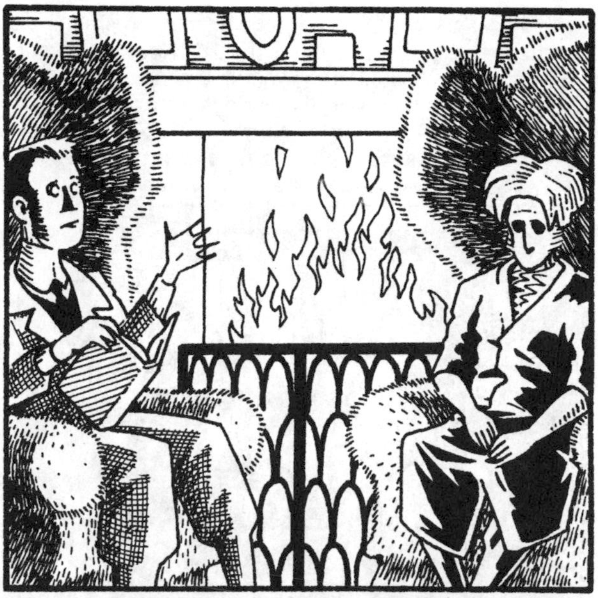

We painted and read together; or I listened, as if in a dream, to the wild improvisations of his guitar. And thus, as a closer intimacy admitted me more unreservedly into the recesses of his spirit, the more bitterly did I perceive the futility of all attempt at cheering a mind from which darkness, as if an inherent positive quality, poured forth upon all objects of the moral and physical universe.

I shall ever bear a memory of the solemn hours I thus spent alone with the master of the House of Usher.

His long, improvised dirges will ring forever in my ears. Among other things, I hold painfully in mind a particular piece entitled "The Haunted Palace." I was, perhaps, the more forcibly impressed with it because, in the undercurrent of its meaning, I fancied that I perceived for the first time a full consciousness on the part of Usher of the tottering of his lofty reason upon her throne.

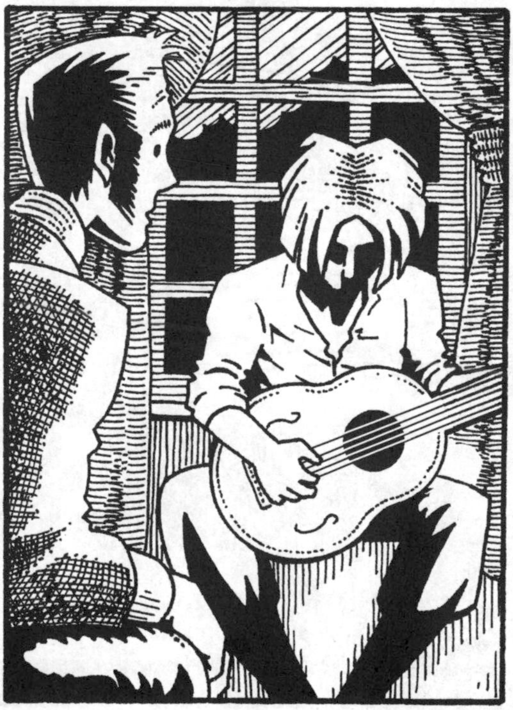

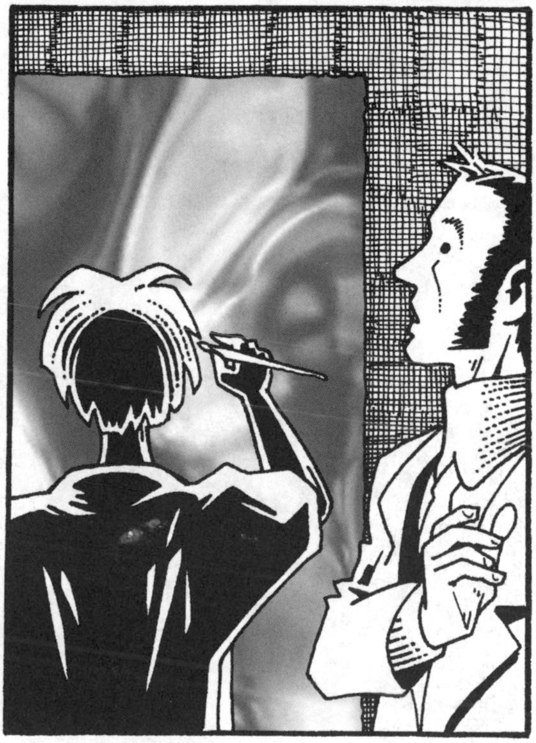

The paintings over which his elaborate fancy brooded grew, touch by touch, into vaguenesses at which I shuddered thrillingly.

There arose out of the abstractions which the hypochondriac contrived to throw upon his canvas, an intensity of intolerable awe.

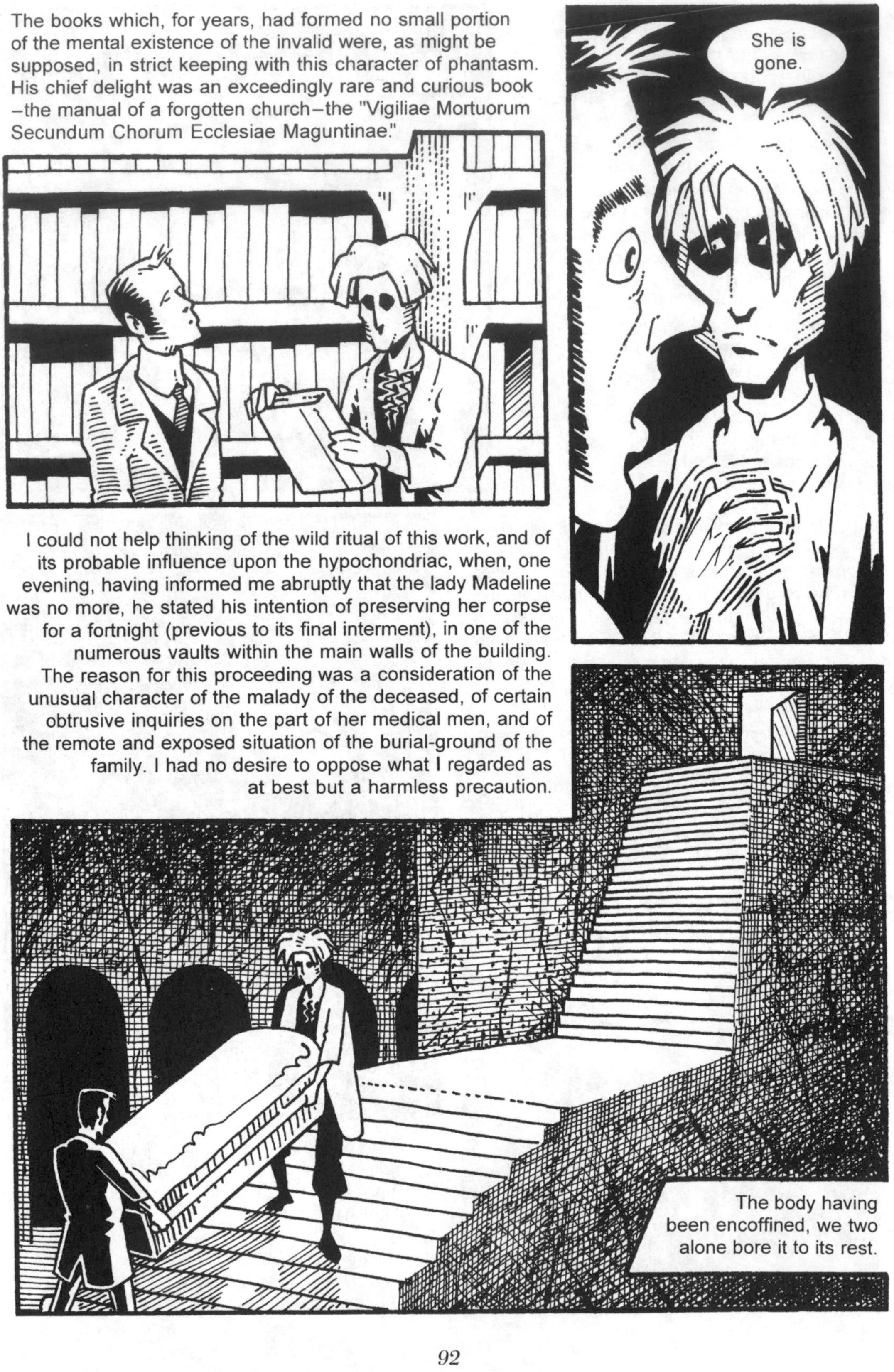
The books which, for years, had formed no small portion of the mental existence of the invalid were, as might be supposed, in strict keeping with this character of phantasm. His chief delight was an exceedingly rare and curious book –the manual of a forgotten church–the "Vigiliae Mortuorum Secundum Chorum Ecclesiae Maguntinae."
She is gone.
I could not help thinking of the wild ritual of this work, and of its probable influence upon the hypochondriac, when, one evening, having informed me abruptly that the lady Madeline was no more, he stated his intention of preserving her corpse for a fortnight (previous to its final interment), in one of the numerous vaults within the main walls of the building. The reason for this proceeding was a consideration of the unusual character of the malady of the deceased, of certain obtrusive inquiries on the part of her medical men, and of the remote and exposed situation of the burial-ground of the family. I had no desire to oppose what I regarded as at best but a harmless precaution.
The body having been encoffined, we two alone bore it to its rest.

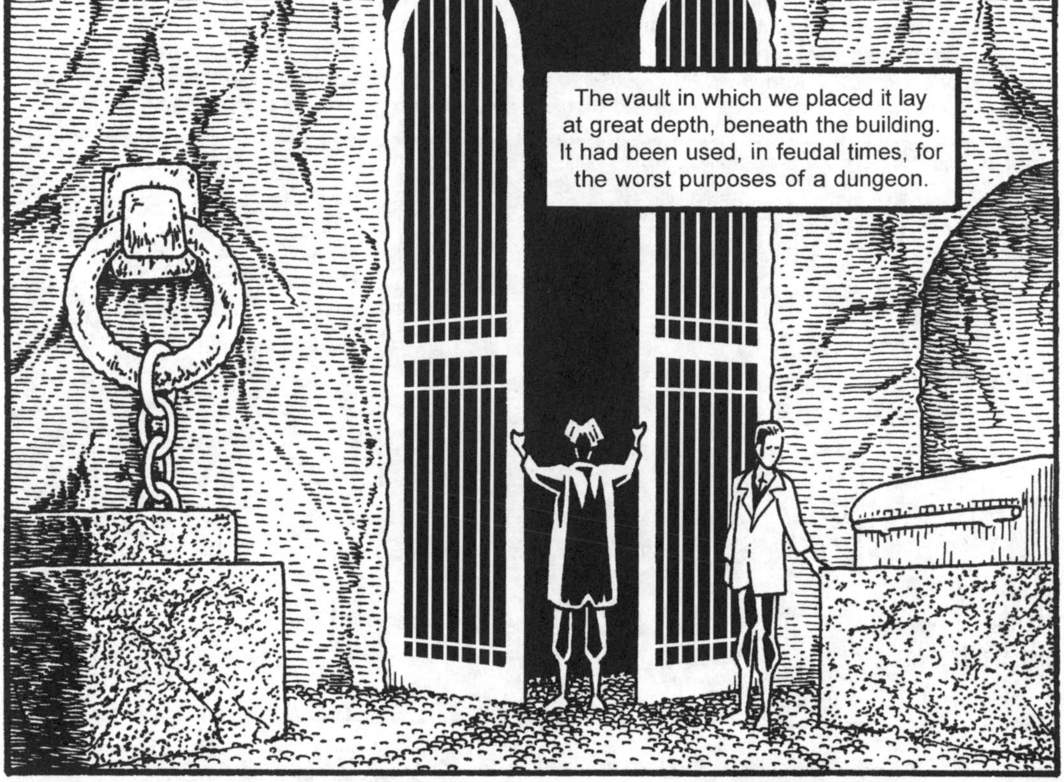
The vault in which we placed it lay at great depth, beneath the building. It had been used, in feudal times, for the worst purposes of a dungeon.

Having deposited our mournful burden within this region of horror, we partially turned aside the lid of the coffin, and looked upon the face of the tenant. A striking similitude between the brother and sister arrested my attention; and Usher, divining my thoughts, murmured that the deceased and himself had been twins, and that sympathies of a scarcely intelligible nature had always existed between them.

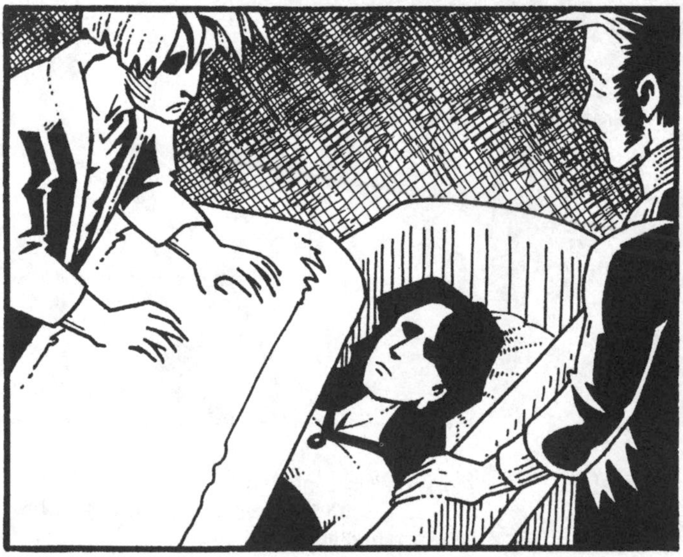

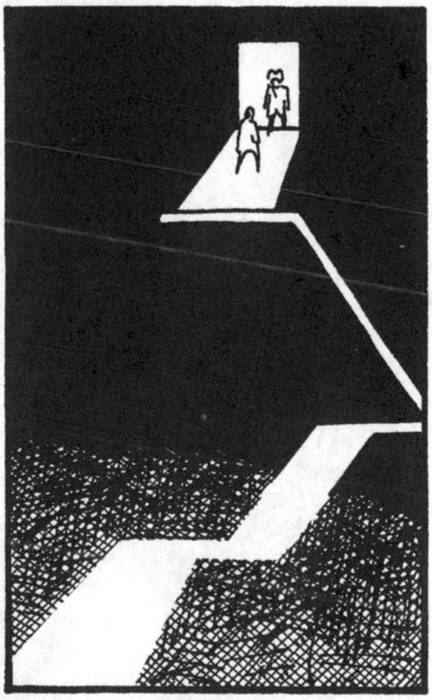

We replaced and screwed down the lid, and, having secured the door of iron, made our way into the scarcely less gloomy apartments of the upper portion of the house.

And now, some days of bitter grief having elapsed, my friend's ordinary manner had vanished. He roamed from chamber to chamber with hurried and objectless step. The pallor of his countenance had assumed, if possible, a more ghastly hue, and the luminousness of his eye had utterly gone out. There were times, indeed, when I thought his unceasingly agitated mind was laboring with some oppressive secret, to divulge which he struggled for the necessary courage.

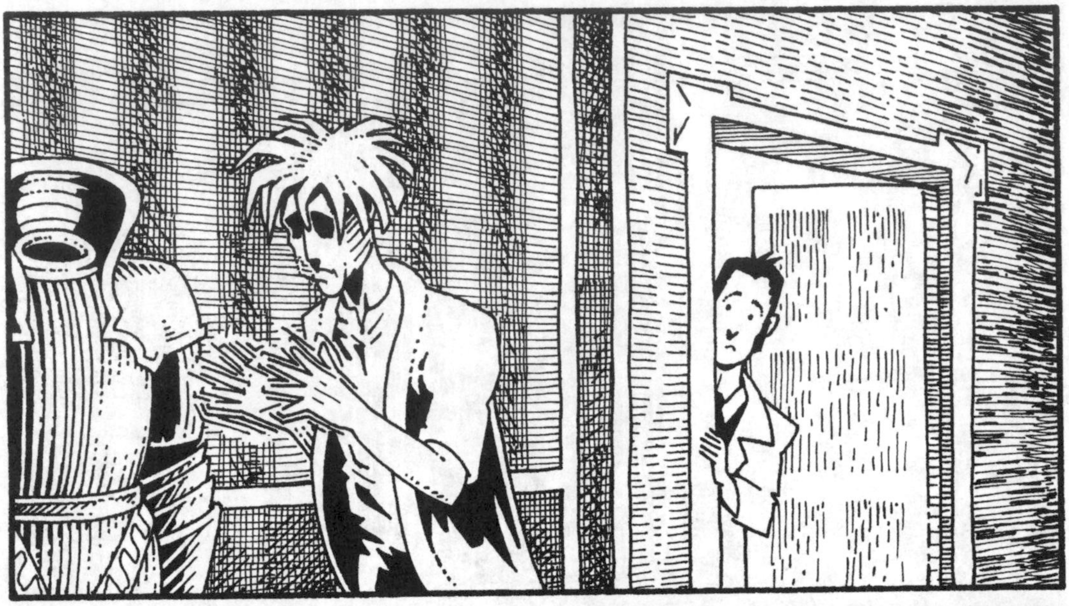

At times, I beheld him gazing upon vacancy for long hours, in an attitude of the profoundest attention, as if listening to some imaginary sound.

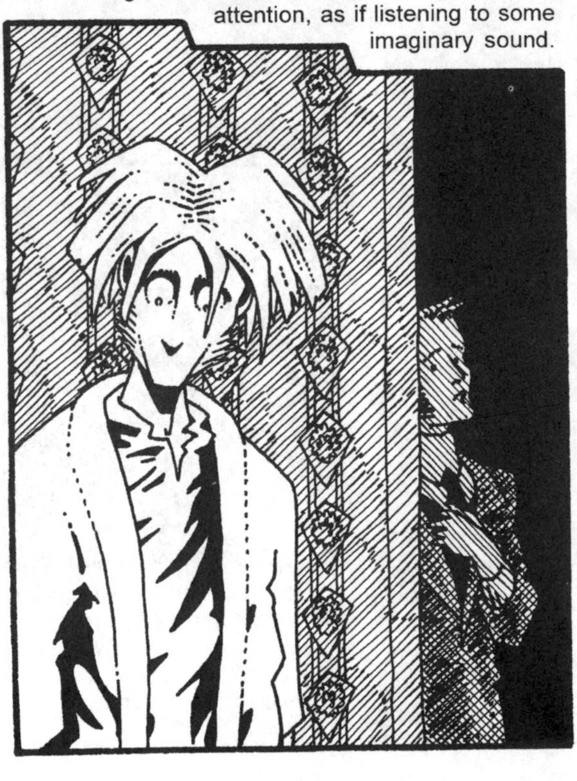

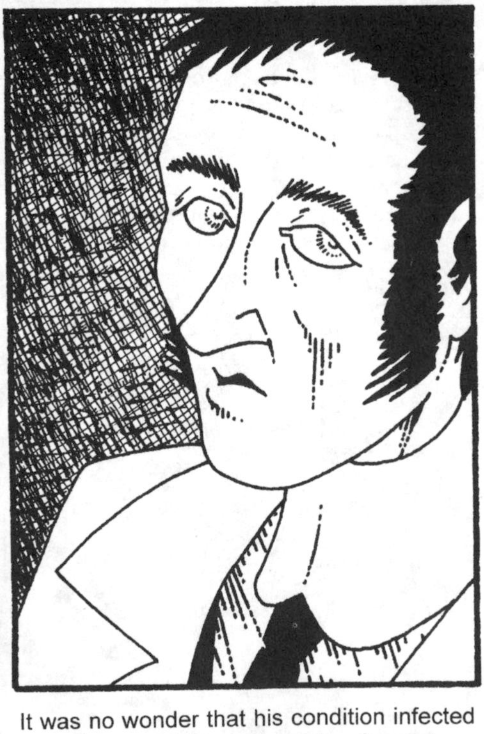

It was no wonder that his condition infected me. I felt creeping upon me, by slow yet certain degrees, the wild influences of his own fantastic superstitions.

It was upon retiring to bed late in the night of the seventh or eighth day after the placing of the lady Madeline within the dungeon, that sleep came not near my couch. I struggled to reason off the nervousness which had dominion over me. I endeavored to believe that much, if not all of what I felt, was due to the bewildering influence of the gloomy furniture of the room—of the dark and tattered draperies, which, tortured into motion by the breath of a rising tempest, swayed fitfully upon the walls. I listened earnestly, within the intense darkness of the chamber, to low and indefinite sounds which came, through the pauses of the storm, at long intervals, I knew not whence.

Overpowered by an intense sentiment of horror, I threw on my clothes and endeavored to arouse myself by pacing to and fro through the apartment.

I had taken but few turns in this manner when Usher rapped at my door and entered, bearing a lamp. His countenance was, as usual, cadaverously wan—but, moreover, there was a restrained hysteria in his whole demeanor which appalled me.

95

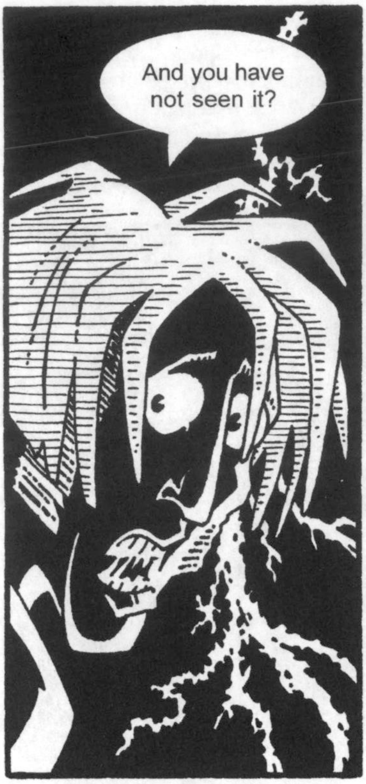
And you have not seen it?

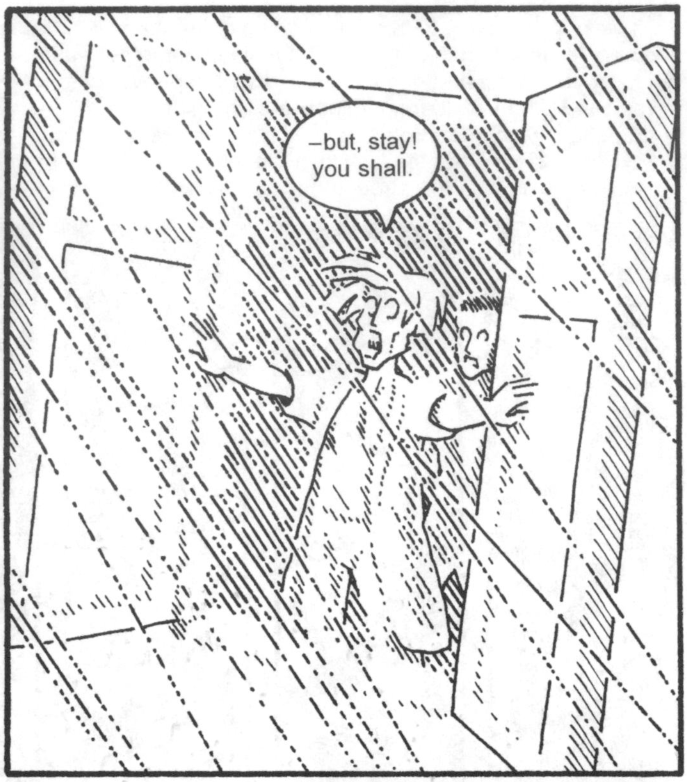
–but, stay! you shall.

The impetuous fury of the entering gust nearly lifted us from our feet. It was, indeed, a tempestuous night, wildly singular in its terror and its beauty. There were frequent and violent alterations in the direction of the wind; and the clouds flew with life-like velocity.

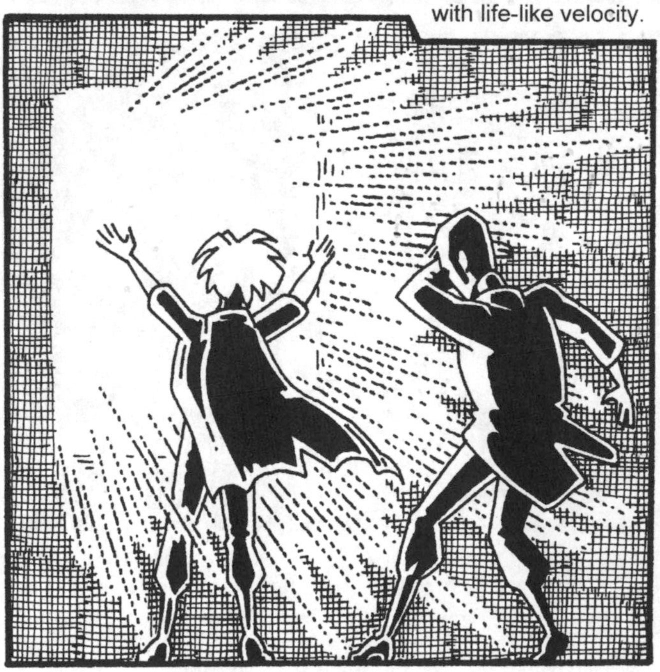

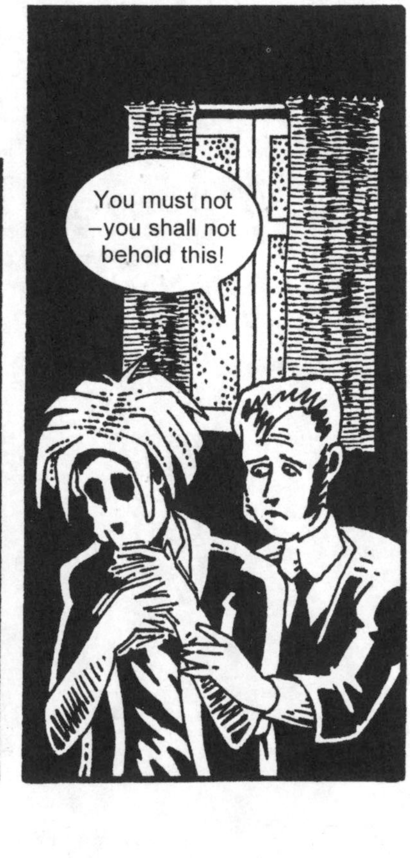
You must not –you shall not behold this!

Here is a romance. I will read, and you shall listen; and so we will pass away this terrible night together.

The antique volume which I had taken up was the "Mad Trist" of Sir Launcelot Canning. It was the only book immediately at hand; and I indulged a vague hope that the excitement which now agitated the hypochondriac, might find relief even in the extremeness of the folly which I should read.

I had arrived at that well-known portion of the story where Ethelred, the hero, having sought in vain for peaceable admission into the dwelling of the hermit, proceeds to make an entrance by force:

"And Ethelred uplifted his mace and, with blows, tore all asunder the plankings of the door, and the noise reverberated throughout the forest."

At the termination of this sentence I started, and for a moment, paused; for it appeared to me (although I at once concluded that my excited fancy had deceived me)–that, from some very remote portion of the mansion, there came what might have been the echo of the sound which Sir Launcelot had described.

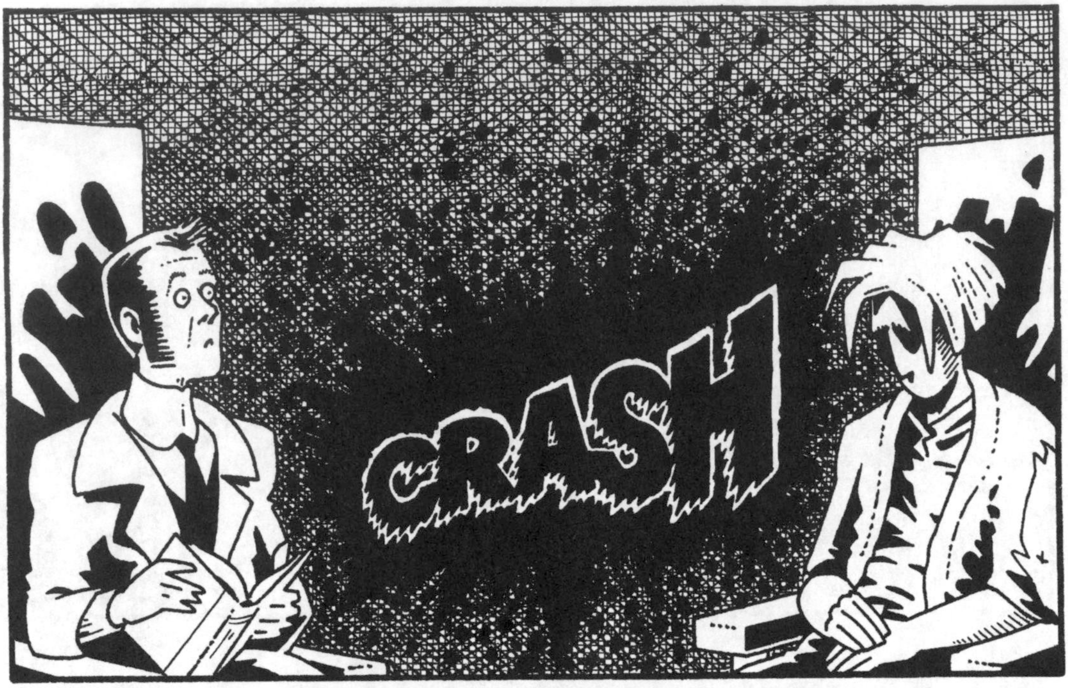
CRASH

It was, beyond doubt, the coincidence alone which had arrested my attention; for, amid the rattling of the sashes of the casements, and the ordinary noises of the still-increasing storm, the sound, in itself, had nothing which should have disturbed me.

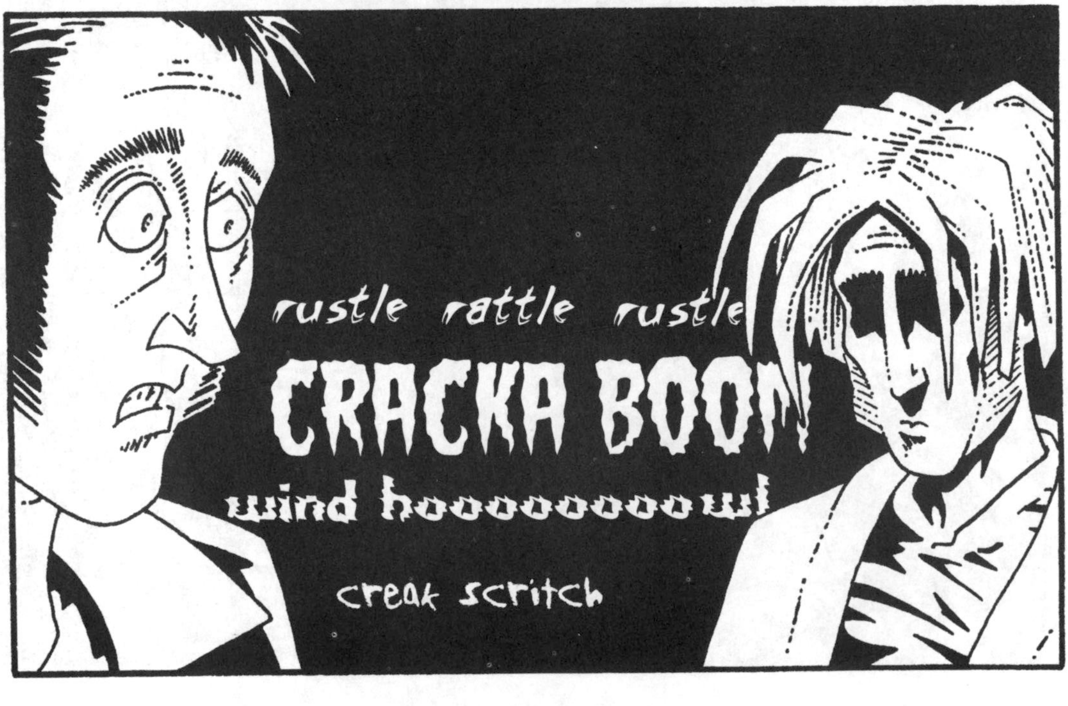
rustle rattle rustle
CRACKA BOOM
wind hooooooooowl
creak scritch

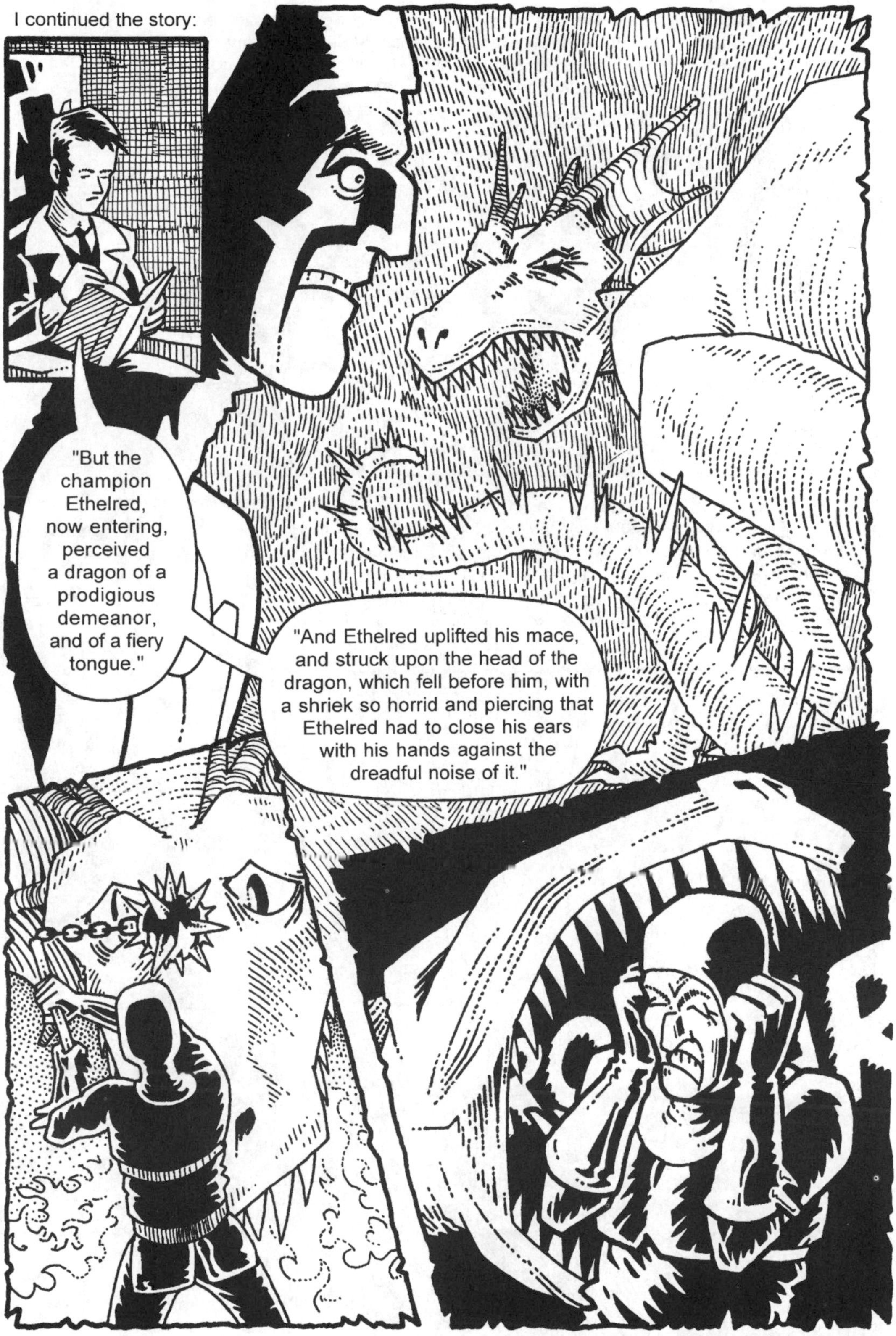
I continued the story:
"But the champion Ethelred, now entering, perceived a dragon of a prodigious demeanor, and of a fiery tongue."
"And Ethelred uplifted his mace, and struck upon the head of the dragon, which fell before him, with a shriek so horrid and piercing that Ethelred had to close his ears with his hands against the dreadful noise of it."

Here again I paused abruptly, and now with a feeling of amazement–for there could be no doubt whatever that I did actually hear a distant screaming sound–the exact counterpart of what my fancy had already conjured up for the dragon's unnatural shriek as described by the romancer.

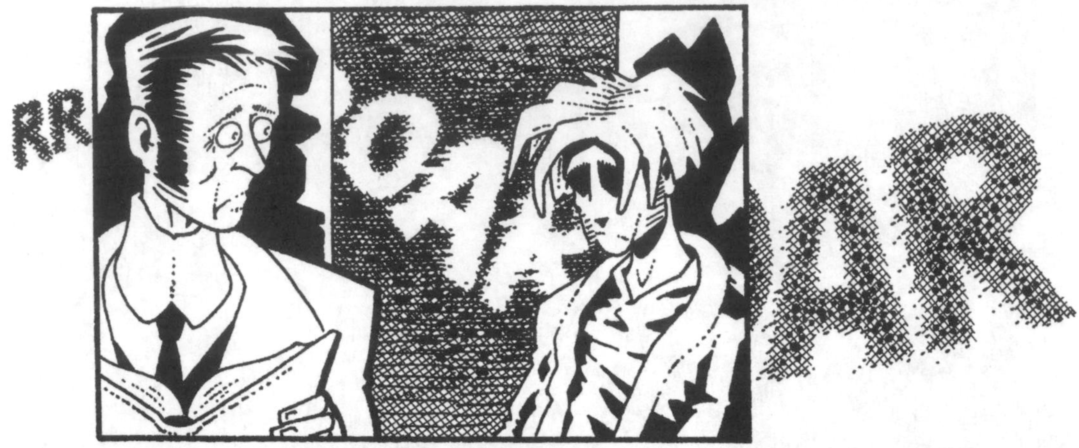
RR
OA
AR

Oppressed with fear as I certainly was, upon the occurrence of this second and most extraordinary coincidence, I still retained sufficient presence of mind to avoid exciting the sensitive nervousness of my companion. I was by no means certain that he had noticed the sounds in question. He had gradually brought round his chair, so as to sit with his face to the door of the chamber.

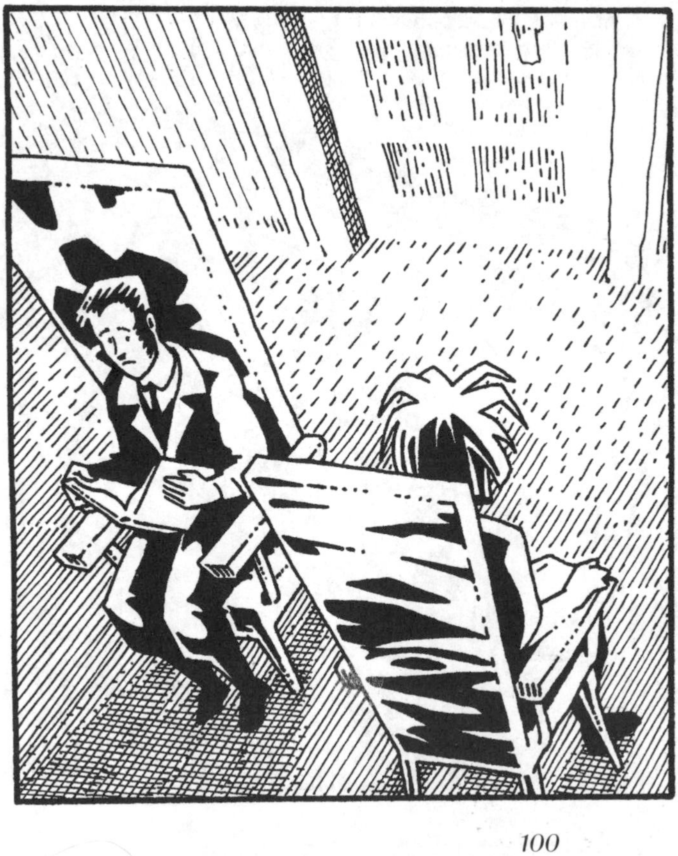

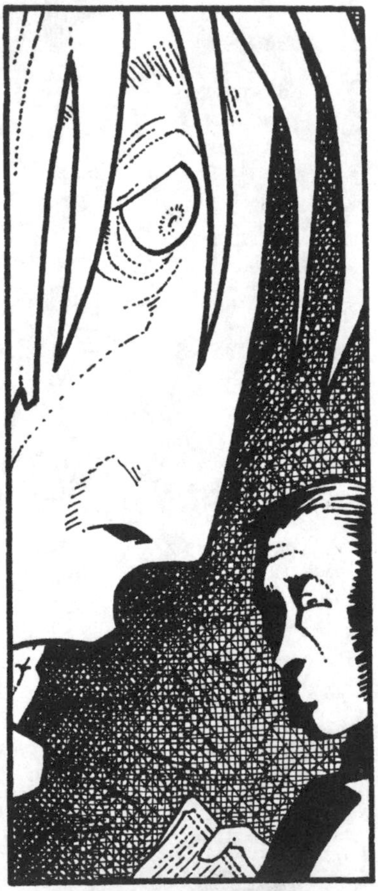

Thus I could but partially perceive his features, although I saw that his lips trembled as if he were murmuring inaudibly.

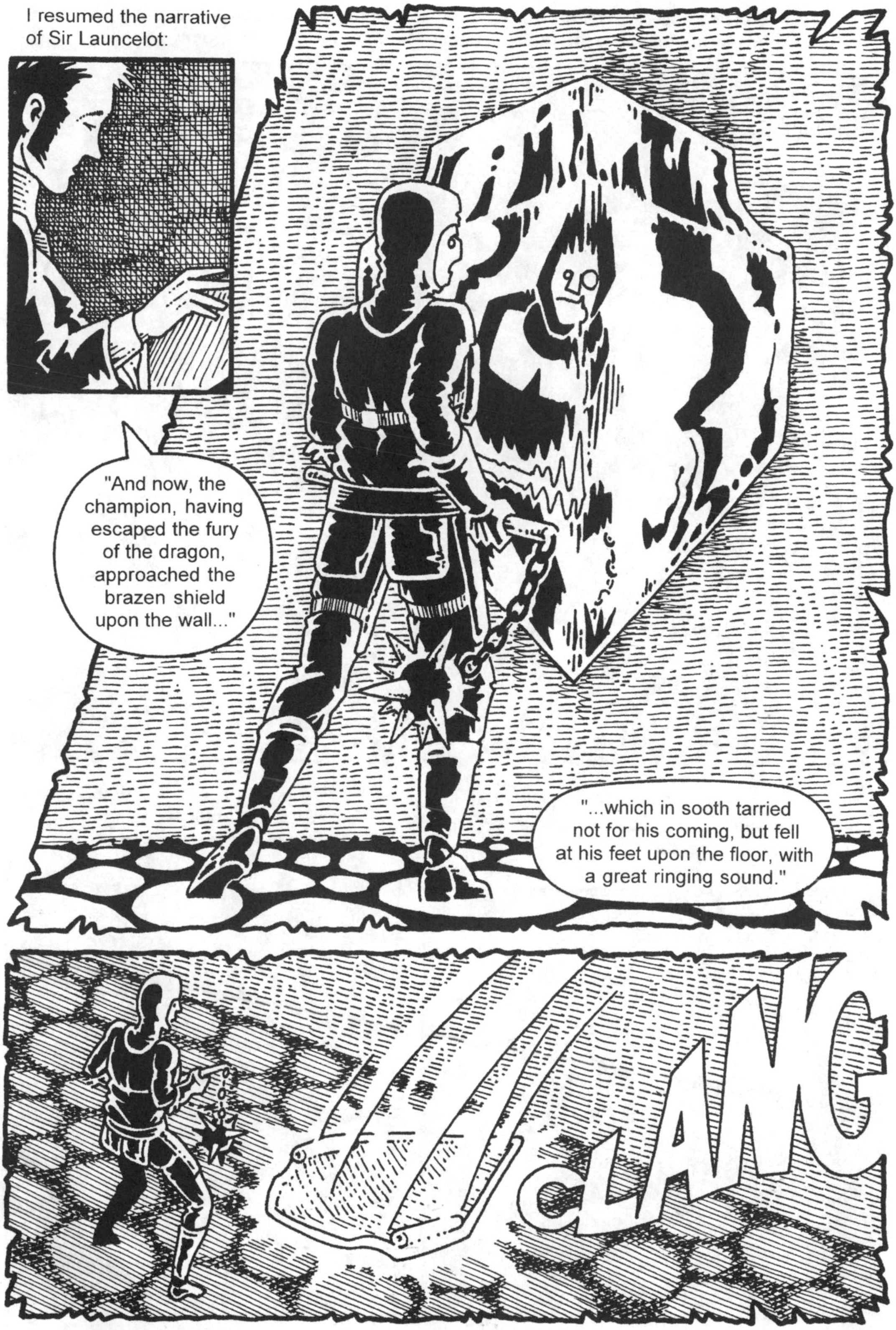
I resumed the narrative of Sir Launcelot:
"And now, the champion, having escaped the fury of the dragon, approached the brazen shield upon the wall..."
"...which in sooth tarried not for his coming, but fell at his feet upon the floor, with a great ringing sound."
CLANG

No sooner had these syllables passed my lips, than I became aware of a distinct, hollow, metallic, reverberation. Completely unnerved, I leaped to my feet.

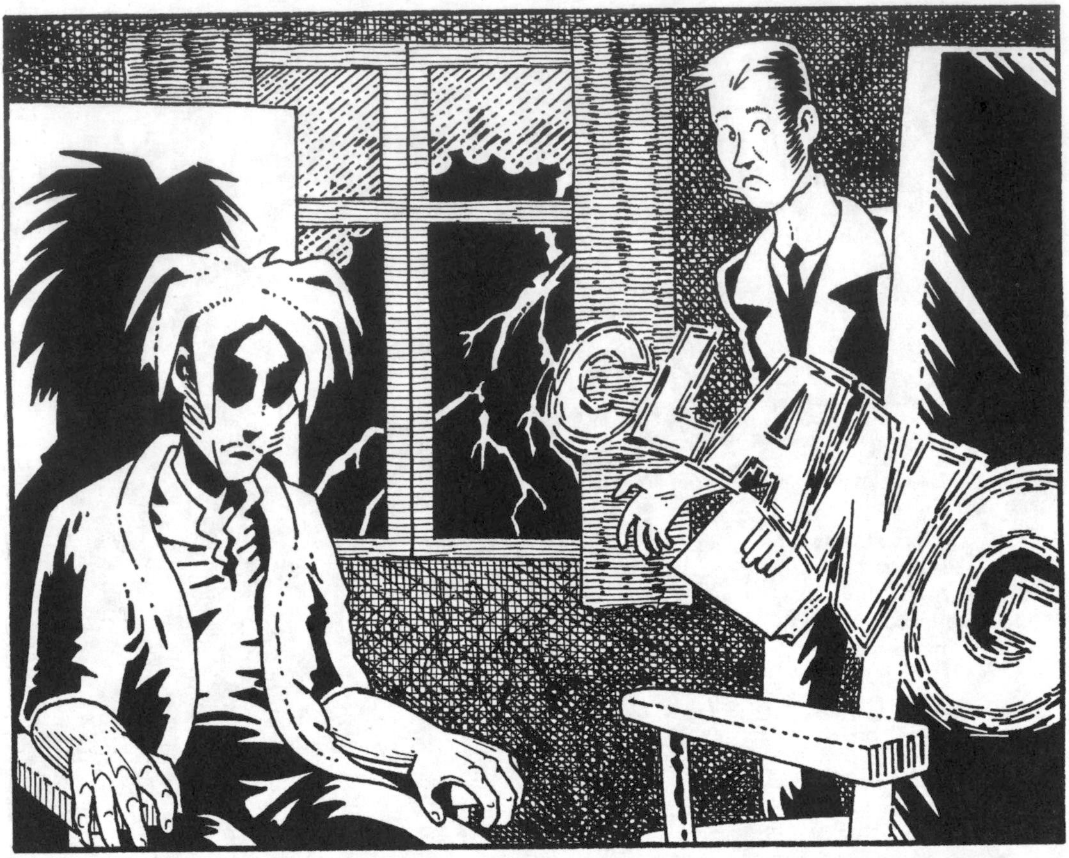
CLANG

As I placed my hand upon his shoulder, there came a strong shudder over his whole person; and he spoke in a gibbering murmur, as if unconscious of my presence.

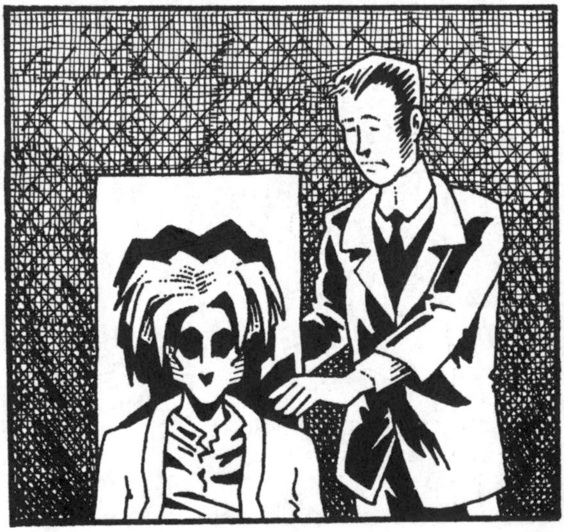

Bending closely over him, I drank in the hideous import of his words.

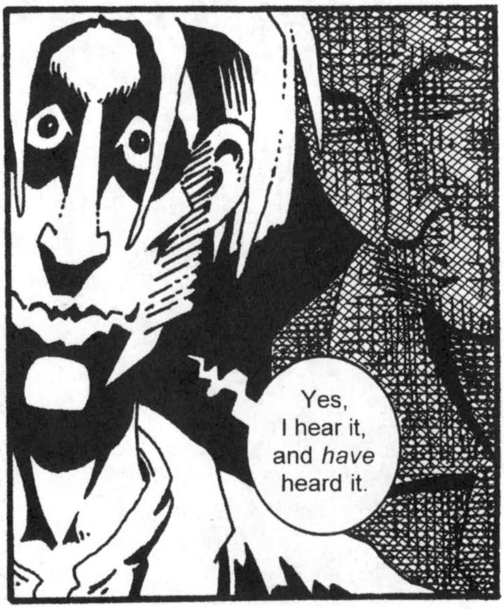
Yes, I hear it, and *have* heard it.

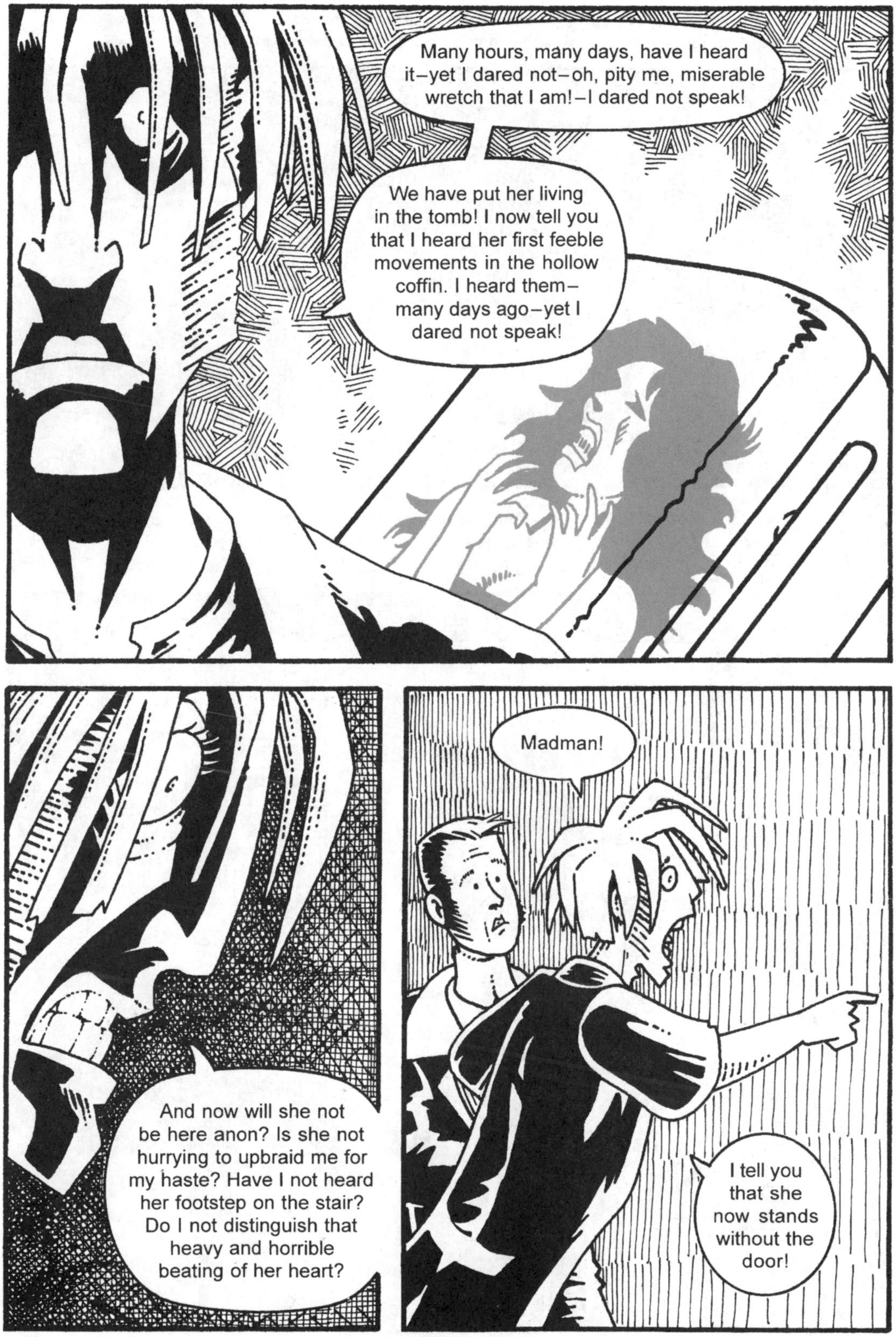
Many hours, many days, have I heard it–yet I dared not–oh, pity me, miserable wretch that I am!–I dared not speak!
We have put her living in the tomb! I now tell you that I heard her first feeble movements in the hollow coffin. I heard them–many days ago–yet I dared not speak!
And now will she not be here anon? Is she not hurrying to upbraid me for my haste? Have I not heard her footstep on the stair? Do I not distinguish that heavy and horrible beating of her heart?
Madman!
I tell you that she now stands without the door!

As if in the superhuman energy of his utterance there had been found the potency of a spell, the huge antique panels to which the speaker pointed threw back their ebony jaws.

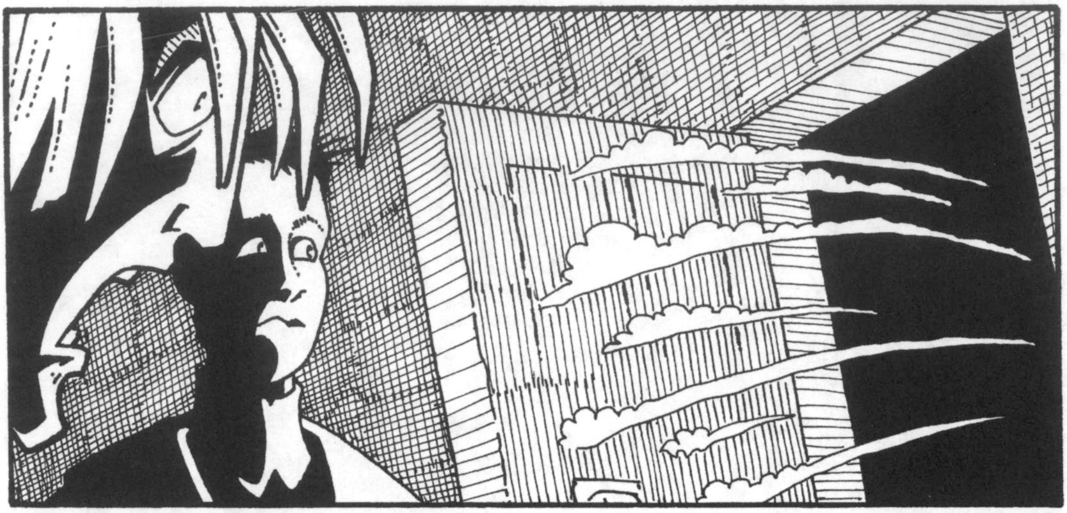

It was the work of the rushing gust–but then without those doors there did stand the lofty and enshrouded figure of the lady Madeline of Usher. There was blood upon her white robes, and the evidence of some bitter struggle upon every portion of her emaciated frame.

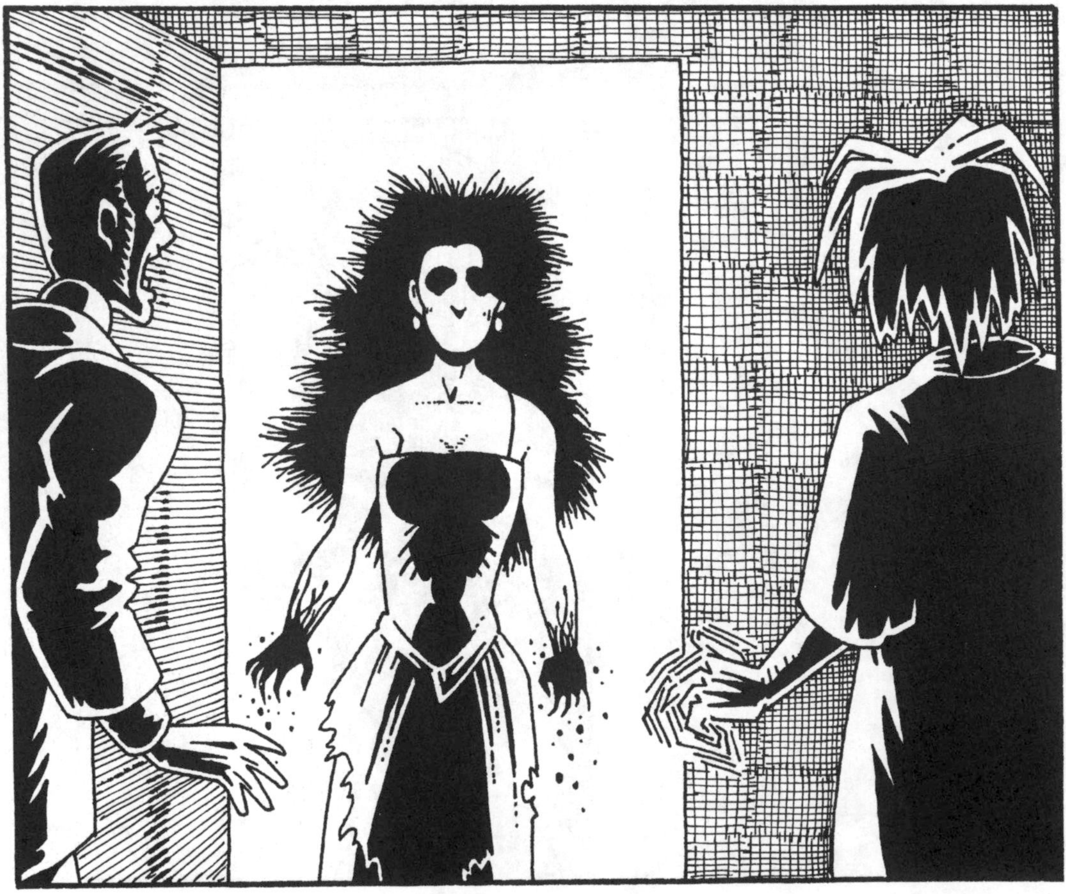

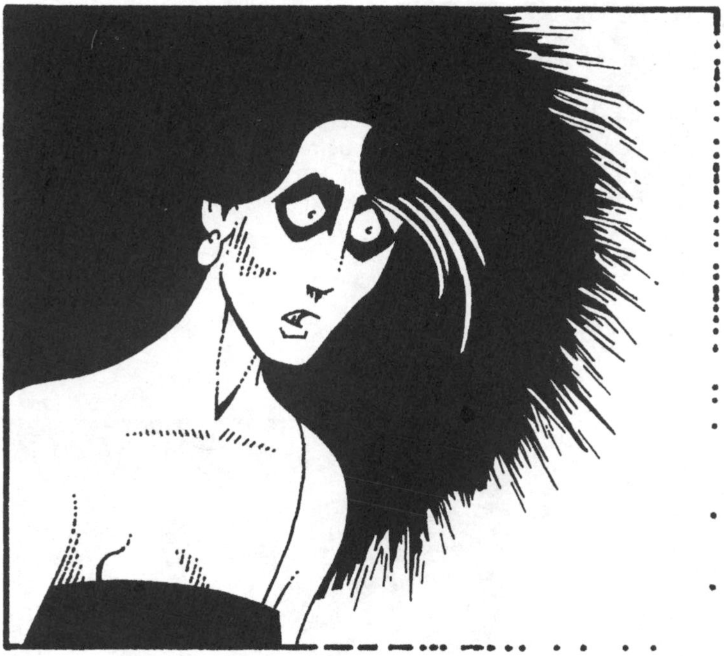

For a moment
she remained trembling
and reeling to and fro
upon the threshold.

Then, with a low moaning cry, fell heavily inward upon the person of her brother,
and in her violent and now final death-agonies, bore him to the floor a corpse!

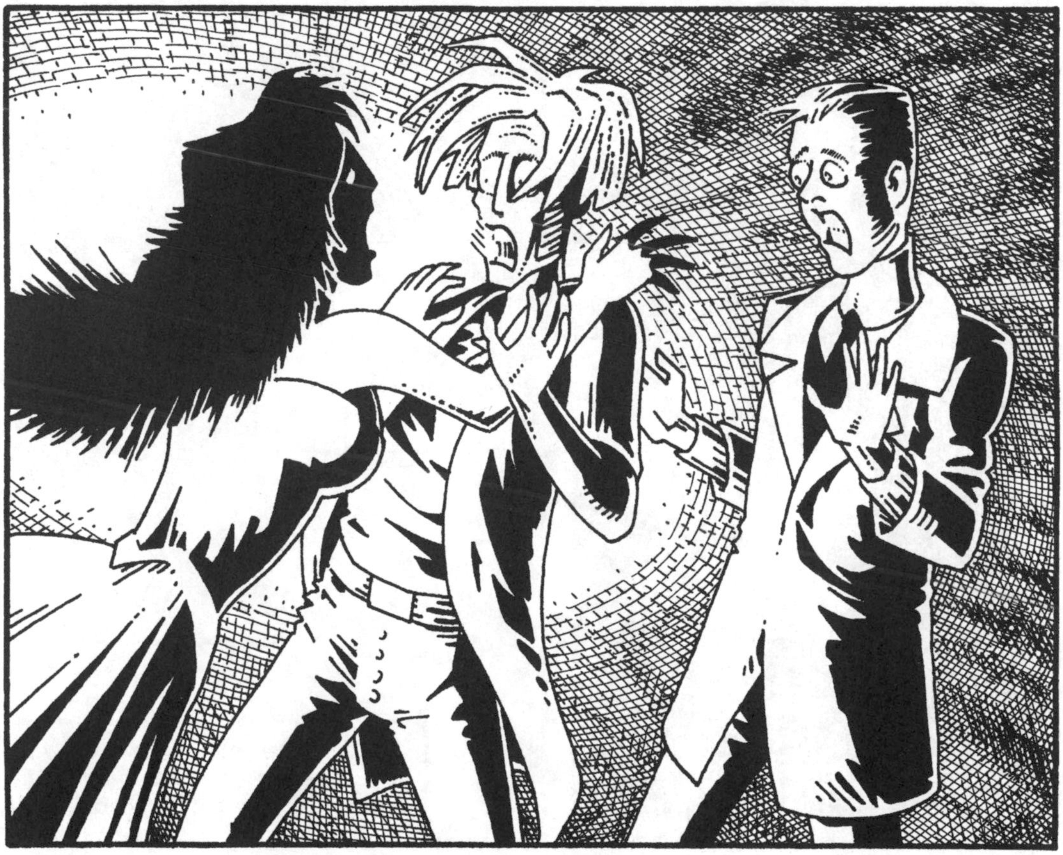

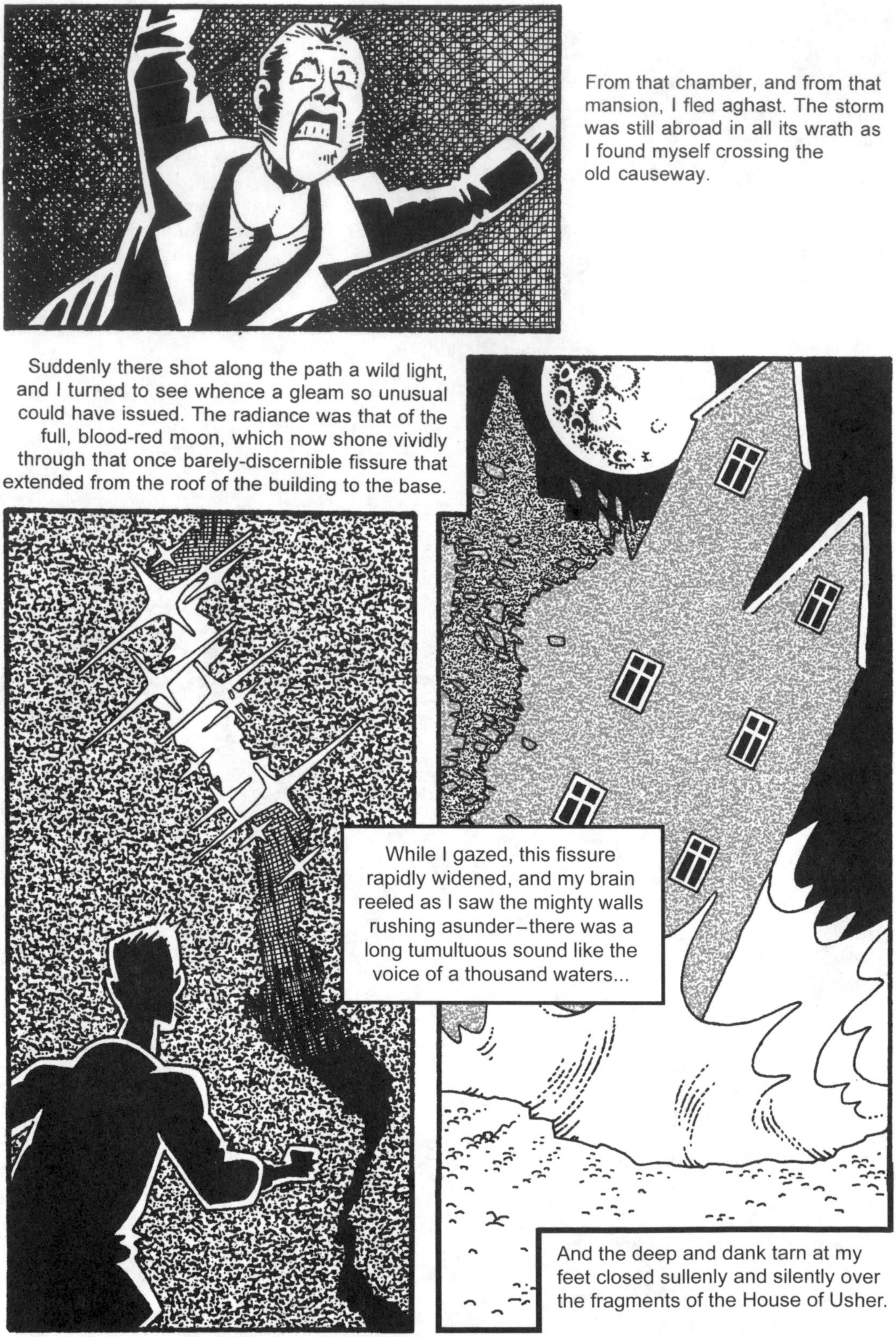
From that chamber, and from that mansion, I fled aghast. The storm was still abroad in all its wrath as I found myself crossing the old causeway.
Suddenly there shot along the path a wild light, and I turned to see whence a gleam so unusual could have issued. The radiance was that of the full, blood-red moon, which now shone vividly through that once barely-discernible fissure that extended from the roof of the building to the base.
While I gazed, this fissure rapidly widened, and my brain reeled as I saw the mighty walls rushing asunder–there was a long tumultuous sound like the voice of a thousand waters...
And the deep and dank tarn at my feet closed sullenly and silently over the fragments of the House of Usher.
©2004 MATT HOWARTH

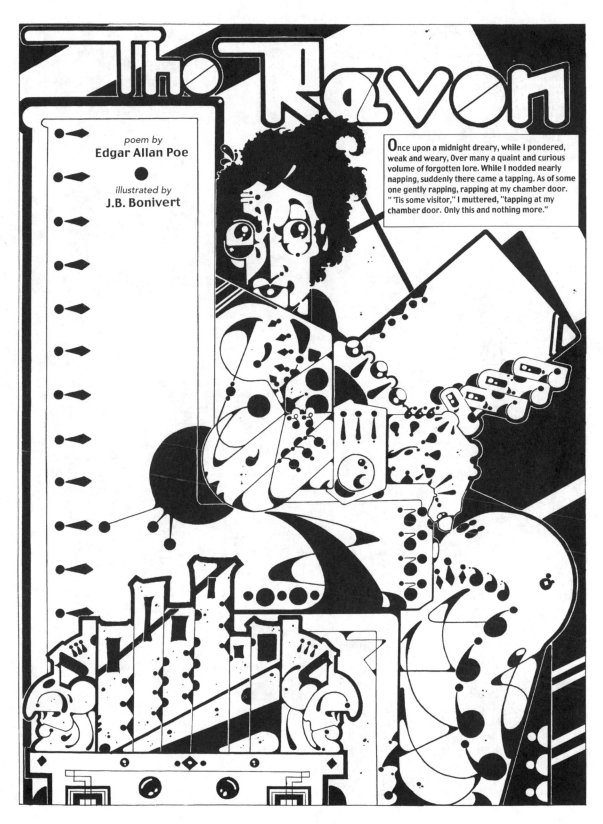

The Raven

poem by
Edgar Allan Poe

illustrated by
J.B. Bonivert

Once upon a midnight dreary, while I pondered, weak and weary, Over many a quaint and curious volume of forgotten lore. While I nodded nearly napping, suddenly there came a tapping. As of some one gently rapping, rapping at my chamber door. "'Tis some visitor," I muttered, "tapping at my chamber door. Only this and nothing more."

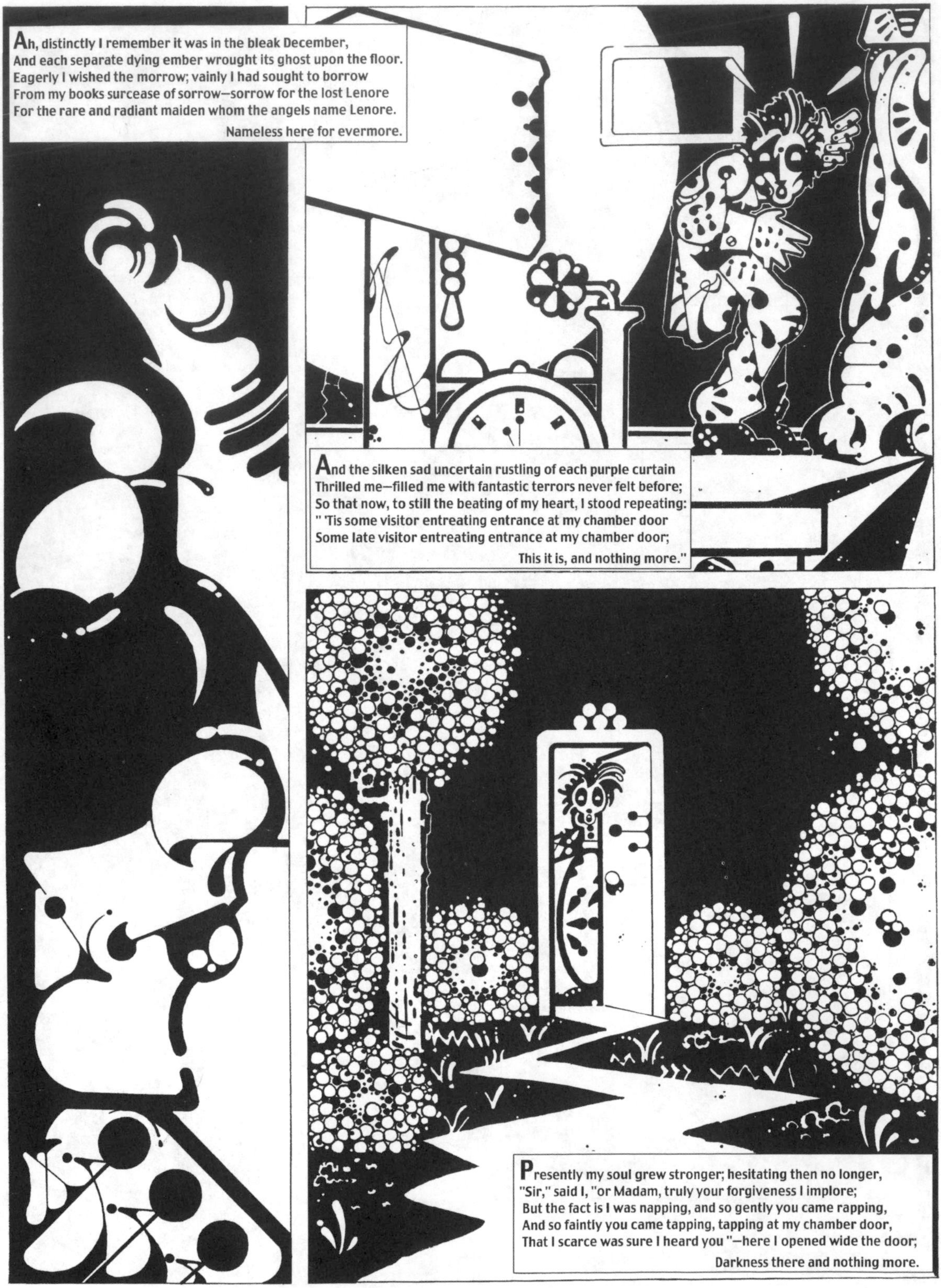
Ah, distinctly I remember it was in the bleak December,
And each separate dying ember wrought its ghost upon the floor.
Eagerly I wished the morrow; vainly I had sought to borrow
From my books surcease of sorrow—sorrow for the lost Lenore
For the rare and radiant maiden whom the angels name Lenore.
Nameless here for evermore.
And the silken sad uncertain rustling of each purple curtain
Thrilled me—filled me with fantastic terrors never felt before;
So that now, to still the beating of my heart, I stood repeating:
" 'Tis some visitor entreating entrance at my chamber door
Some late visitor entreating entrance at my chamber door;
This it is, and nothing more."
Presently my soul grew stronger; hesitating then no longer,
"Sir," said I, "or Madam, truly your forgiveness I implore;
But the fact is I was napping, and so gently you came rapping,
And so faintly you came tapping, tapping at my chamber door,
That I scarce was sure I heard you"—here I opened wide the door;
Darkness there and nothing more.

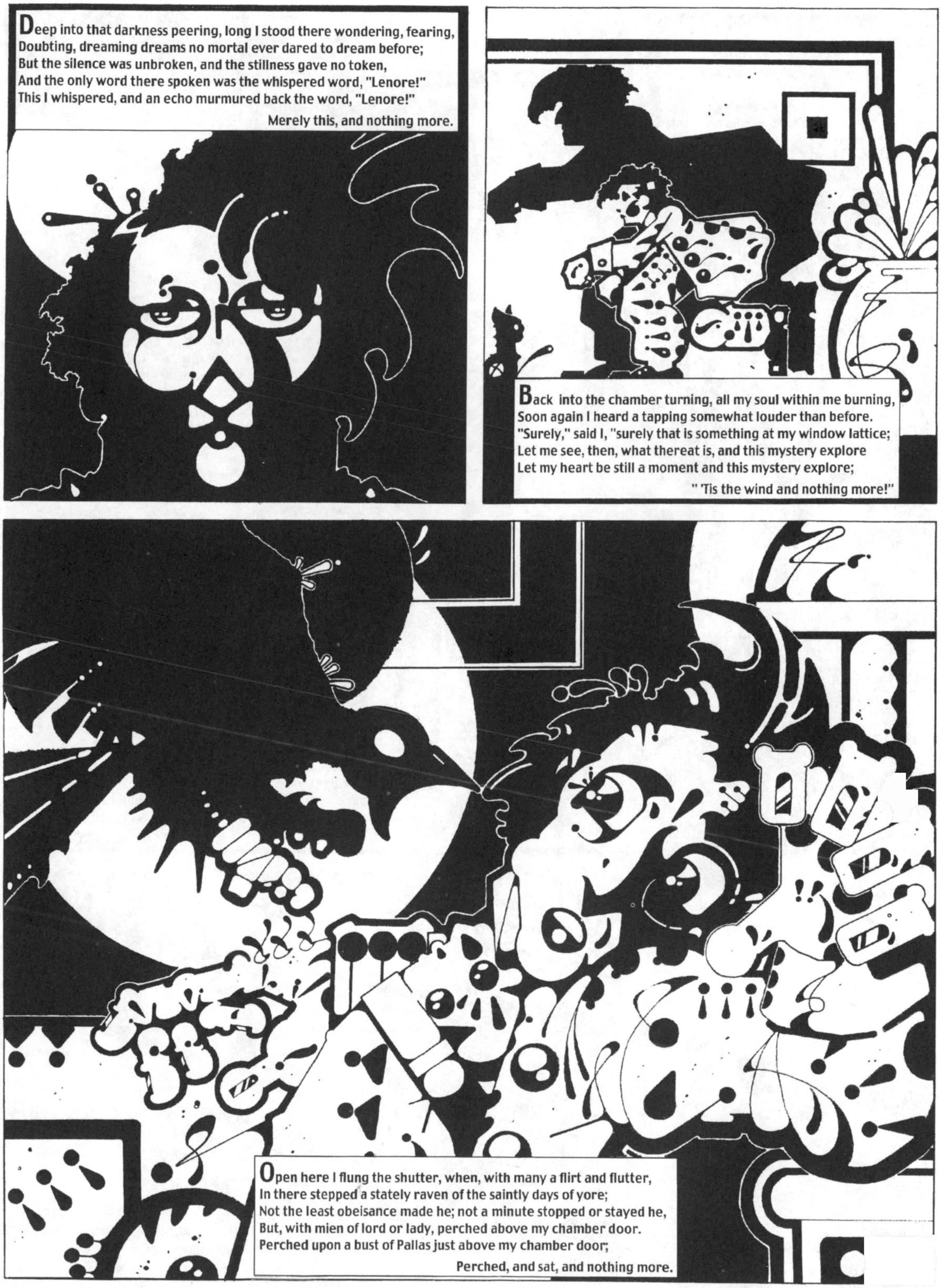
Deep into that darkness peering, long I stood there wondering, fearing,
Doubting, dreaming dreams no mortal ever dared to dream before;
But the silence was unbroken, and the stillness gave no token,
And the only word there spoken was the whispered word, "Lenore!"
This I whispered, and an echo murmured back the word, "Lenore!"
Merely this, and nothing more.
Back into the chamber turning, all my soul within me burning,
Soon again I heard a tapping somewhat louder than before.
"Surely," said I, "surely that is something at my window lattice;
Let me see, then, what thereat is, and this mystery explore
Let my heart be still a moment and this mystery explore;
" 'Tis the wind and nothing more!"
Open here I flung the shutter, when, with many a flirt and flutter,
In there stepped a stately raven of the saintly days of yore;
Not the least obeisance made he; not a minute stopped or stayed he,
But, with mien of lord or lady, perched above my chamber door.
Perched upon a bust of Pallas just above my chamber door;
Perched, and sat, and nothing more.

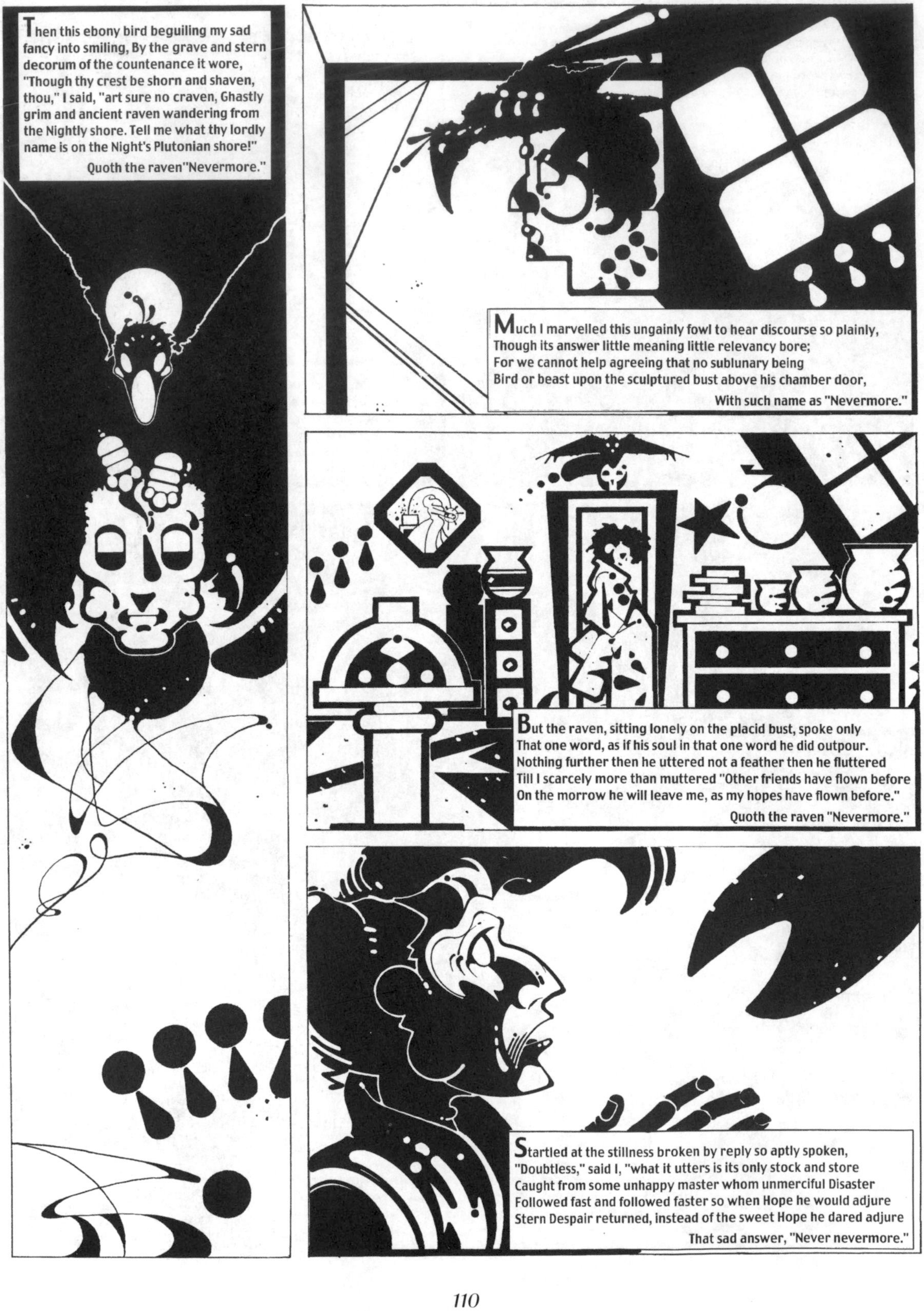
Then this ebony bird beguiling my sad fancy into smiling, By the grave and stern decorum of the countenance it wore, "Though thy crest be shorn and shaven, thou," I said, "art sure no craven, Ghastly grim and ancient raven wandering from the Nightly shore. Tell me what thy lordly name is on the Night's Plutonian shore!"
Quoth the raven"Nevermore."
Much I marvelled this ungainly fowl to hear discourse so plainly,
Though its answer little meaning little relevancy bore;
For we cannot help agreeing that no sublunary being
Bird or beast upon the sculptured bust above his chamber door,
With such name as "Nevermore."
But the raven, sitting lonely on the placid bust, spoke only
That one word, as if his soul in that one word he did outpour.
Nothing further then he uttered not a feather then he fluttered
Till I scarcely more than muttered "Other friends have flown before
On the morrow he will leave me, as my hopes have flown before."
Quoth the raven "Nevermore."
Startled at the stillness broken by reply so aptly spoken,
"Doubtless," said I, "what it utters is its only stock and store
Caught from some unhappy master whom unmerciful Disaster
Followed fast and followed faster so when Hope he would adjure
Stern Despair returned, instead of the sweet Hope he dared adjure
That sad answer, "Never nevermore."

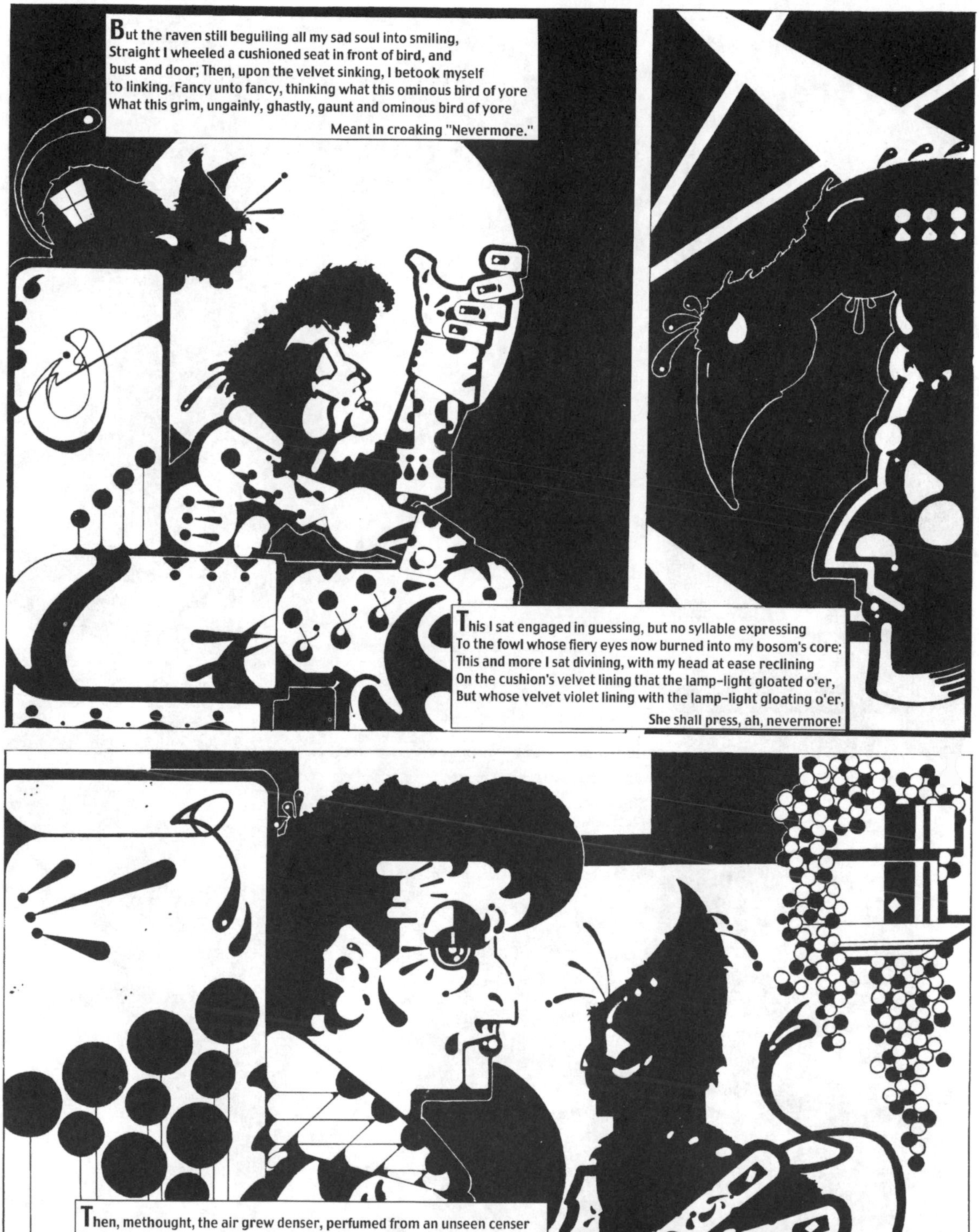
But the raven still beguiling all my sad soul into smiling,
Straight I wheeled a cushioned seat in front of bird, and
bust and door; Then, upon the velvet sinking, I betook myself
to linking. Fancy unto fancy, thinking what this ominous bird of yore
What this grim, ungainly, ghastly, gaunt and ominous bird of yore
Meant in croaking "Nevermore."
This I sat engaged in guessing, but no syllable expressing
To the fowl whose fiery eyes now burned into my bosom's core;
This and more I sat divining, with my head at ease reclining
On the cushion's velvet lining that the lamp-light gloated o'er,
But whose velvet violet lining with the lamp-light gloating o'er,
She shall press, ah, nevermore!
Then, methought, the air grew denser, perfumed from an unseen censer
Swung by Angels whose faint foot-falls tinkled on the tufted floor.
"Wretch," I cried, "thy God hath lent thee by these angels he hath sent thee.
Respite respite and nepenthe, from thy memories of Lenore;
Let me quaff this kind nepenthe and forget this lost Lenore!"
Quoth the raven "Nevermore."

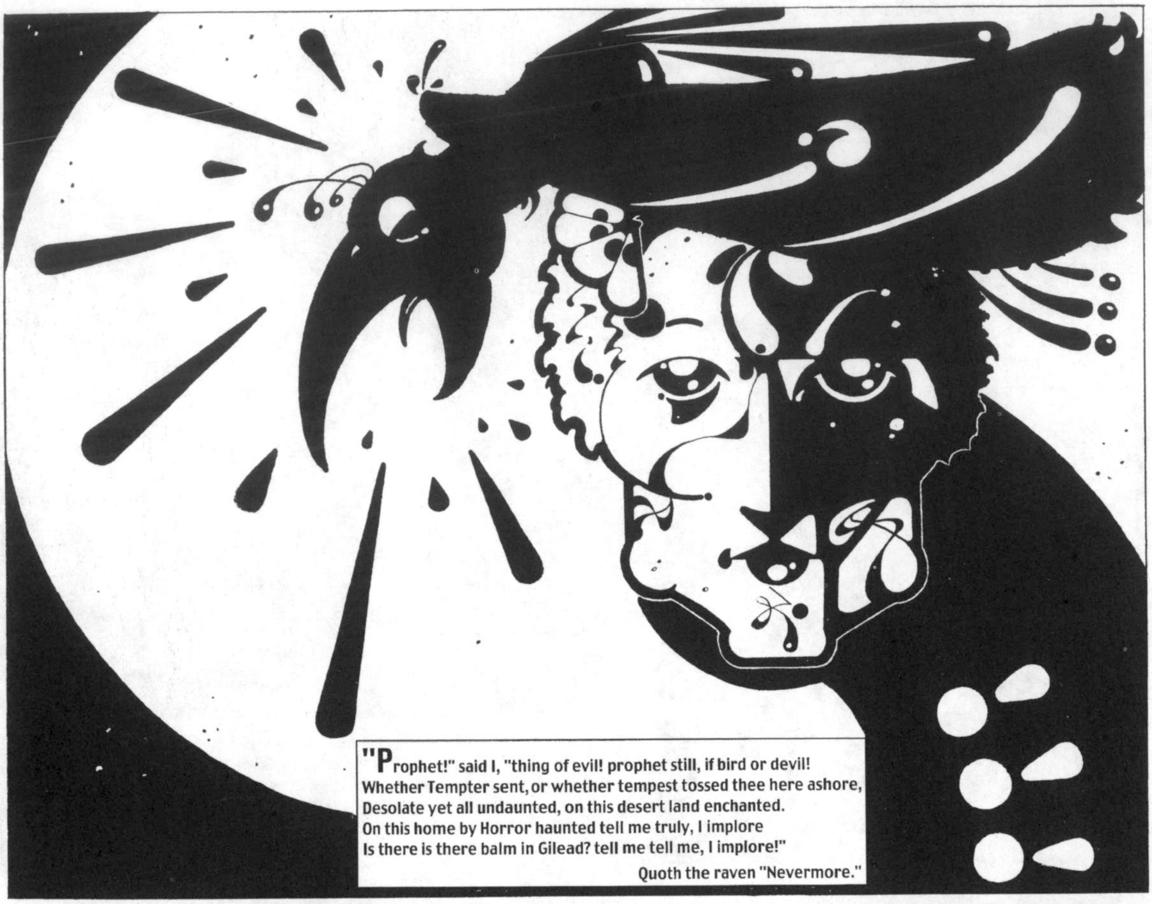
"Prophet!" said I, "thing of evil! prophet still, if bird or devil!
Whether Tempter sent, or whether tempest tossed thee here ashore,
Desolate yet all undaunted, on this desert land enchanted.
On this home by Horror haunted tell me truly, I implore
Is there is there balm in Gilead? tell me tell me, I implore!"
Quoth the raven "Nevermore."

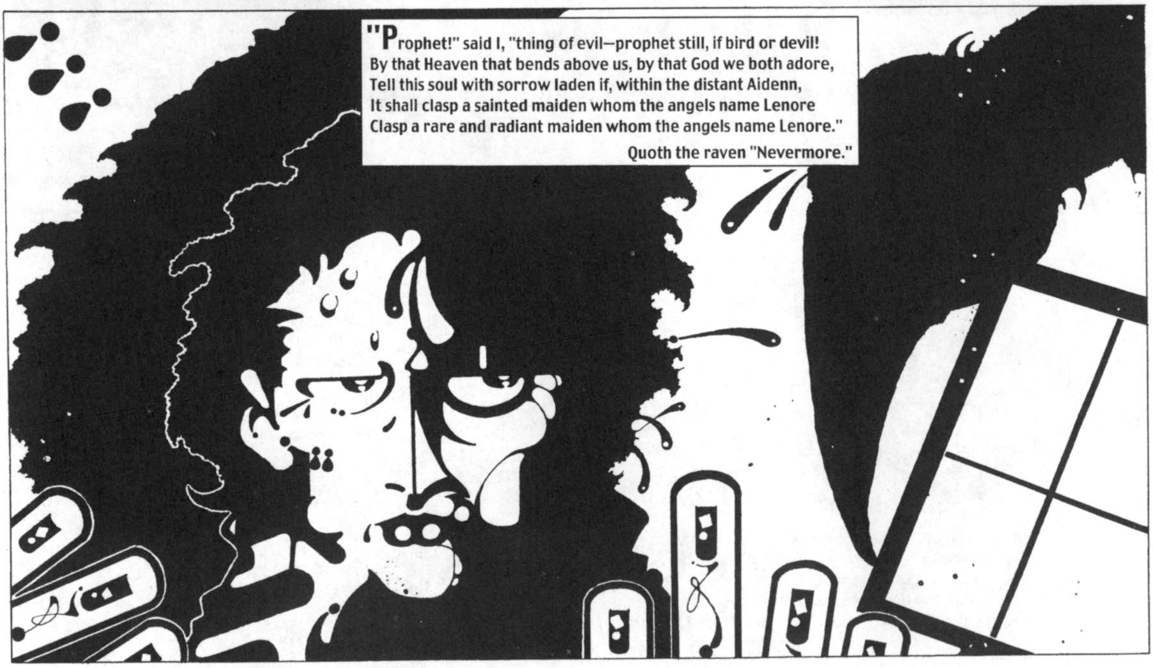
"Prophet!" said I, "thing of evil—prophet still, if bird or devil!
By that Heaven that bends above us, by that God we both adore,
Tell this soul with sorrow laden if, within the distant Aidenn,
It shall clasp a sainted maiden whom the angels name Lenore
Clasp a rare and radiant maiden whom the angels name Lenore."
Quoth the raven "Nevermore."

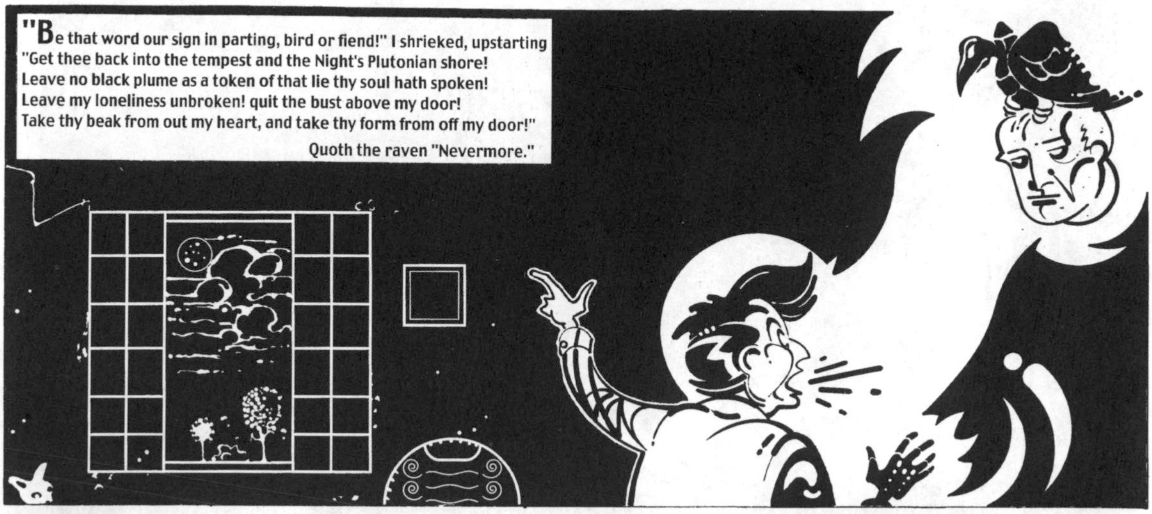
"Be that word our sign in parting, bird or fiend!" I shrieked, upstarting
"Get thee back into the tempest and the Night's Plutonian shore!
Leave no black plume as a token of that lie thy soul hath spoken!
Leave my loneliness unbroken! quit the bust above my door!
Take thy beak from out my heart, and take thy form from off my door!"
Quoth the raven "Nevermore."

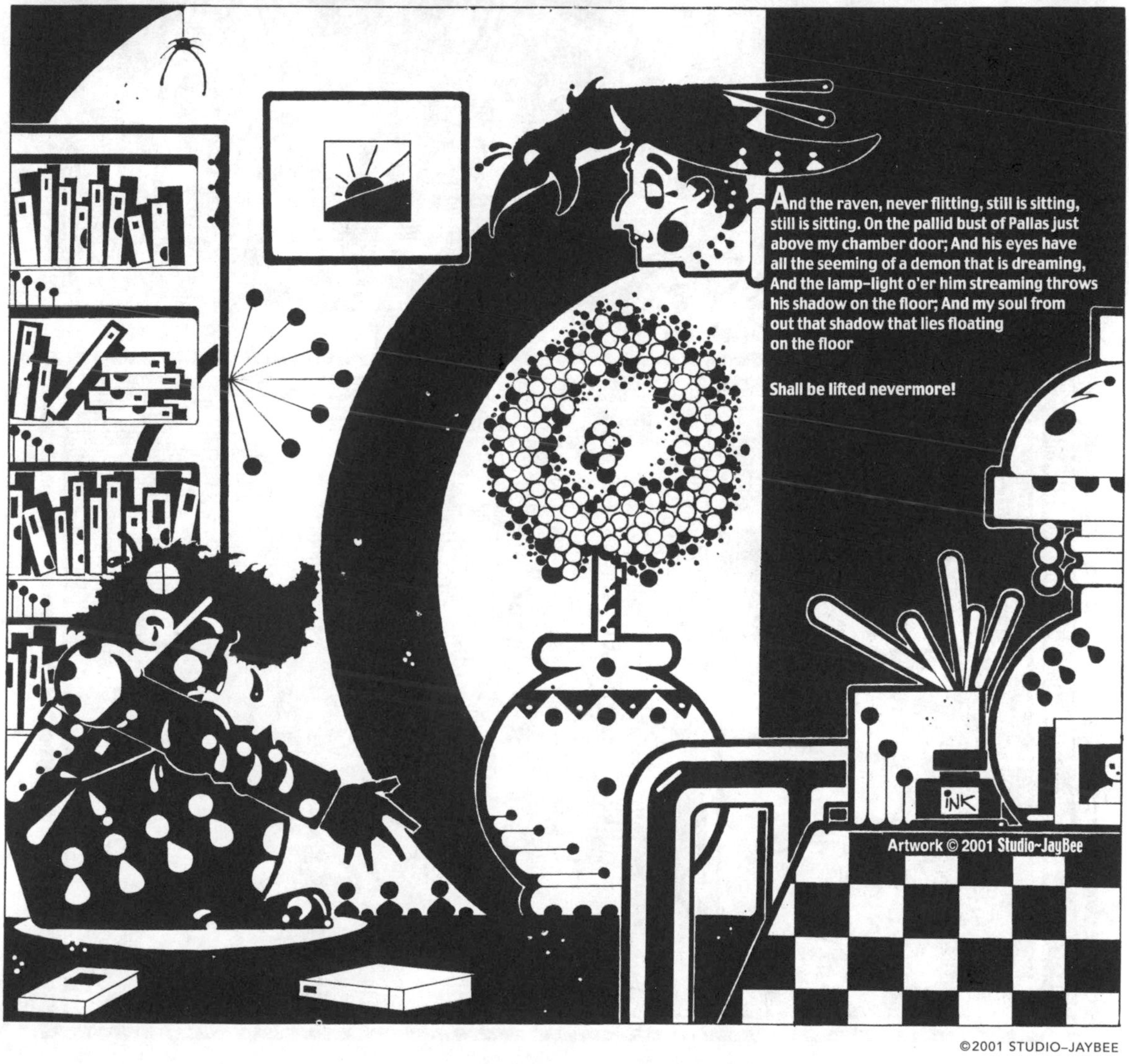
And the raven, never flitting, still is sitting, still is sitting. On the pallid bust of Pallas just above my chamber door; And his eyes have all the seeming of a demon that is dreaming, And the lamp-light o'er him streaming throws his shadow on the floor; And my soul from out that shadow that lies floating on the floor
Shall be lifted nevermore!
INK
Artwork © 2001 Studio~JayBee

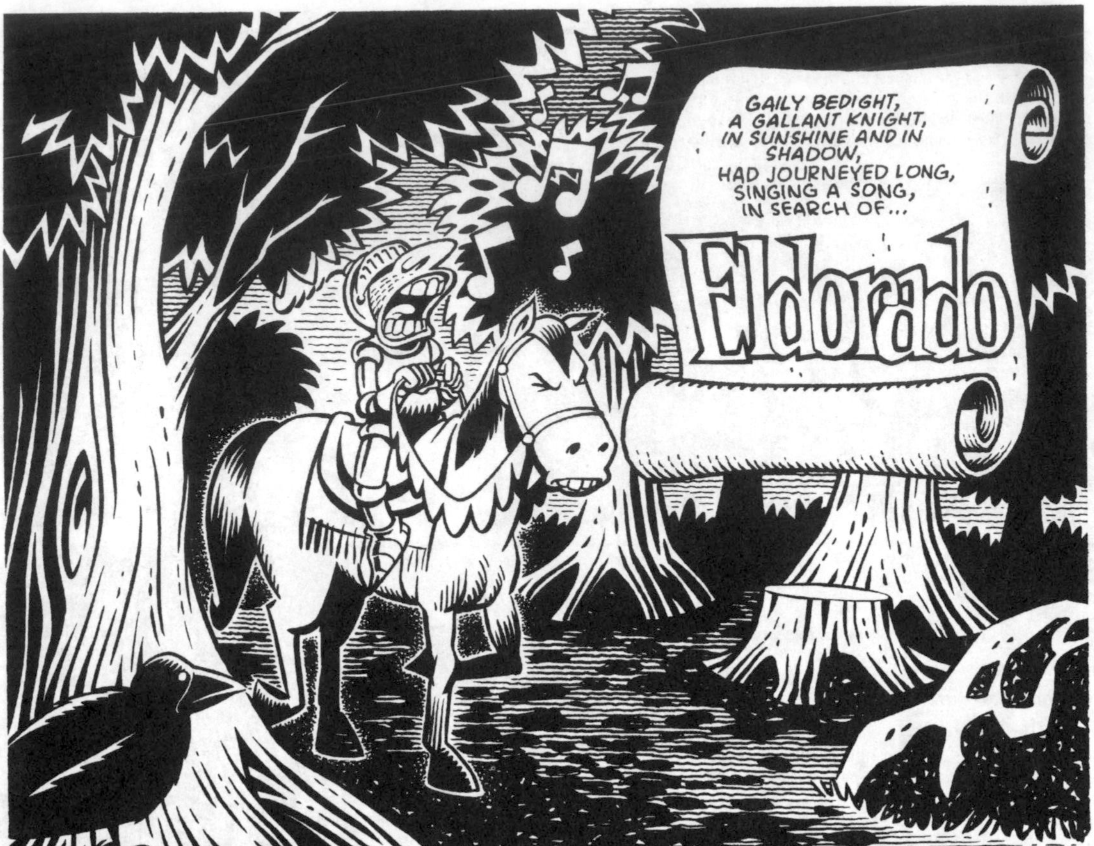
GAILY BEDIGHT,
A GALLANT KNIGHT,
IN SUNSHINE AND IN
SHADOW,
HAD JOURNEYED LONG,
SINGING A SONG,
IN SEARCH OF...
Eldorado

WORDS BY **EDGAR ALLAN POE** PICTURES BY ROGER LANGRIDGE

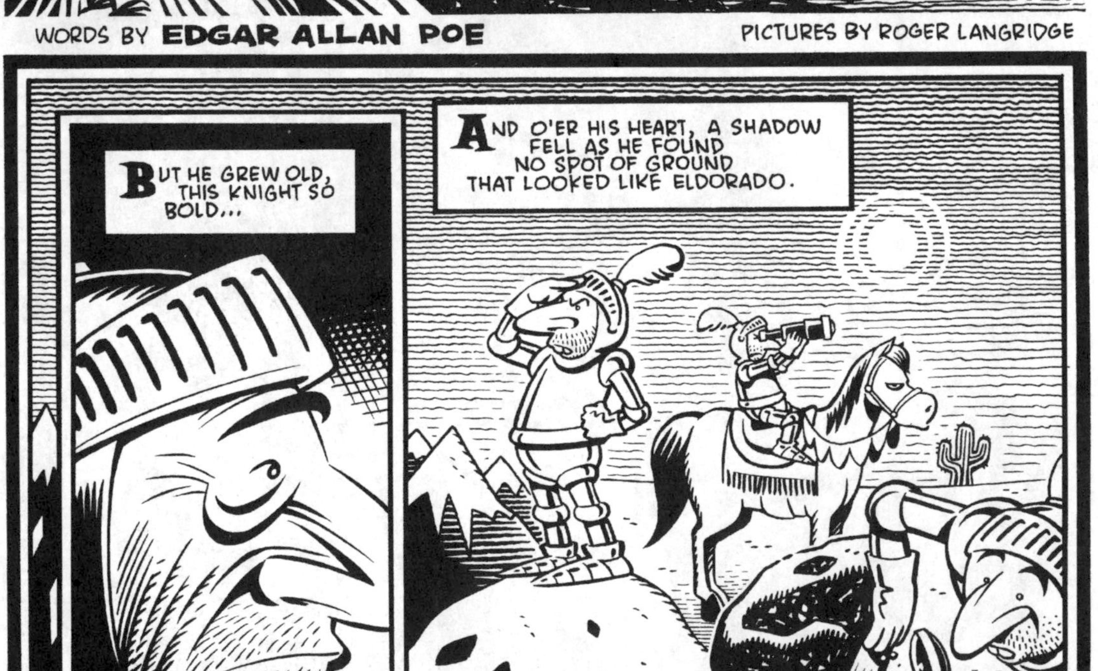
BUT HE GREW OLD,
THIS KNIGHT SO
BOLD...
AND O'ER HIS HEART, A SHADOW
FELL AS HE FOUND
NO SPOT OF GROUND
THAT LOOKED LIKE ELDORADO.

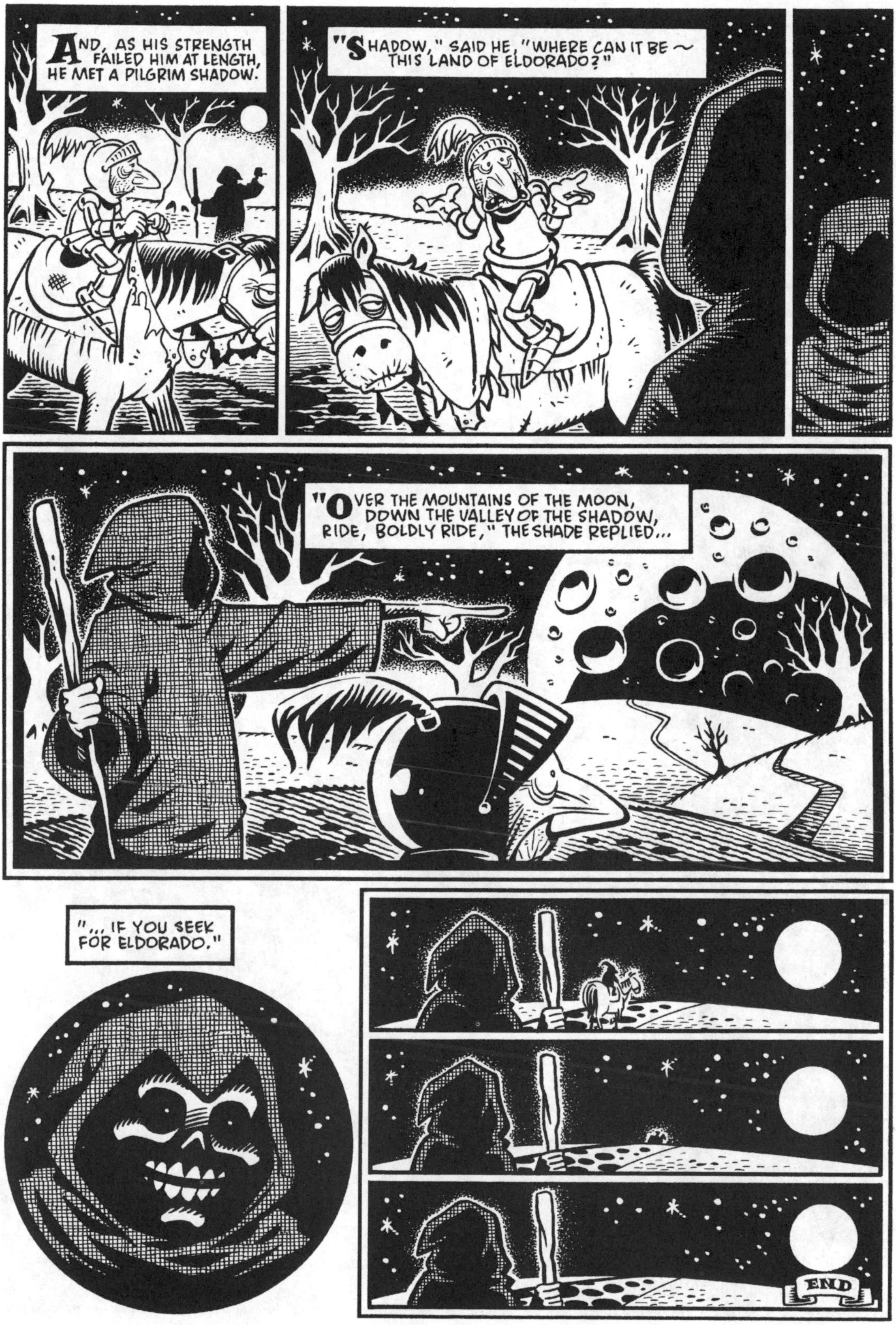
AND, AS HIS STRENGTH FAILED HIM AT LENGTH, HE MET A PILGRIM SHADOW.
"SHADOW," SAID HE, "WHERE CAN IT BE ~ THIS LAND OF ELDORADO?"
"OVER THE MOUNTAINS OF THE MOON, DOWN THE VALLEY OF THE SHADOW, RIDE, BOLDLY RIDE," THE SHADE REPLIED...
"... IF YOU SEEK FOR ELDORADO."
END

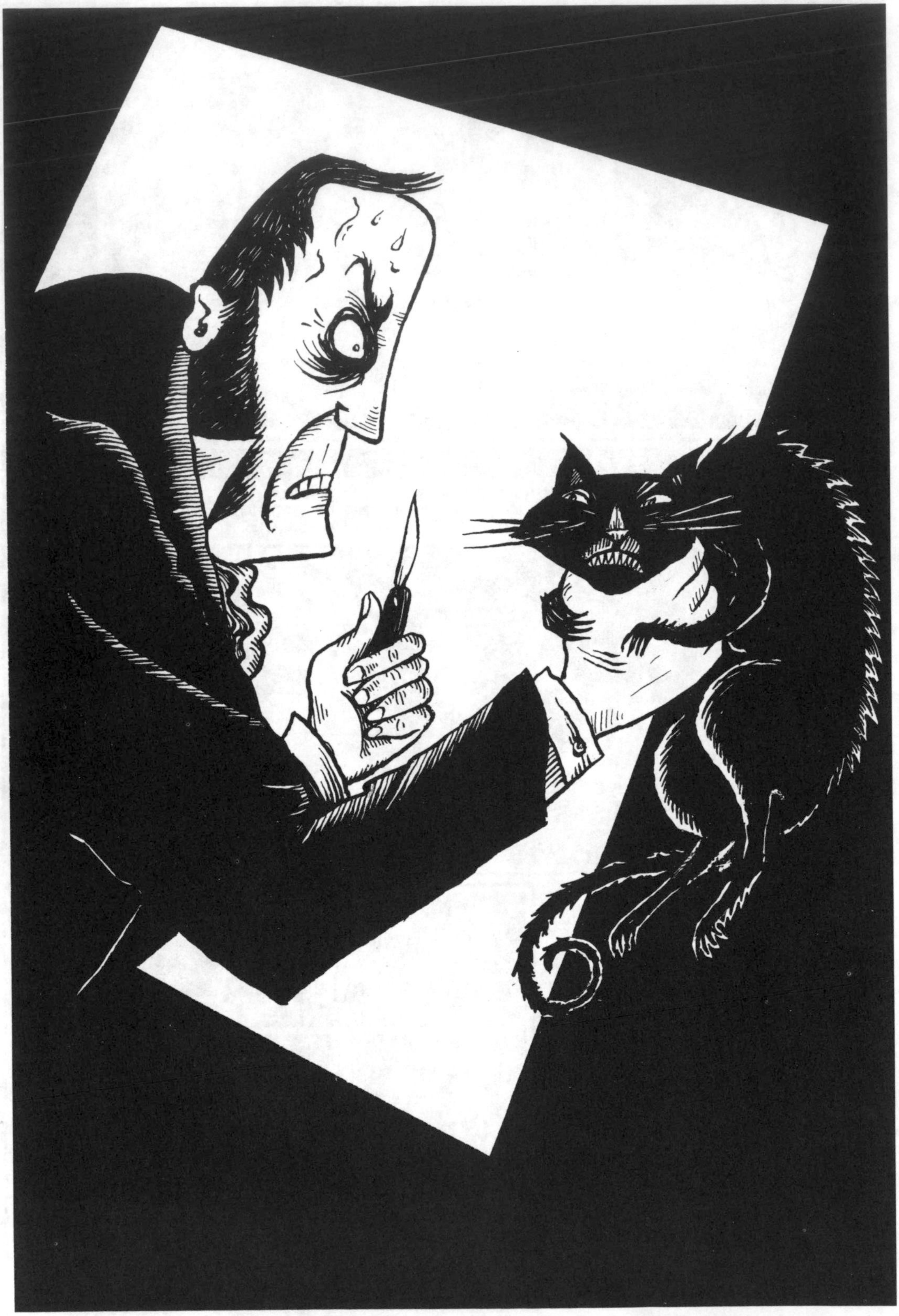

The Black Cat

illustrated by RICHARD SALA

For the most wild, yet most homely narrative which I am about to pen, I neither expect nor solicit belief. Mad indeed would I be to expect it, in a case where my very senses reject their own evidence. Yet, mad am I not — and very surely do I not dream. But tomorrow I die, and today I would unburden my soul. My immediate purpose is to place before the world, plainly, succinctly, and without comment, a series of mere household events.

In their consequences, these events have terrified — have tortured — have destroyed me. Yet I will not attempt to expound them. To me, they have presented little but horror — to many they will seem less terrible than *baroques*. Hereafter, perhaps, some intellect may be found which will reduce my phantasm to the commonplace — some intellect more calm, more logical, and far less excitable than my own, which will perceive, in the circumstances I detail with awe, nothing more than an ordinary succession of very natural causes and effects.

From my infancy I was noted for the docility and humanity of my disposition. My tenderness of heart was even so conspicuous as to make me the jest of my companions. I was especially fond of animals, and was indulged by my parents with a great variety of pets. With these I spent most of my time, and never was so happy as when feeding and caressing them. This peculiarity of character grew with my growth, and, in my manhood, I derived from it one of my principal sources of pleasure. To those who have cherished an affection for a faithful and sagacious dog, I need hardly be at the trouble of explaining the nature of the intensity of the gratification thus derivable. There is something in the unselfish and self-sacrificing love of a brute, which goes directly to the heart of him who has had frequent occasion to test the paltry friendship and gossamer fidelity of mere *Man*.

I married early, and was happy to find in my wife a disposition not uncongenial with my own. Observing my partiality for domestic pets, she lost no opportunity of procuring those of the most agreeable kind. We had birds, goldfish, a fine dog, rabbits, a small monkey, and a *cat*.

This latter was a remarkably large and beautiful animal, entirely black, and sagacious to an astonishing degree. In speaking of his intelligence, my wife, who at heart was not a little tinctured with superstition, made frequent allusion to the ancient popular notion, which regarded all black cats as witches in disguise. Not that she was ever *serious* upon this point — and I mention the matter at all for no better reason than that it happens, just now, to be remembered.

Pluto — this was the cat's name — was my favourite pet and playmate. I alone fed him, and he attended me wherever I went about the house. It was even with difficulty that I could prevent him from following me through the streets.

Our friendship lasted, in this manner, for several years, during which my general temperament and character—through the instrumentality of the fiend Intemperance — had (I blush to confess it) experienced a radical alteration for the worse. I grew, day by day, more moody, more irritable, more regardless of the feelings of others.

I suffered myself to use intemperate language to my wife. At length, I even offered her personal violence. My pets, of course, were made to feel the change in my disposition. I not only neglected, but ill-used them. For Pluto, however, I still retained sufficient regard to restrain me from maltreating him, as I made no scruple of maltreating the rabbits, the monkey, or even the dog, when by accident, or through affection, they came in my way. But my disease grew upon me — for what disease is like alcohol? — and at length even Pluto, who was now becoming old, and consequently somewhat peevish — even Pluto began to experience the effects of my ill-temper.

One night, returning home, much intoxicated, from one of my haunts about town, I fancied that the cat avoided my presence. I seized him; when, in his fright at my violence, he inflicted a slight wound upon my hand with his teeth. The fury of a demon instantly possessed me. I knew myself no longer. My original soul seemed, at once, to take its flight from my body; and a more than fiendish malevolence, gin-nurtured, thrilled every fibre of my frame. I took from my waistcoat pocket a pen-knife, opened it, grasped the poor beast by the throat, and deliberately cut one of its eyes from the socket! I blush, I burn, I shudder, while I pen the damnable atrocity.

When reason returned with the morning — when I had slept off the fumes of the night's debauch — I experienced a sentiment half of horror, half of remorse, for the crime of which I had been guilty; but it was, at best, a feeble and equivocal feeling, and the soul remained untouched. I again plunged into excess, and soon drowned in wine all memory of the deed.

In the meantime the cat slowly recovered. The socket of the lost eye presented, it is true, a frightful appearance, but he no longer appeared to suffer any pain. He went about the house as usual, but, as might be expected, fled in extreme terror at my approach. I had so much of my old heart left, as to be at first grieved by this evident dislike on the part of a creature which had once so loved me. But this feeling soon gave place to irritation. And then came, as if to my final and irrevocable overthrow, the spirit of PERVERSENESS. Of this spirit philosophy takes no account. Yet I am not more sure that my soul lives, than I am that perverseness is one of the primitive impulses of the human heart — one of the indivisible primary faculties, or sentiments, which give direction to the character of man. Who has not, a hundred times, found himself committing a vile or a silly action, for no other reason than because he knows he should *not*? Have we not a perpetual inclination, in the teeth of our best judgment, to violate that which is *Law*, merely because we understand it to be such? This spirit of perverseness, I say, came to my final overthrow. It was this unfathomable longing of the soul to *vex itself* — to offer violence to its own nature — to do wrong for the wrong's sake only — that urged me to continue and finally to consummate the injury I had inflicted upon the unoffending brute. One morning, in cool blood, I slipped a noose about its neck and hung it to the limb of a tree — hung it with the tears streaming from my eyes, and with the bitterest remorse at my heart — hung it *because* I knew that it had loved me, and *because* I felt it had given me no reason of offence — hung it *because* I knew that in so doing I was committing a sin — a deadly sin that would so jeopardize my immortal soul as to place it — if such a thing were possible — even beyond the reach of the infinite mercy of the Most Merciful and Most Terrible God.

On the night of the day on which this cruel deed was done, I was aroused from sleep by the cry of "Fire!" The curtains of my bed were in flames. The whole house was blazing. It was with great difficulty that my wife, a servant, and myself, made our escape from the conflagration. The destruction was complete. My entire worldly wealth was swallowed up, and I resigned myself thenceforward to despair.

I am above the weakness of seeking to establish a sequence of cause and effect between the disaster and the atrocity. But I am detailing a chain of facts, and wish not to leave even a possible link imperfect. On the day succeeding the fire, I visited the ruins. The walls, with one exception, had fallen in. This exception was found in a compartment wall, not very thick, which stood about the middle of the house, and against which had rested the head of my bed. The plastering had here, in great measure, resisted the action of the fire — a fact which I attributed to its having been recently spread. About this wall a dense crowd were collected, and many persons seemed to be examining a particular portion of it with very minute and eager attention. The words 'strange!' 'singular!' and other similar expressions, excited my curiosity. I approached and saw, as if graven in *bas-relief* upon the white surface, the figure of a gigantic *cat*. The impression was given with an accuracy truly marvellous. There was a rope about the animal's neck.

When I first beheld this apparition — for I could scarcely regard it as less — my wonder and my terror were extreme. But at length reflection came to my aid. The cat, I remembered, had been hung in a garden adjacent to the house. Upon the alarm of fire, this garden had been immediately filled by the crowd — by some one of whom the animal must have been cut from the tree and thrown, through an open window, into my chamber. This had probably been done with the view of arousing me from sleep. The falling of other walls had compressed the victim of my cruelty into the substance of the freshly-spread plaster; the lime of which, with the flames and the *ammonia* from the carcass, had then accomplished the portraiture as I saw it.

Although I thus readily accounted to my reason, if not altogether to my conscience, for the startling fact just detailed, it did not the less fail to make a deep impression upon my fancy. For months I could not rid myself of the phantasm of the cat; and, during this period, there came back into my spirit a half-sentiment that seemed, but was not, remorse. I went so far as to regret the loss of the animal, and to look about me, among the vile haunts which I now habitually frequented, for another pet of the same species, and of somewhat similar appearance, with which to supply its place.

One night as I sat, half-stupefied, in a den of more than infamy, my attention was suddenly drawn to some black object, reposing upon the head of one of the immense hogsheads of gin, or of rum, which constituted the chief furniture of the apartment. I had been looking steadily at the top of this hogshead for some minutes, and what now caused me surprise was the fact that I had not sooner perceived the object thereupon. I approached it, and touched it with my hand. It was a black cat — a very large one — fully as large as Pluto, and closely resembling him in every respect but one. Pluto had not a white hair upon any portion of his body; but this cat had a large, although indefinite, splotch of white, covering nearly the whole region of the breast.

Upon my touching him, he immediately arose, purred loudly, rubbed against my hand, and appeared delighted with my notice. This, then, was the very creature of which I was in search. I at once offered to purchase it of the landlord; but this person made no claim to it — knew nothing of it — had never seen it before.

I continued my caresses, and when I prepared to go home, the animal evinced a disposition to accompany me. I permitted it to do so; occasionally stooping and patting it as I proceeded. When it reached the house it domesticated itself at once, and became immediately a great favourite with my wife.

For my own part, I soon found a dislike to it arising within me. This was just the reverse of what I had anticipated; but — I know not how or why it was — its evident fondness for myself rather disgusted and annoyed me. By slow degrees, these feelings of disgust and annoyance rose into the bitterness of hatred. I avoided the creature; a certain sense of shame, and the remembrance of my former deed of cruelty, preventing me from physically abusing it. I did not, for some weeks, strike, or otherwise violently ill-use it; but gradually — very gradually — I came to look upon it with unutterable loathing, and to flee silently from its odious presence, as from the breath of a pestilence.

What added, no doubt, to my hatred of the beast, was the discovery, on the morning after I brought it home, that, like Pluto, it also had been deprived of one of its eyes. This circumstance, however, only endeared it to my wife, who, as I have already said, possessed, in a high degree, that humanity of feeling which had once been my distinguishing trait, and the source of many of my simplest and purest pleasures.

With my aversion to this cat, however, its partiality for myself seemed to increase. It followed my footsteps with a pertinacity which it would be difficult to make the reader comprehend. Whenever I sat, it would crouch beneath my chair, or spring upon my knees, covering me with its loathsome caresses. If I arose to walk, it would get between my feet, and thus nearly throw me down, or, fastening its long and sharp claws in my dress, clamber,

in this manner, to my breast. At such times, although I longed to destroy it with a blow, I was yet withheld from so doing, partly by a memory of my former crime, but chiefly — let me confess it at once — by absolute *dread* of the beast.

This dread was not exactly a dread of physical evil — and yet I should be at a loss how otherwise to define it. I am almost ashamed to own — yes, even in this felon's cell, I am almost ashamed to own — that the terror and horror with which the animal inspired me, had been heightened by one of the merest chimeras it would be possible to conceive. My wife had called my attention, more than once, to the character of the mark of white hair, of which I have spoken, and which constituted the sole visible difference between the strange beast and the one I had destroyed. The reader will remember that this mark, although large, had been originally very indefinite; but, by slow degrees — degrees nearly imperceptible, and which for a long time my reason struggled to reject as fanciful — it had, at length, resumed a rigorous distinctness of outline. It was now the representation of an object that I shudder to name — and for this, above all, I loathed, and dreaded, and would have rid myself of the monster *had I dared* — it was now, I say, the image of a hideous — of a ghastly thing — of the GALLOWS! — oh, mournful and terrible engine of horror and of crime — of agony and death!

And now was I indeed wretched beyond the wretchedness of mere humanity. And a *brute beast* — whose fellow I had contemptuously destroyed — *a brute beast* to work out for *me* — for me, a man, fashioned in the image of the High God — so much of insufferable woe! Alas! neither by day nor by night knew I the blessing of rest any more! During the former the creature left me no moment alone; and, in the latter, I started, hourly, from dreams of unutterable fear, to find the hot breath of *the thing* upon my face, and its vast weight — an incarnate nightmare that I had no power to shake off — incumbent eternally upon my *heart!*

Beneath the pressure of torments such as these, the feeble remnant of the good within me succumbed. Evil thoughts became my sole intimates — the darkest and most evil of thoughts. The moodiness of my usual temper increased to hatred of all things and of all mankind; while, from the sudden, frequent, and ungovernable outbursts of a fury to which I now blindly abandoned myself, my uncomplaining wife, alas! was the most usual and the most patient of sufferers.

One day she accompanied me, upon some household errand, into the cellar of the old building which our poverty compelled us to inhabit. The cat followed me down the steep stairs, and, nearly throwing me headlong, exasperated me to madness. Uplifting an axe, and forgetting, in my wrath, the childish dread which had hitherto stayed my hand, I aimed a blow at the animal which, of course, would have proved instantly fatal had it descended as I wished. But this blow was arrested by the hand of my wife. Goaded, by the interference, into a rage more than demoniacal, I withdrew my arm from her grasp, and buried the axe in her brain. She fell dead upon the spot, without a groan.

This hideous murder accomplished, I set myself forthwith, and with entire deliberation, to the task of concealing the body. I knew that I could not remove it from the house, either by day or by night, without the risk of being observed by the neighbors. Many projects entered my mind. At one period I thought of cutting the corpse into minute fragments and destroying them by fire. At another, I resolved to dig a grave for it in the floor of the cellar. Again, I deliberated about casting it into the well in the yard — about packing it in a box, as if merchandise, with the usual arrangements, and so getting a porter to take it from the house. Finally I hit upon what I considered a far better expedient than either of these. I determined to wall it up in the cellar — as the monks of the Middle Ages are recorded to have walled up their victims.

For a purpose such as this the cellar was well adapted. Its walls were loosely constructed, and had lately been plastered throughout with a rough plaster, which the dampness of the atmosphere had prevented from hardening. Moreover, in one of the walls was a projection, caused by a false chimney, or fire-place, that had been filled up and made to resemble the rest of the cellar. I made no doubt that I could readily displace the bricks at this point, insert the corpse, and wall the whole up as before, so that no eye could detect anything suspicious.

And in this calculation I was not deceived. By means of a crowbar I easily dislodged the bricks, and having carefully deposited the body against the inner wall, I propped it in that position, while, with little trouble, I relaid the whole structure as it originally stood. Having procured mortar, sand, and hair, with every possible precaution, I prepared a plaster which could not be distinguished from the old, and with this I very carefully went over the new brickwork. When I had finished, I felt satisfied that all was right. The wall did not present the slightest appearance of having been disturbed. The rubbish on the floor was picked up with the minutest care. I looked around triumphantly, and said to myself, "Here at least, then, my labour has not been in vain."

My next step was to look for the beast which had been the cause of so much wretchedness; for I had, at length, firmly resolved to put it to death. Had I been able

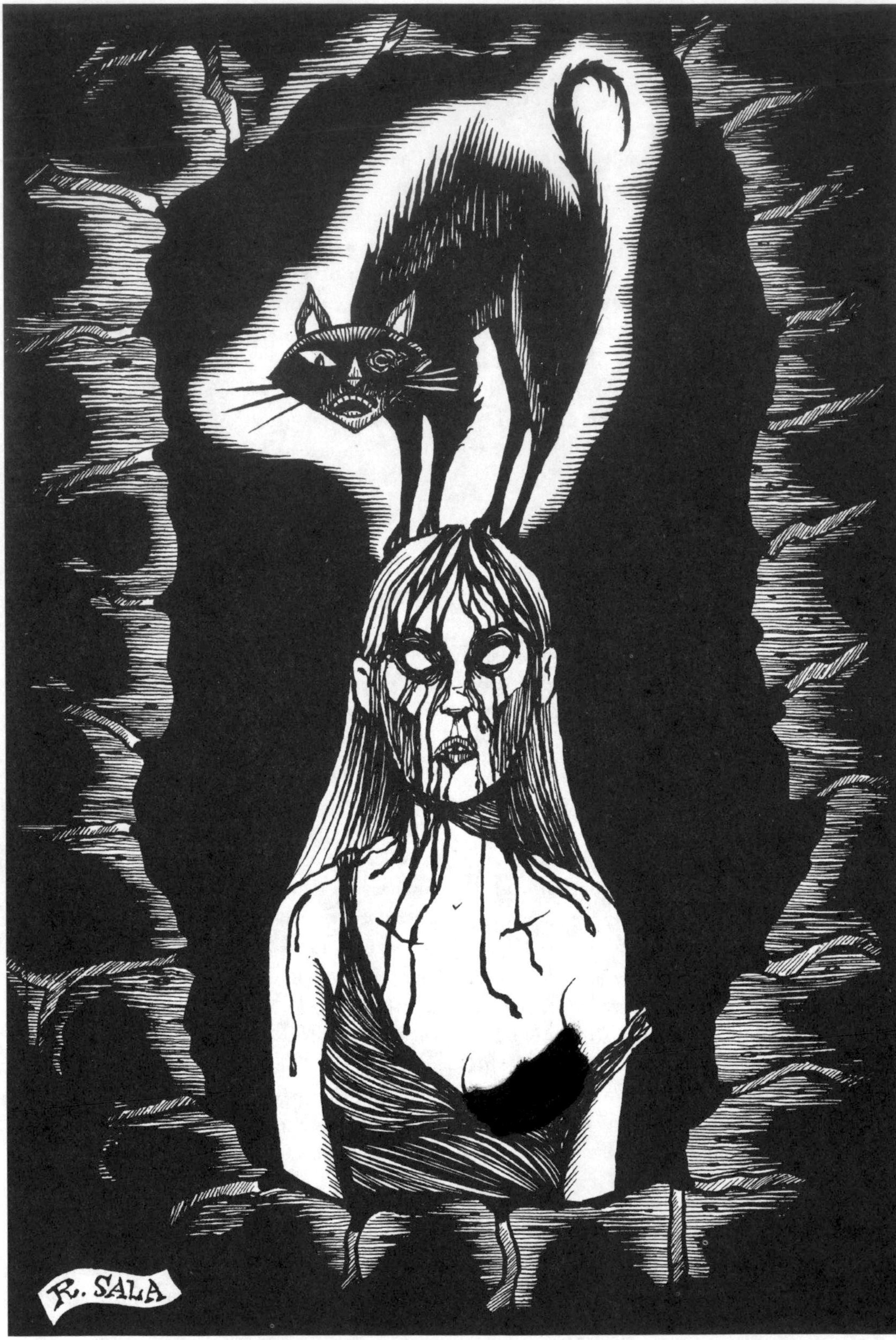
R. SALA

to meet with it at the moment, there could have been no doubt of its fate; but it appeared that the crafty animal had been alarmed at the violence of my previous anger, and forbore to present itself in my present mood. It is impossible to describe, or to imagine, the deep, the blissful sense of relief which the absence of the detested creature occasioned in my bosom. It did not make its appearance during the night — and thus for one night at least, since its introduction into the house, I soundly and tranquilly slept; aye, *slept* even with the burden of murder upon my soul!

The second and the third day passed, and still my tormentor came not. Once again I breathed as a free man. The monster, in terror, had fled the premises forever! I should behold it no more! My happiness was supreme! The guilt of my dark deed disturbed me but little. Some few inquiries had been made, but these had been readily answered. Even a search had been instituted — but of course nothing was to be discovered. I looked upon my future felicity as secured.

Upon the fourth day of the assassination, a party of the police came, very unexpectedly, into the house, and proceeded again to make rigorous investigation of the premises. Secure, however, in the inscrutability of my place of concealment, I felt no embarrassment whatever. The officers bade me accompany them in their search. They left no nook or corner unexplored. At length, for the third or fourth time, they descended into the cellar. I quivered not in a muscle. My heart beat calmly as that of one who slumbers in innocence. I walked the cellar from end to end. I folded my arms upon my bosom, and roamed easily to and fro. The police were thoroughly satisfied, and prepared to depart. The glee at my heart was too strong to be restrained. I burned to say if but one word, by way of triumph, and to render doubly sure their assurance of my guiltlessness.

"Gentlemen," I said at last, as the party ascended the steps, "I delight to have allayed your suspicions. I wish you all health, and a little more courtesy. By the by, gentlemen, this — this is a very well-constructed house." (In the rabid desire to say something easily, I scarcely knew what I uttered at all.) "I may say an *excellently* well-constructed house. These walls — are you going, gentlemen?— these walls are solidly put together"; and here, through the mere frenzy of bravado, I rapped heavily, with a cane which I held in my hand, upon that very portion of the brickwork behind which stood the corpse of the wife of my bosom.

But may God shield and deliver me from the fangs on the Arch-Fiend! No sooner had the reverberation of my blows sunk into silence, than I was answered by a voice from within the tomb! — by a cry, at first muffled and broken, like the sobbing of a child, and then quickly swelling into one long, loud, and continuous scream, half of horror and half of triumph, such as might have arisen only out of hell, conjointly from the throats of the damned in their agony and of the demons that exult in the damnation.

Of my own thoughts it is folly to speak. Swooning, I staggered to the opposite wall. For one instant the party upon the stairs remained motionless, through extremity of terror and of awe. In the next, a dozen stout arms were toiling at the wall. It fell bodily. The corpse, already greatly decayed and clotted with gore, stood erect before the eyes of the spectators. Upon its head, with red extended mouth and solitary eye of fire, sat the hideous beast whose craft had seduced me into murder, and whose informing voice had consigned me to the hangman. I had walled the monster up within the tomb!

THE INHERITANCE OF RUFUS GRISWOLD

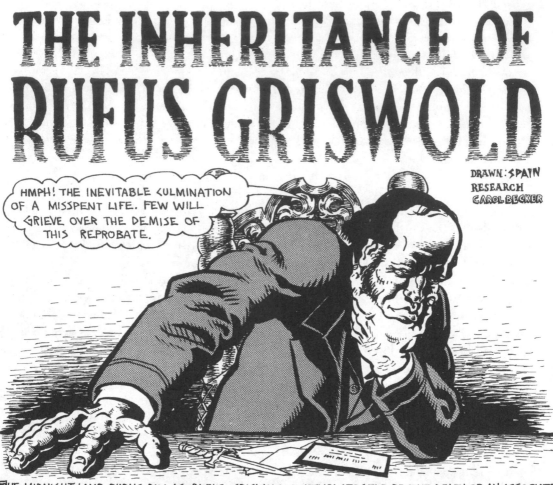

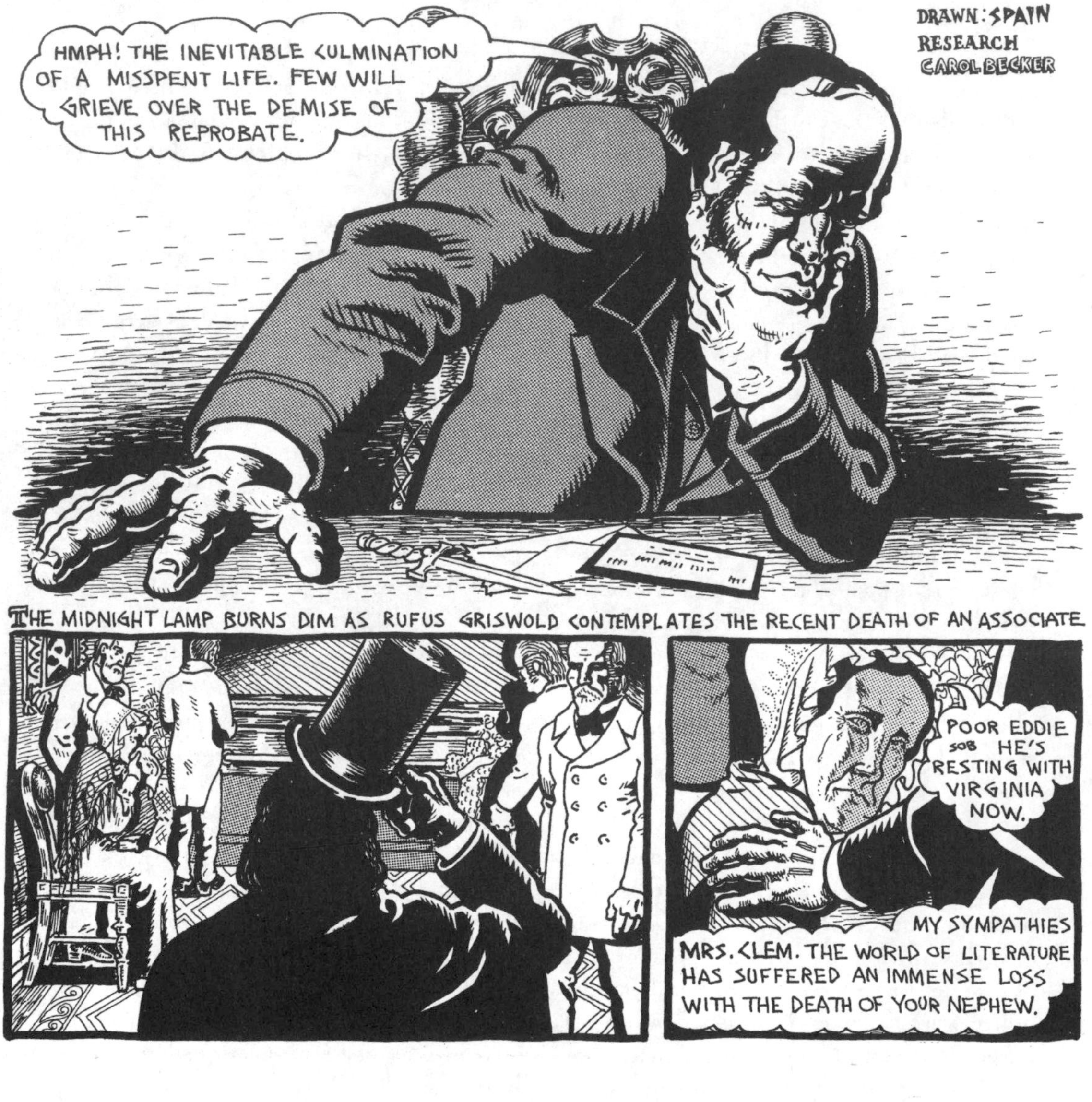
DRAWN: SPAIN
RESEARCH CAROL BECKER
HMPH! THE INEVITABLE CULMINATION OF A MISSPENT LIFE. FEW WILL GRIEVE OVER THE DEMISE OF THIS REPROBATE.
THE MIDNIGHT LAMP BURNS DIM AS RUFUS GRISWOLD CONTEMPLATES THE RECENT DEATH OF AN ASSOCIATE
POOR EDDIE SOB HE'S RESTING WITH VIRGINIA NOW.
MY SYMPATHIES MRS. CLEM. THE WORLD OF LITERATURE HAS SUFFERED AN IMMENSE LOSS WITH THE DEATH OF YOUR NEPHEW.

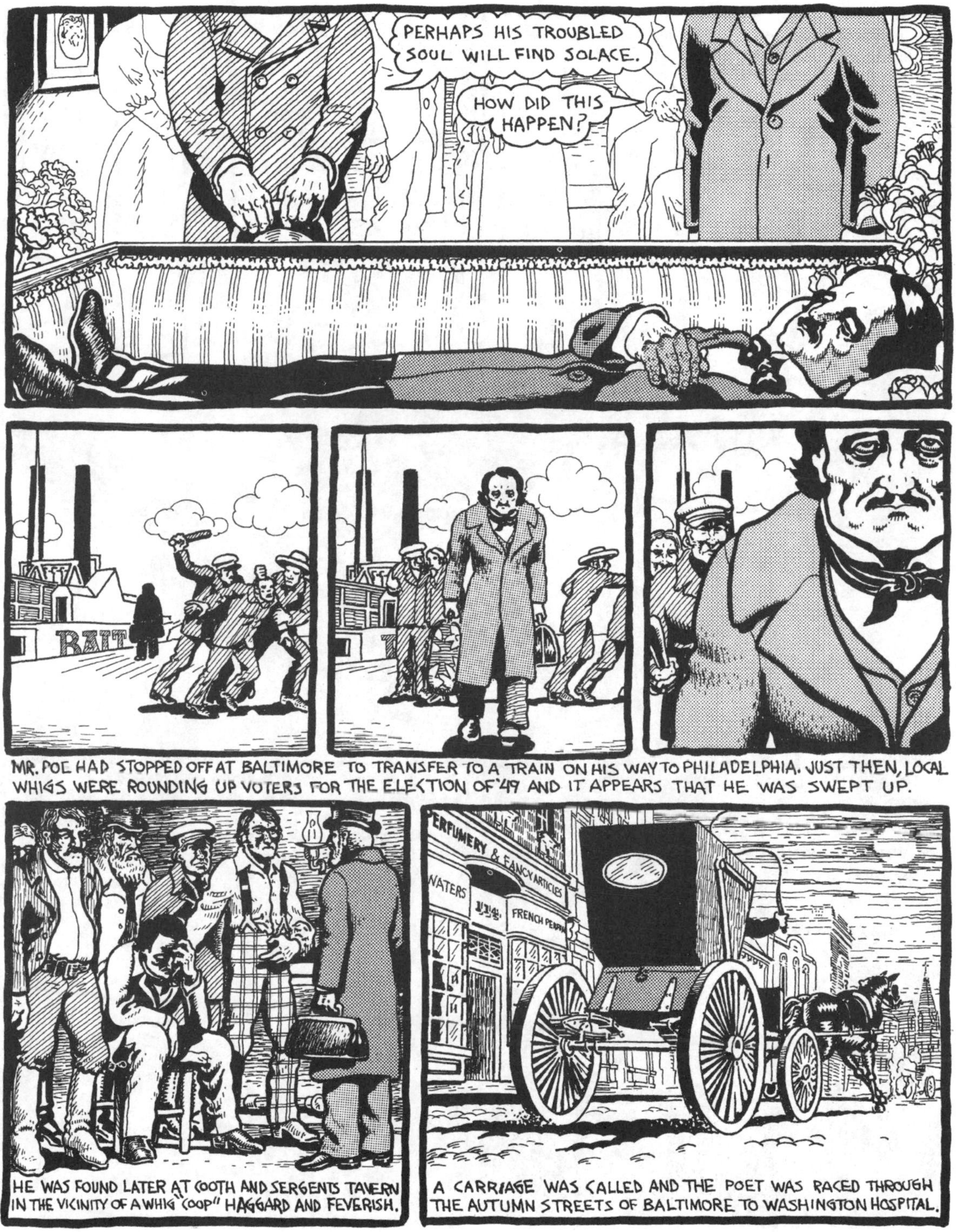
PERHAPS HIS TROUBLED SOUL WILL FIND SOLACE.
HOW DID THIS HAPPEN?
MR. POE HAD STOPPED OFF AT BALTIMORE TO TRANSFER TO A TRAIN ON HIS WAY TO PHILADELPHIA. JUST THEN, LOCAL WHIGS WERE ROUNDING UP VOTERS FOR THE ELECTION OF '49 AND IT APPEARS THAT HE WAS SWEPT UP.
HE WAS FOUND LATER AT COOTH AND SERGENTS TAVERN IN THE VICINITY OF A WHIG "COOP" HAGGARD AND FEVERISH.
A CARRIAGE WAS CALLED AND THE POET WAS RACED THROUGH THE AUTUMN STREETS OF BALTIMORE TO WASHINGTON HOSPITAL.

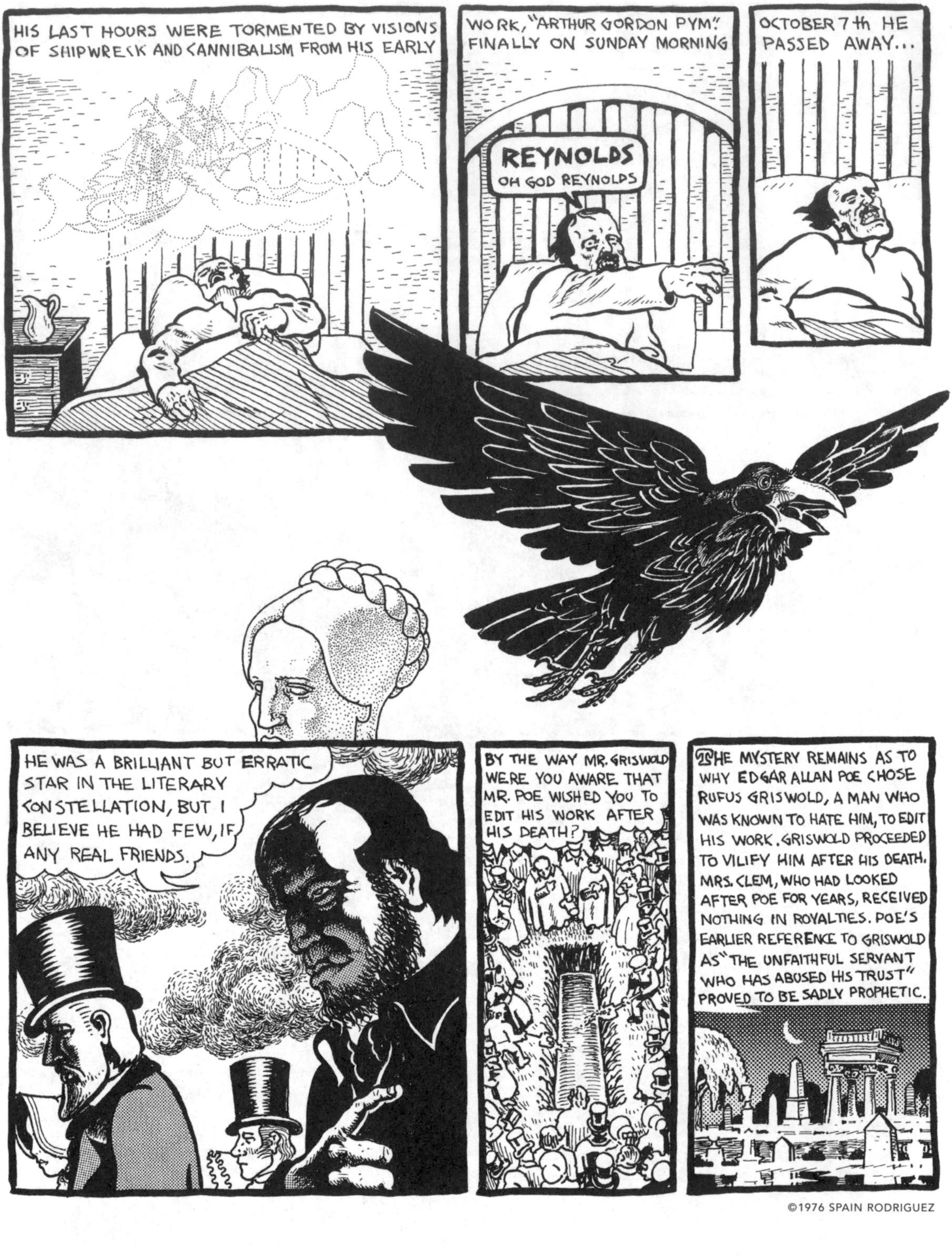
HIS LAST HOURS WERE TORMENTED BY VISIONS OF SHIPWRECK AND CANNIBALISM FROM HIS EARLY
WORK, "ARTHUR GORDON PYM." FINALLY ON SUNDAY MORNING
REYNOLDS
OH GOD REYNOLDS
OCTOBER 7th HE PASSED AWAY...
HE WAS A BRILLIANT BUT ERRATIC STAR IN THE LITERARY CONSTELLATION, BUT I BELIEVE HE HAD FEW, IF ANY REAL FRIENDS.
BY THE WAY MR. GRISWOLD WERE YOU AWARE THAT MR. POE WISHED YOU TO EDIT HIS WORK AFTER HIS DEATH?
THE MYSTERY REMAINS AS TO WHY EDGAR ALLAN POE CHOSE RUFUS GRISWOLD, A MAN WHO WAS KNOWN TO HATE HIM, TO EDIT HIS WORK. GRISWOLD PROCEEDED TO VILIFY HIM AFTER HIS DEATH. MRS. CLEM, WHO HAD LOOKED AFTER POE FOR YEARS, RECEIVED NOTHING IN ROYALTIES. POE'S EARLIER REFERENCE TO GRISWOLD AS "THE UNFAITHFUL SERVANT WHO HAS ABUSED HIS TRUST" PROVED TO BE SADLY PROPHETIC.

STORY BY EDGAR ALLAN POE • ADAPTATION BY MILTON KNIGHT

NEVER BET THE DEVIL YOUR HEAD

IT IS NOT MY DESIGN TO VITUPERATE MY DECEASED FRIEND, TOBY DAMMIT.

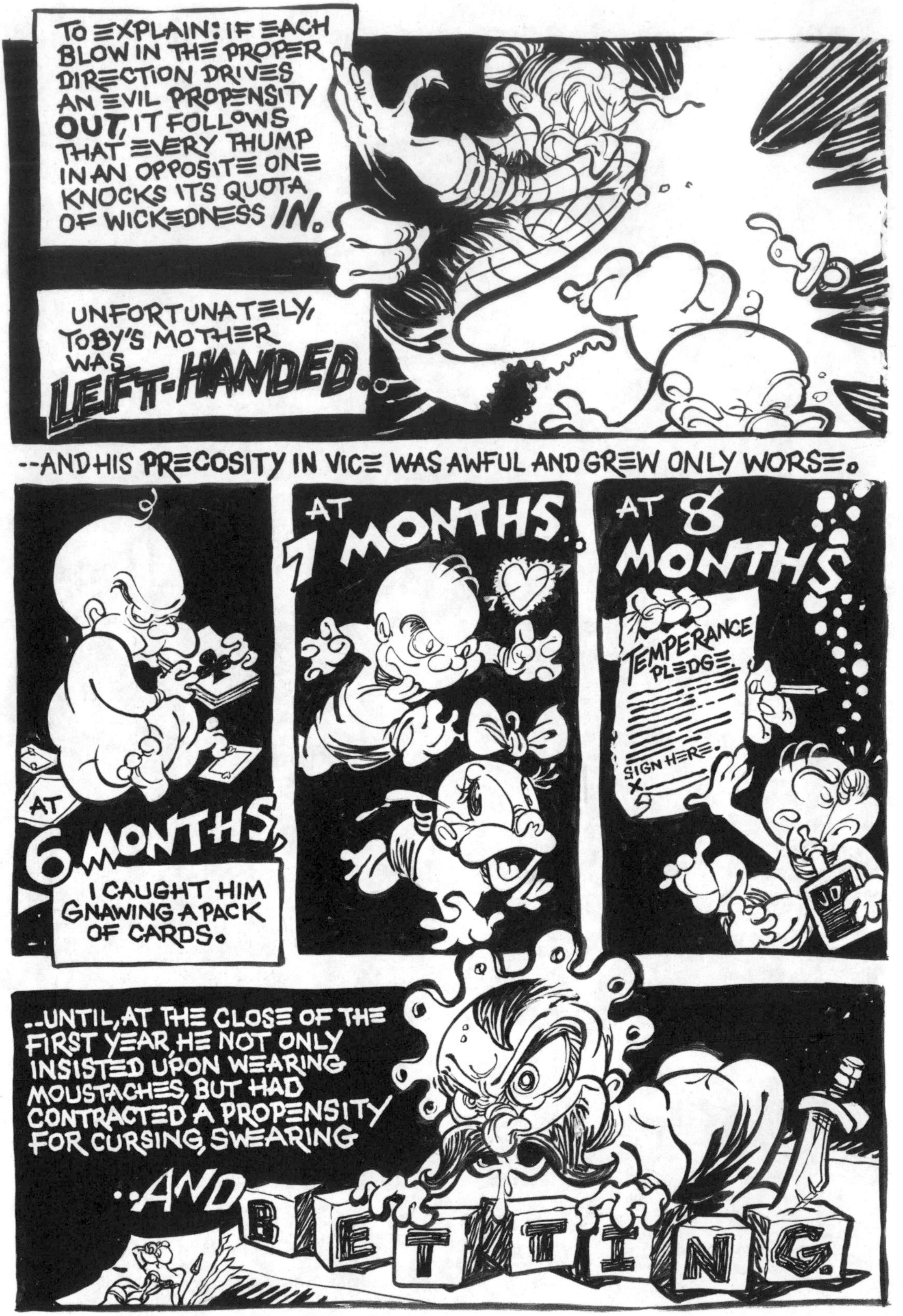
TO EXPLAIN: IF EACH BLOW IN THE PROPER DIRECTION DRIVES AN EVIL PROPENSITY OUT, IT FOLLOWS THAT EVERY THUMP IN AN OPPOSITE ONE KNOCKS ITS QUOTA OF WICKEDNESS IN.
UNFORTUNATELY, TOBY'S MOTHER WAS LEFT-HANDED..
--AND HIS PRECOSITY IN VICE WAS AWFUL AND GREW ONLY WORSE.
AT 6 MONTHS,
I CAUGHT HIM GNAWING A PACK OF CARDS.
AT 7 MONTHS..
AT 8 MONTHS
TEMPERANCE PLEDGE
SIGN HERE
X
JD
..UNTIL, AT THE CLOSE OF THE FIRST YEAR, HE NOT ONLY INSISTED UPON WEARING MOUSTACHES, BUT HAD CONTRACTED A PROPENSITY FOR CURSING, SWEARING
..AND BETTING.

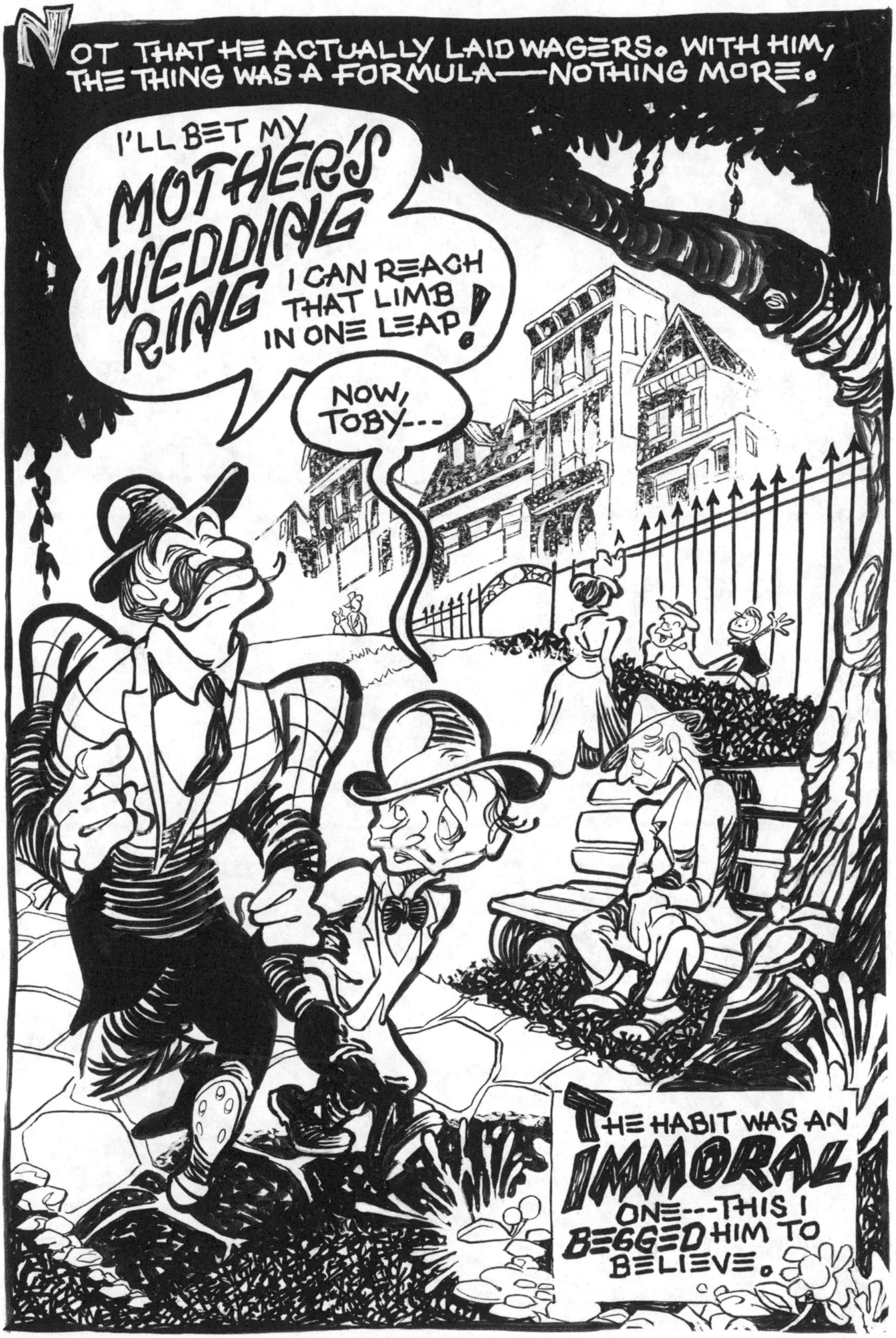
NOT THAT HE ACTUALLY LAID WAGERS. WITH HIM, THE THING WAS A FORMULA—NOTHING MORE.
I'LL BET MY MOTHER'S WEDDING RING I CAN REACH THAT LIMB IN ONE LEAP!
NOW, TOBY---
THE HABIT WAS AN IMMORAL ONE---THIS I BEGGED HIM TO BELIEVE.

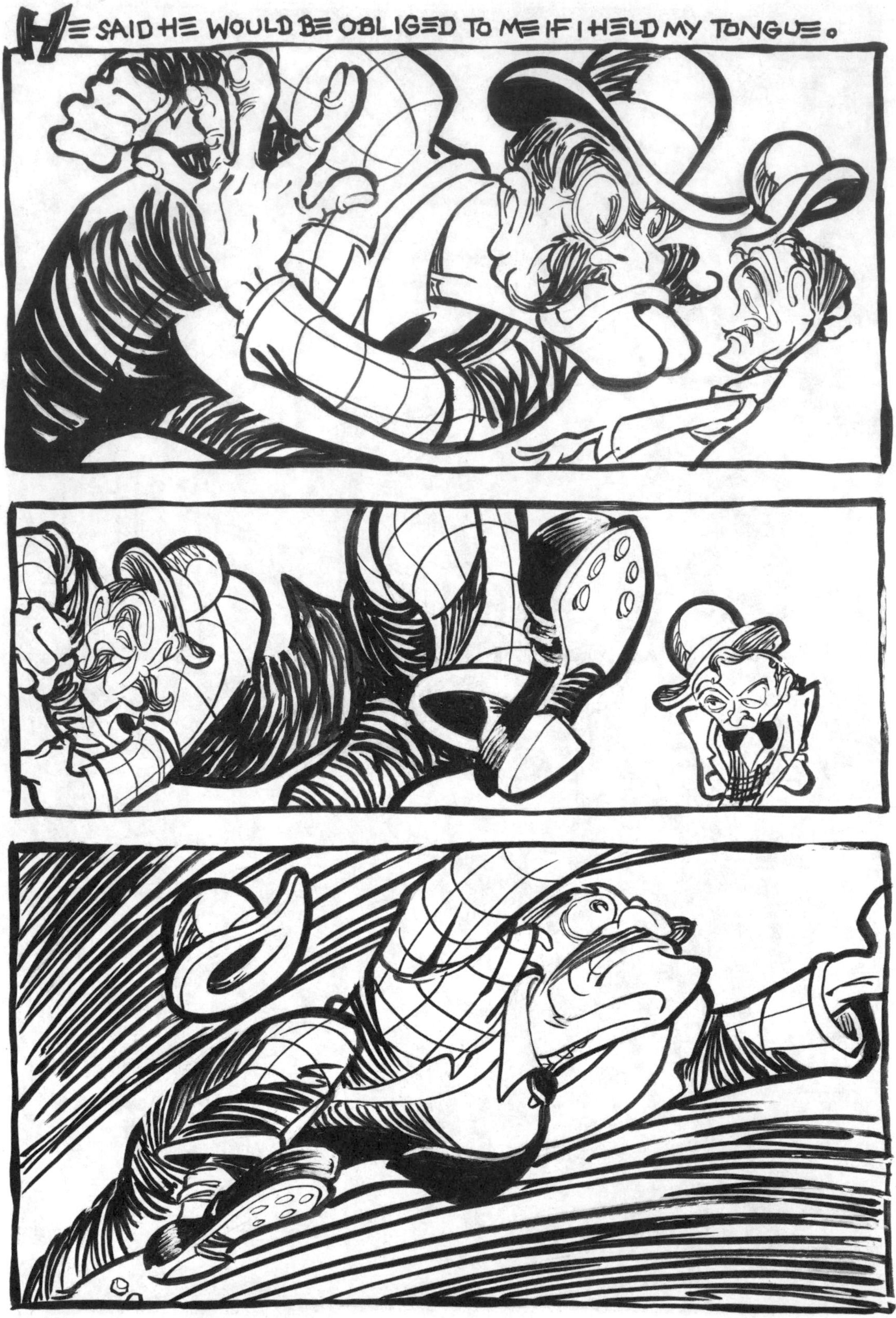
HE SAID HE WOULD BE OBLIGED TO ME IF I HELD MY TONGUE.

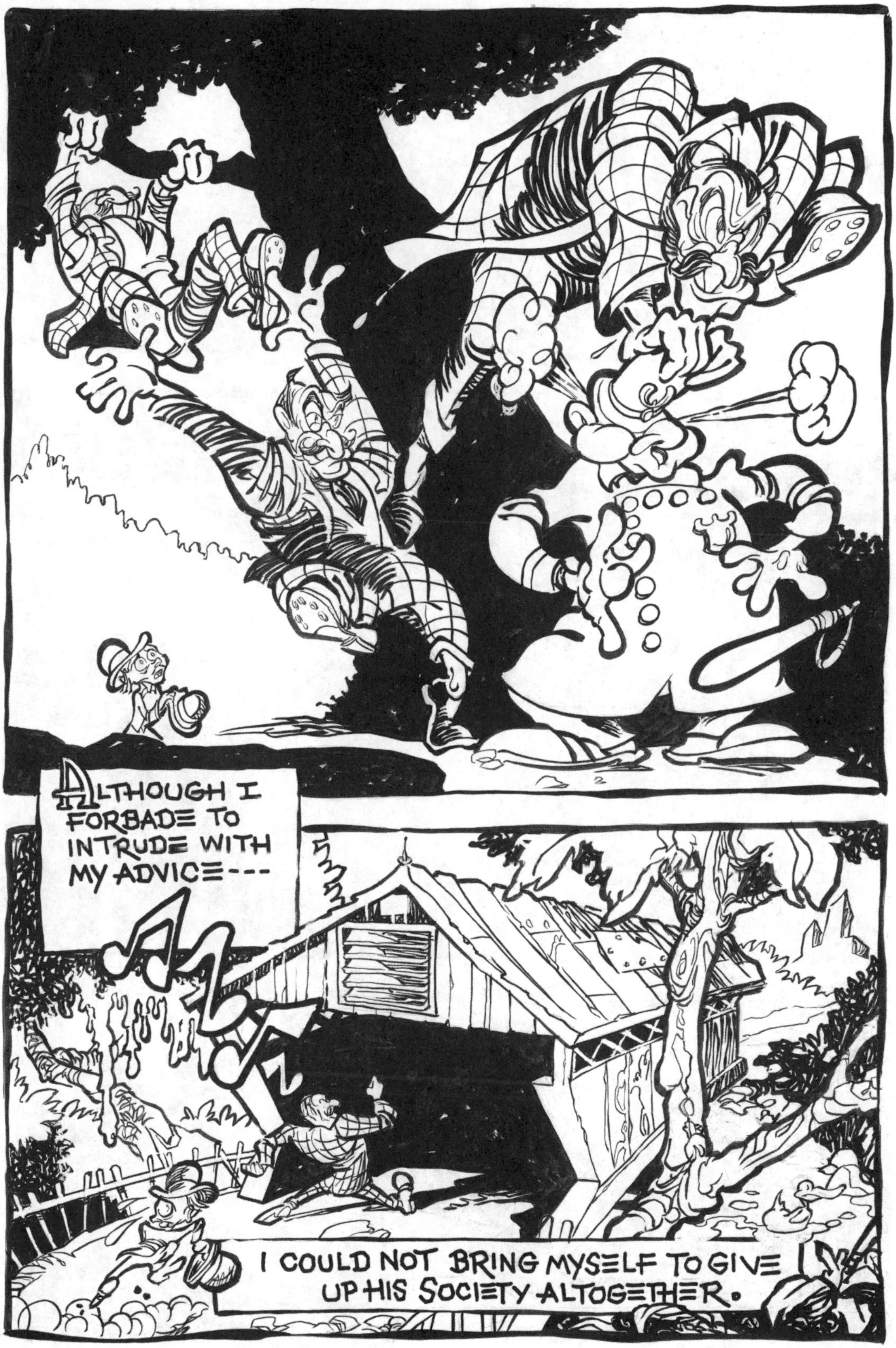
ALTHOUGH I FORBADE TO INTRUDE WITH MY ADVICE---
I COULD NOT BRING MYSELF TO GIVE UP HIS SOCIETY ALTOGETHER.

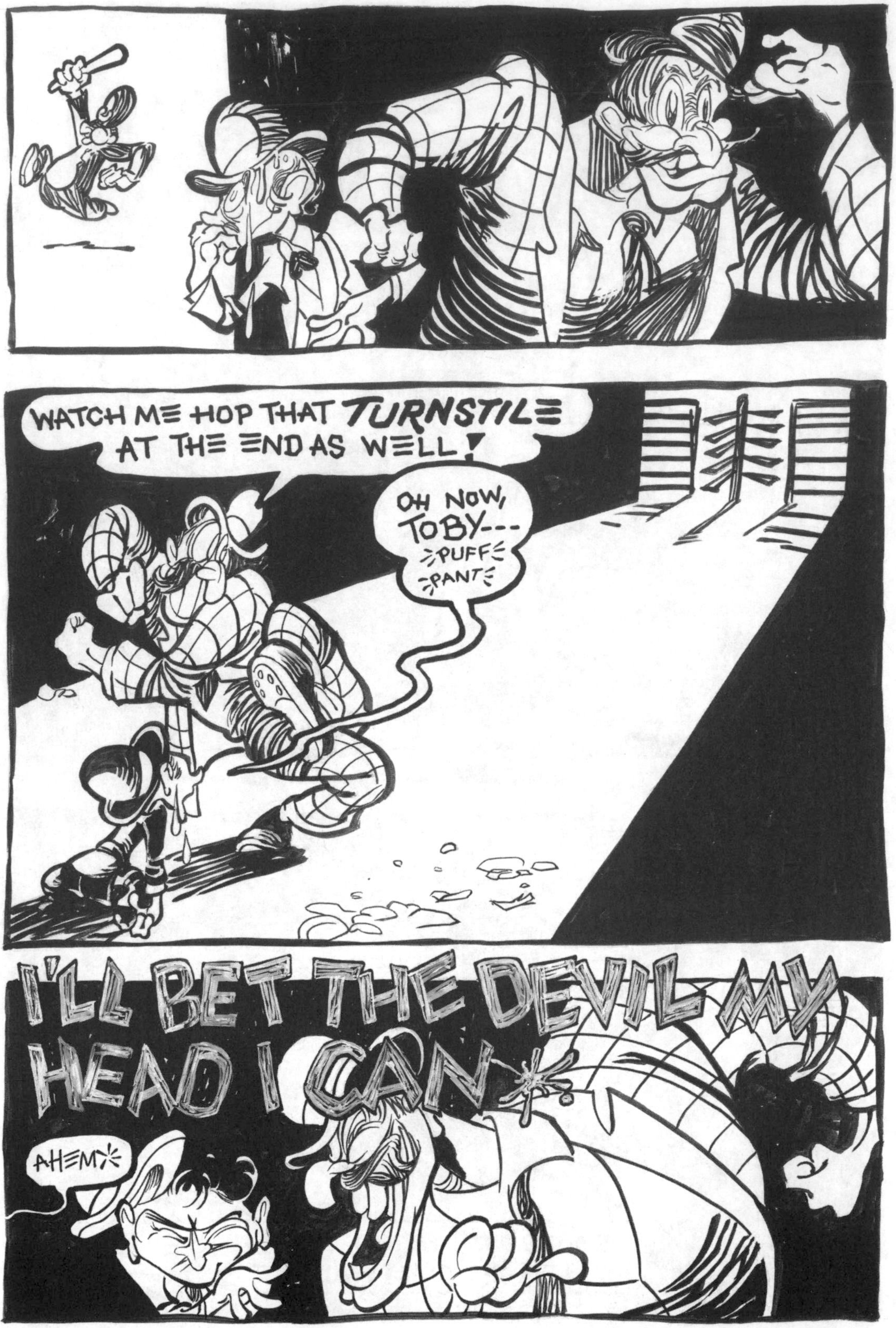
WATCH ME HOP THAT TURNSTILE AT THE END AS WELL!
OH NOW, TOBY--- PUFF PANT
I'LL BET THE DEVIL MY HEAD I CAN*
AHEM*

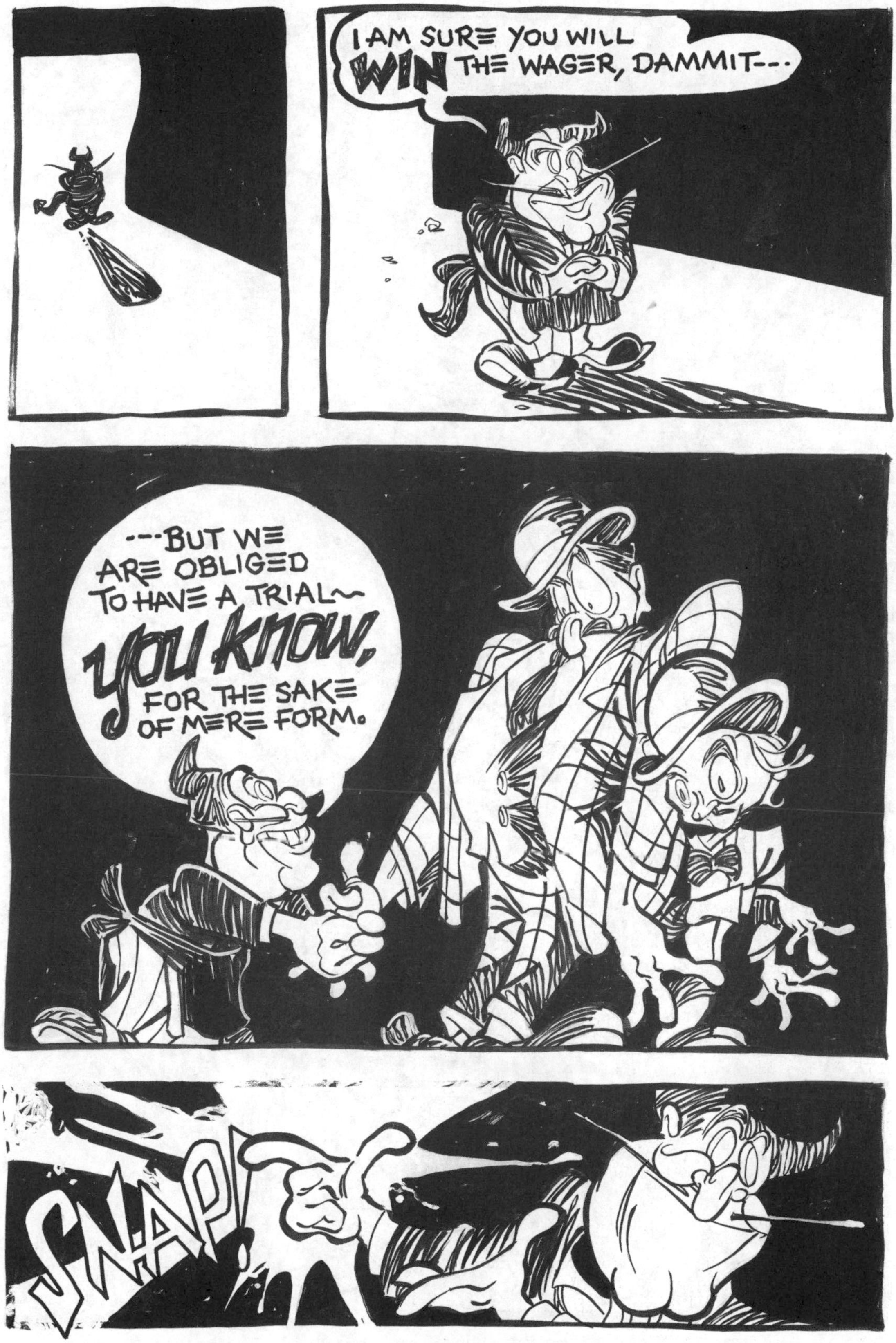
I AM SURE YOU WILL WIN THE WAGER, DAMMIT---.
---BUT WE ARE OBLIGED TO HAVE A TRIAL~ you know, FOR THE SAKE OF MERE FORM.
SNAP!

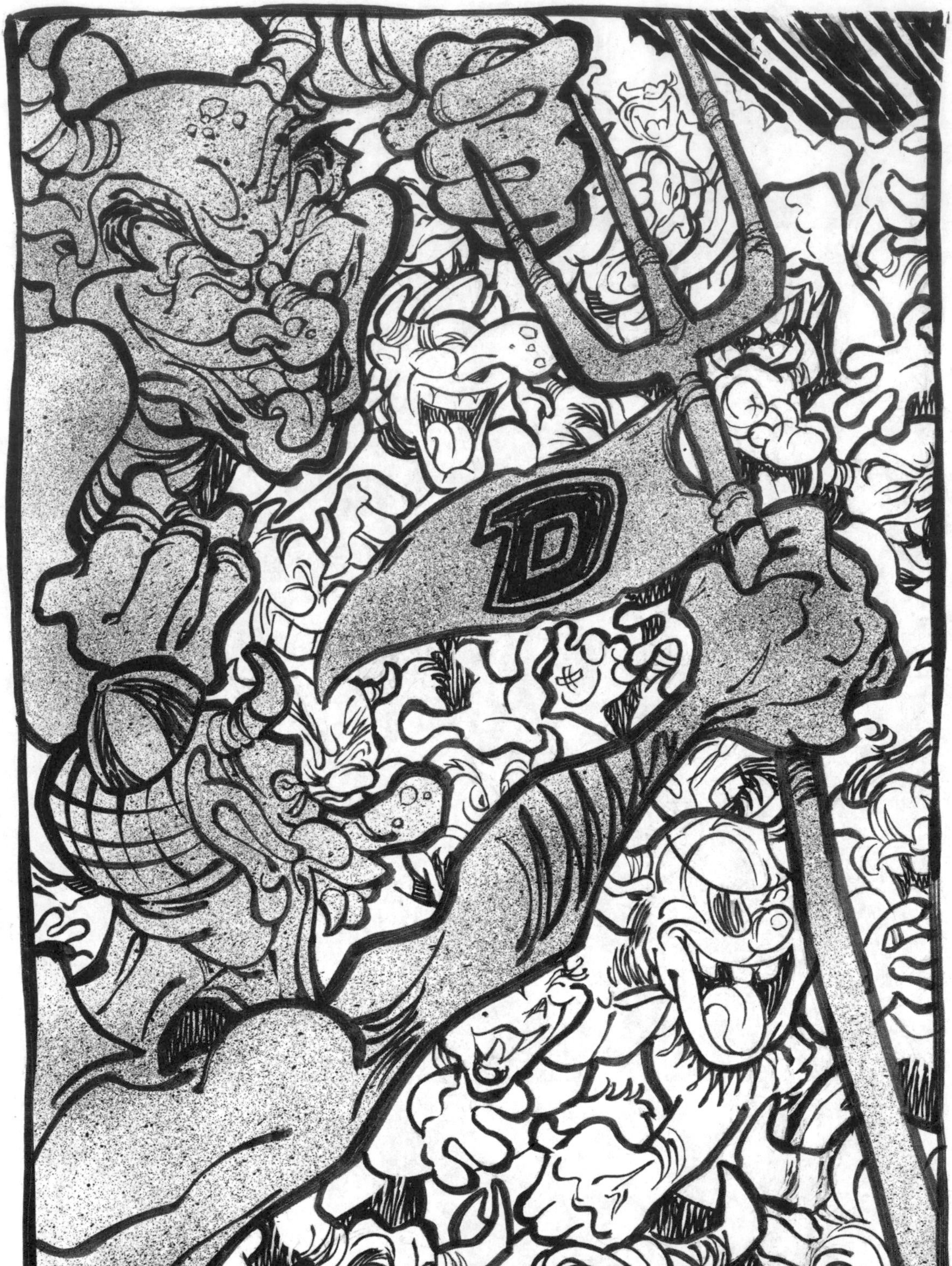
D

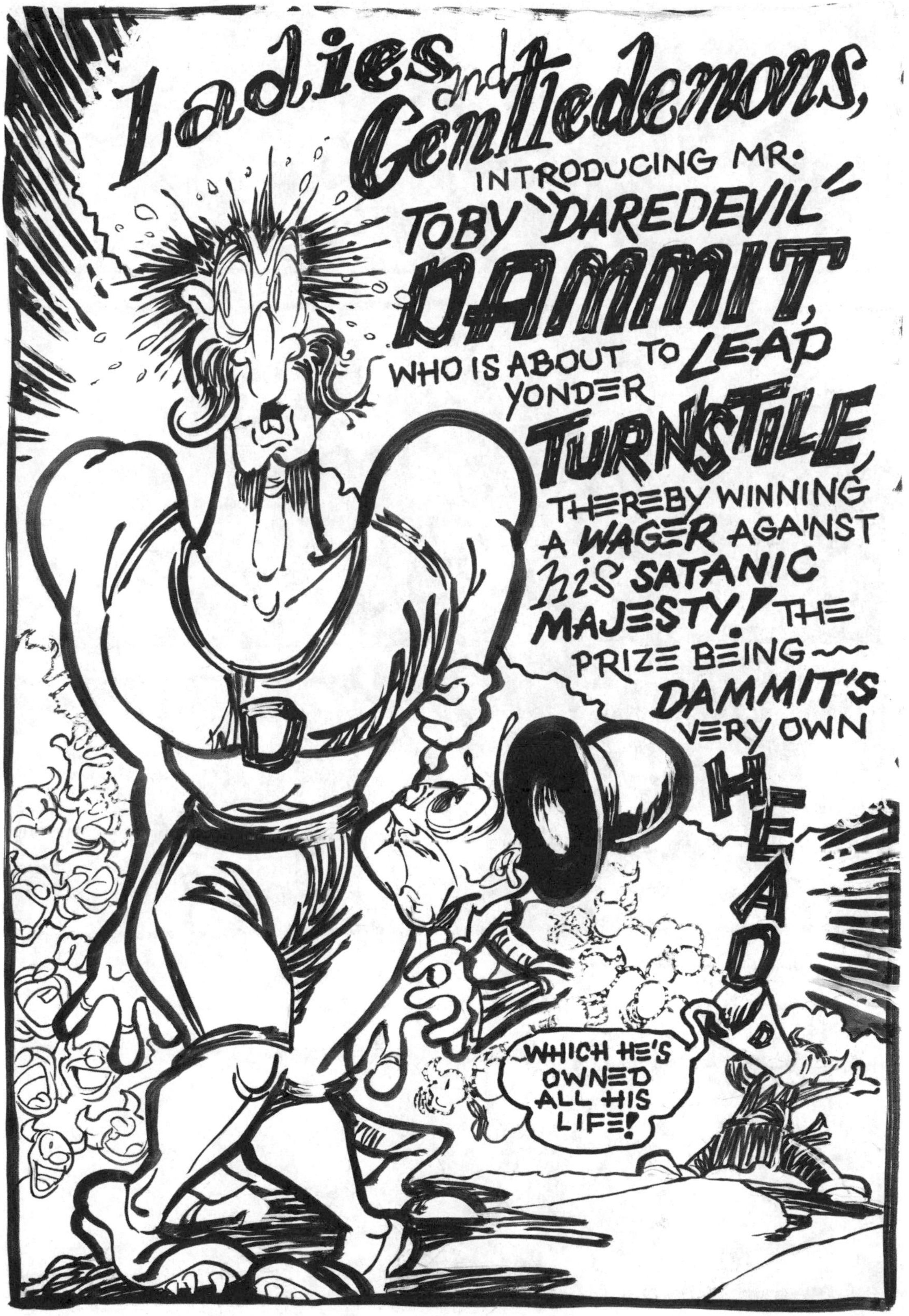
Ladies and Gentledemons,
INTRODUCING MR. TOBY "DAREDEVIL" DAMMIT,
WHO IS ABOUT TO LEAP YONDER TURNSTILE,
THEREBY WINNING A WAGER AGAINST his SATANIC MAJESTY! THE PRIZE BEING~~ DAMMIT'S VERY OWN HEAD
WHICH HE'S OWNED ALL HIS LIFE!

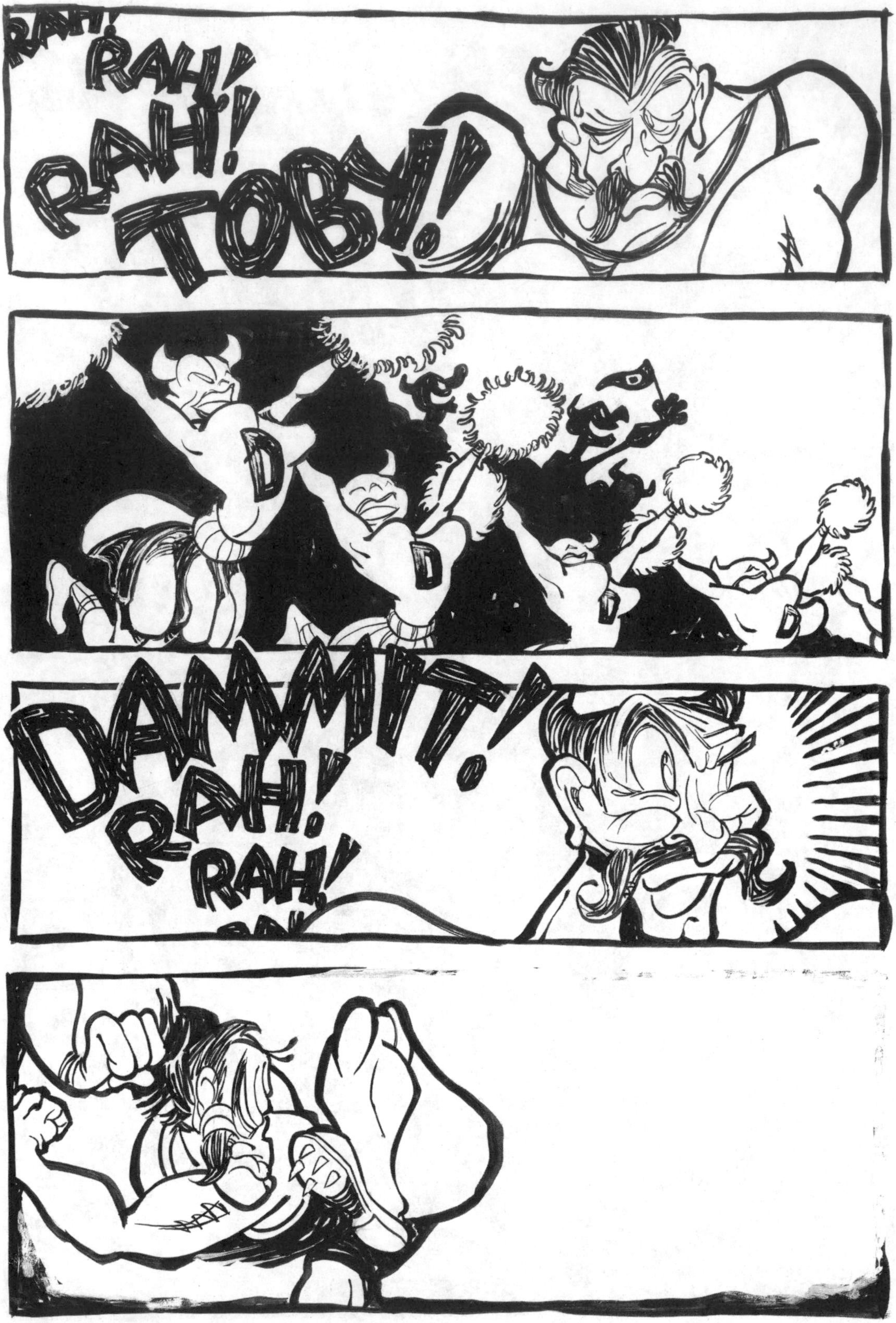
RAH!
RAH!
RAH!
TOBY!
DAMMIT!
RAH!
RAH!

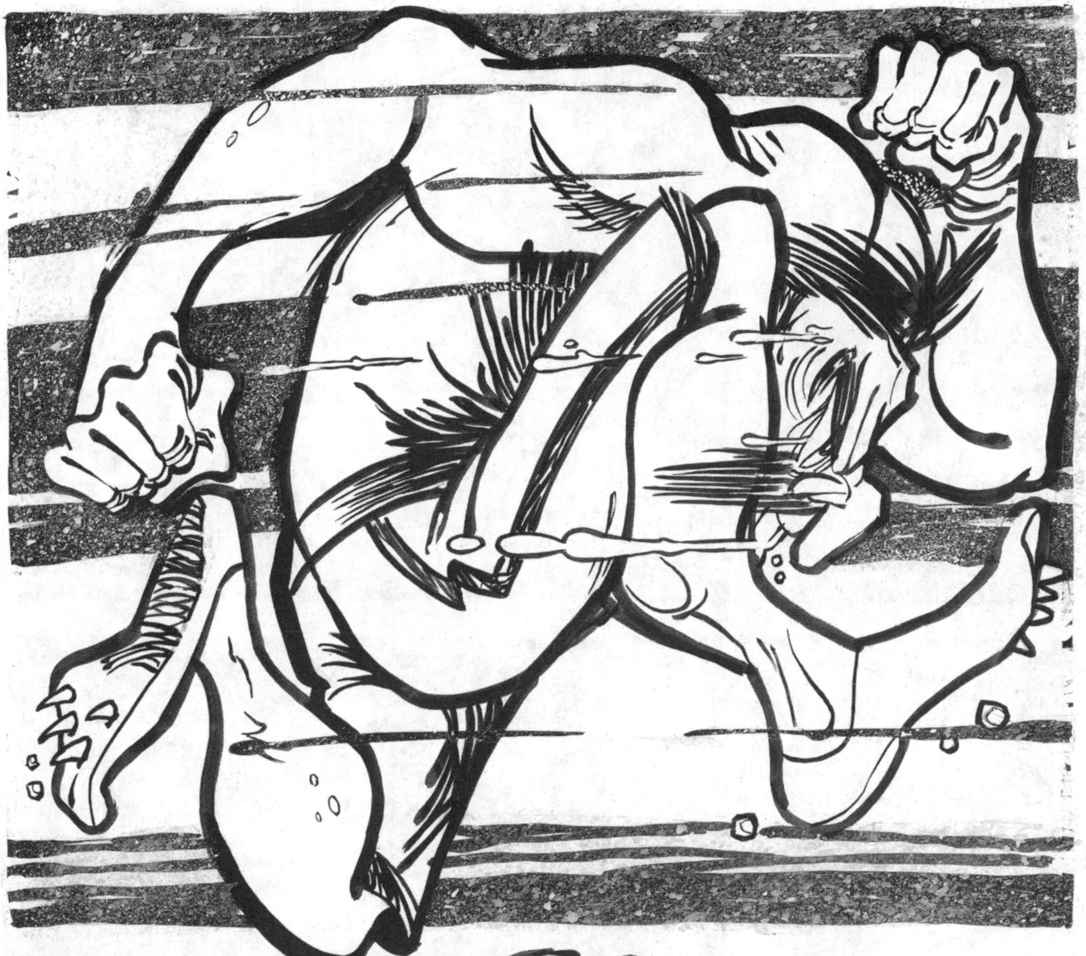

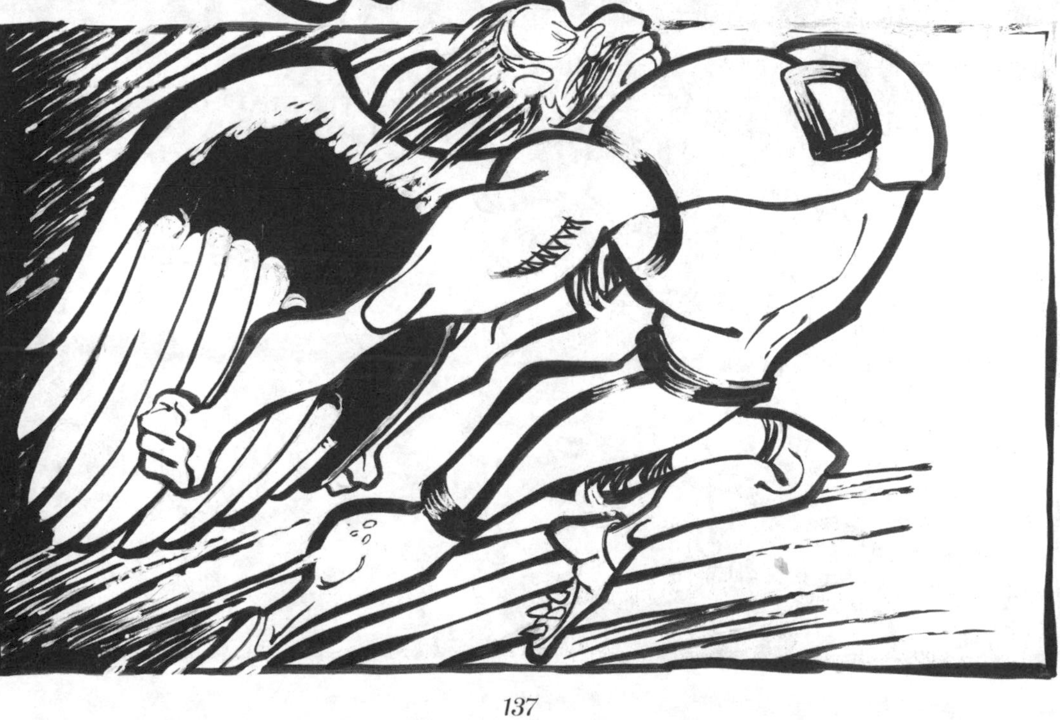

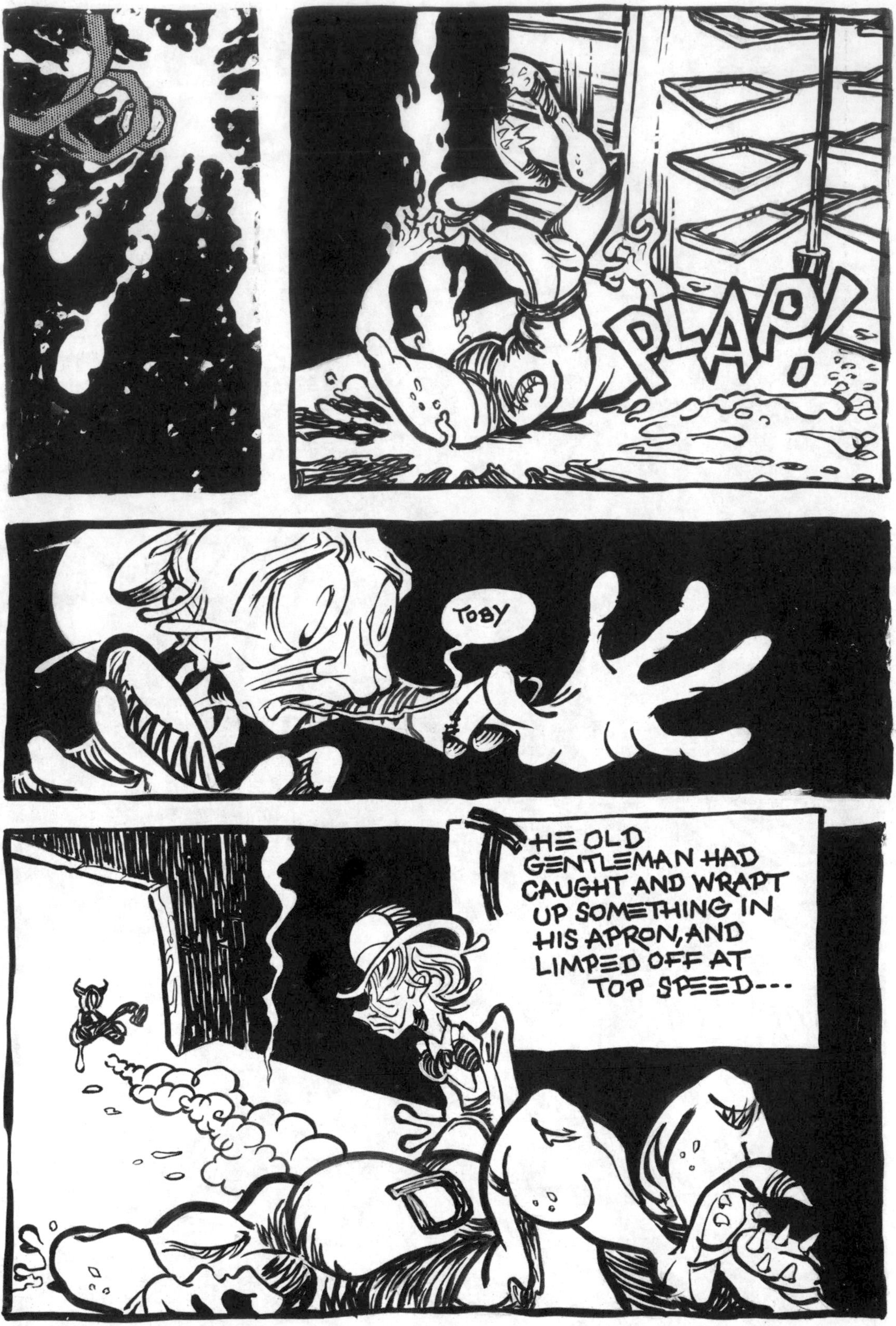
PLAP!
TOBY
THE OLD GENTLEMAN HAD CAUGHT AND WRAPT UP SOMETHING IN HIS APRON, AND LIMPED OFF AT TOP SPEED---

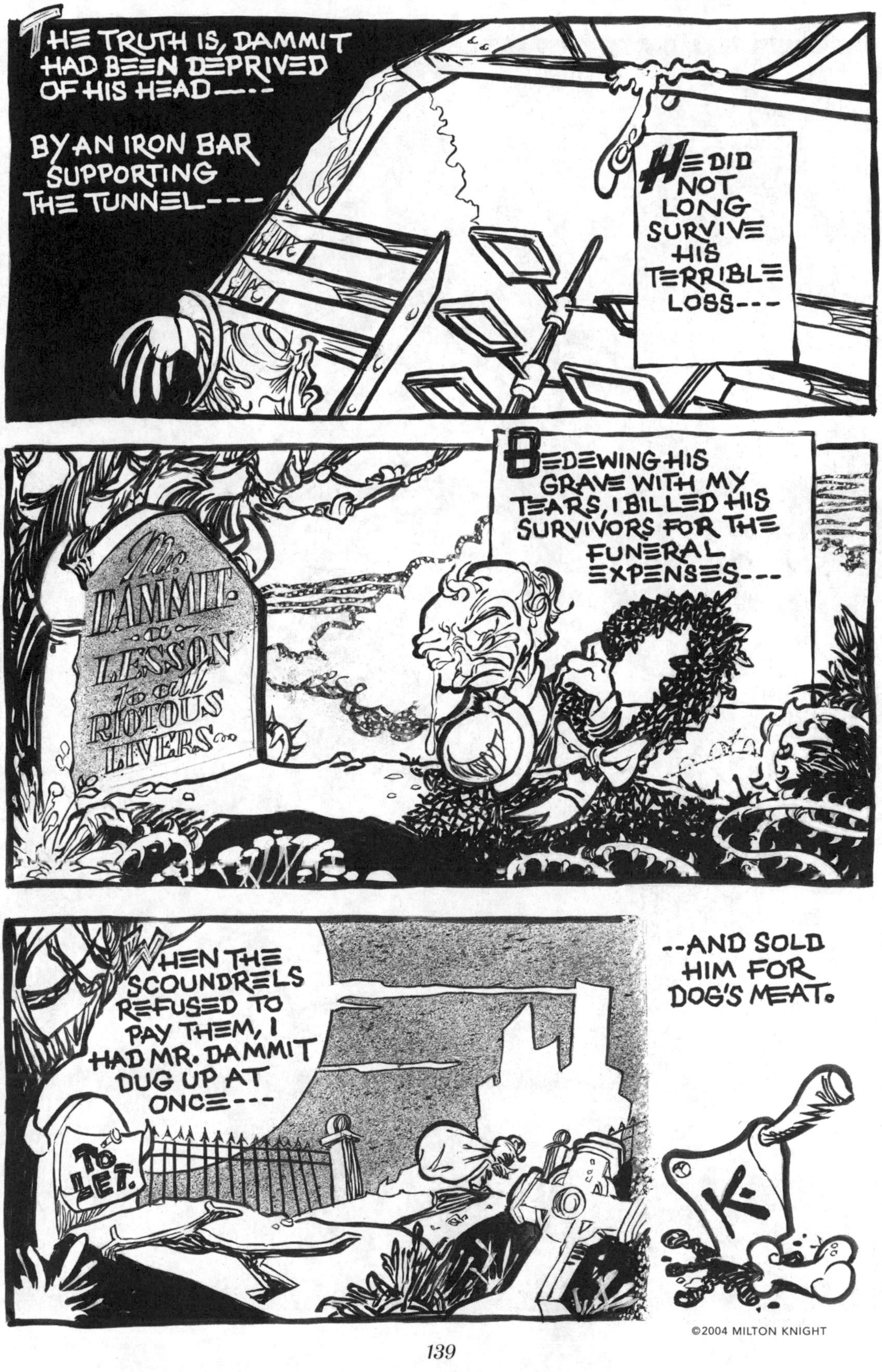
THE TRUTH IS, DAMMIT HAD BEEN DEPRIVED OF HIS HEAD---
BY AN IRON BAR SUPPORTING THE TUNNEL---
HE DID NOT LONG SURVIVE HIS TERRIBLE LOSS---
BEDEWING HIS GRAVE WITH MY TEARS, I BILLED HIS SURVIVORS FOR THE FUNERAL EXPENSES---
Mr. DAMMIT. a LESSON to all RIOTOUS LIVERS...
WHEN THE SCOUNDRELS REFUSED TO PAY THEM, I HAD MR. DAMMIT DUG UP AT ONCE---
TO LET.
--AND SOLD HIM FOR DOG'S MEAT.
K

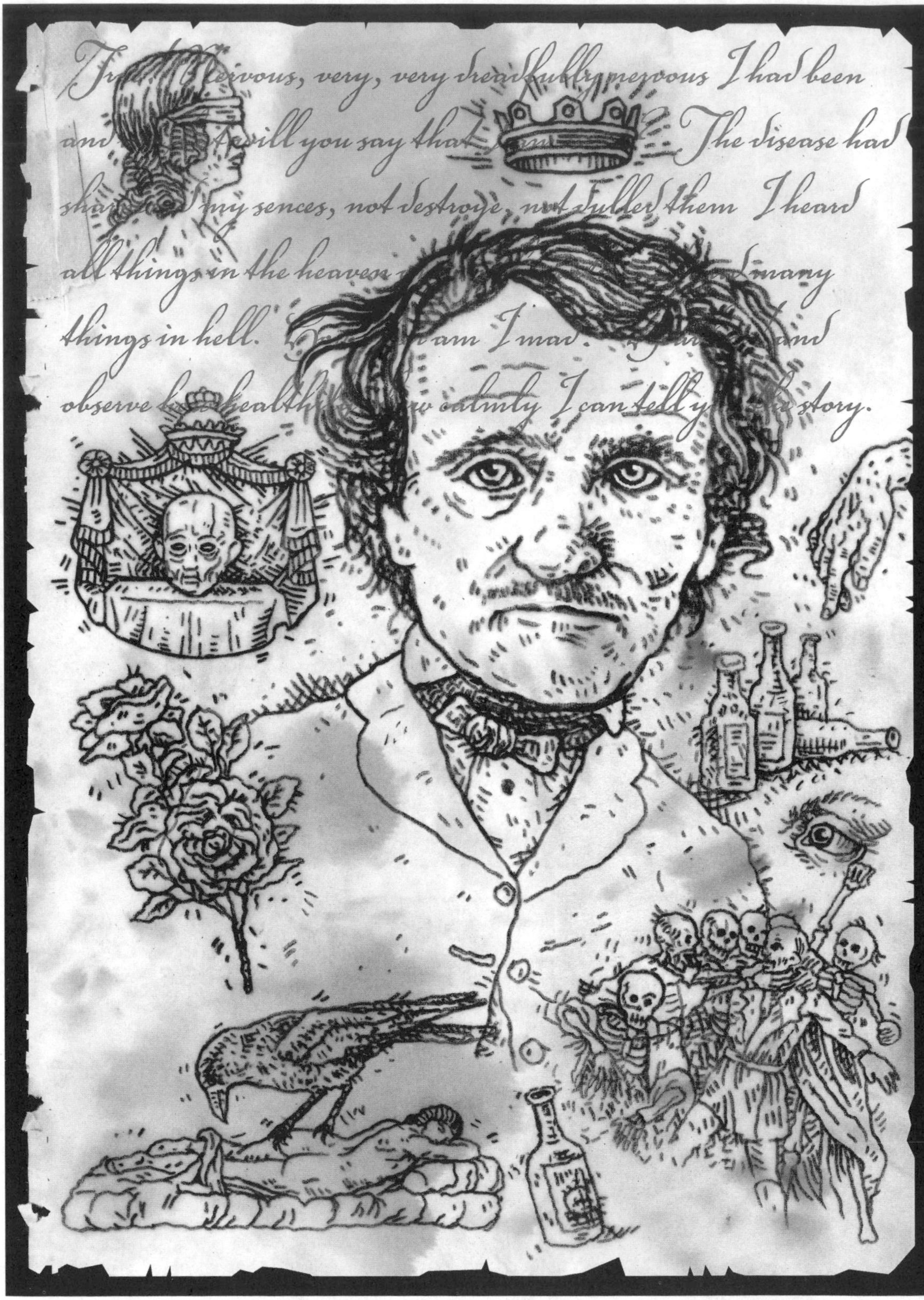
nervous, very, very dreadfully nervous I had been
will you say that
The disease had
my sences, not destroye
I heard
all things in the heaven
many
things in hell.
am I mad
and
observe
calmly I can tell
story.

EDGAR ALLAN POE

Edgar Allan Poe, the orphaned son of itinerant actors, led a tumultuous adolescence of drink and gambling, which resulted in the failure of both his university and military careers. Throughout his life he was plagued by poverty, poor health, insecurity, and depression, much by his own doing and a result of his continuing problems with alcohol. He struggled unsuccessfully as a writer until winning a short story contest in 1833. Poe's subsequent writing ranged from his rigorously metrical poetry to short stories, from journalism and distinguished literary criticism to the pseudo-scientific essays of *Eureka*. Today he is generally acknowledged as the inventor of both the gothic short story and the detective story, a pioneer of early science fiction and the founding father of the horror genre. Fittingly, there is still much mystery associated with his death at age forty in 1849, as told in comics by John Esposito and Roger Langridge in *Rosebud 19*, and even in his choice for an executor of his literary estate, as told by Spain Rodriguez in this volume.

SKOT OLSEN (cover)

While growing up in Connecticut, Skot and his parents spent their summers sailing up and down the coast of New England and all over the West Indies. It was on these long trips that he developed his love for the sea which forms the basis for much of his work. A 1991 graduate of the Joe Kubert School of Cartoon and Graphic Art, Skot now lives on the edge of the Florida Everglades, where he concentrates on paintings which have been featured in numerous publications and exhibited in galleries in Florida, New York and California. His illustrations are printed in *Graphic Classics: H.P. Lovecraft* and *Graphic Classics: Bram Stoker*, and a large collection of his work is online at www.skotolsen.com.

MAXON CRUMB (pages 1, 4, 144)

Maxon will be familiar to many readers from his appearance in Terry Zwigoff's 1994 award-winning film, *Crumb*. While his older brother Robert's work may be more well-known, Maxon is equally talented as both a writer and artist. His gritty fantasy story, *Stigmata*, appears in *Crumb Family Comics*, and his illustrated novel of sex, violence and incest, *Hard Core Mother*, was published in 2000 by CityZen Books. The illustrations reproduced here are from his first book, *Maxon's Poe* (1997, Cottage Classics). New work by Maxon appears in *Graphic Classics: H.P. Lovecraft*, *Graphic Classics: Bram Stoker*, and in the forthcoming *Graphic Classics: Robert Louis Stevenson*.

RICHARD CORBEN (page 2)

One of the most enduring cult favorites in comics, Richard Corben is also an "artist's artist," widely respected by his peers, which made him the perfect choice for the lead spot in *Graphic Classics: H.P. Lovecraft's* unique four-artist adaptation of Herbert West: *Reanimator*. Richard's first underground comic, *Fantagor*, was self-published in 1970. He has since worked for all the major comics publishers including Warren, Métal Hurlant, Dark Horse, Marvel and DC. He has a lifelong interest in film and animation and his "Den" character was adapted in the first *Heavy Metal* movie. Corben's interests in making movies and drawing comics have always complemented each other, and he calls his comic work "a detailed storyboard for a movie." Richard resides in Kansas City, where he continues to work on animation, illustration, and comics. His sketch of Poe's *Masque of the Red Death* was done specifically for this volume.

JOE R. LANSDALE (page 5)

Texas author Joe Lansdale has written over thirty books in the horror, western, fantasy and mystery genres. His versatility extends to comics, where he has written for series including *Batman* and *Jonah Hex*, and animation, where he has scripted episodes of the *Batman* and *Superman* TV series. As Joe declares, "I am my own genre." Two short films have been made of his stories, *The Job*, and *Drive-In Date*. A number of other books have been optioned by Hollywood, and *Bubba Ho-Tep*, a tale of a seventy-year-old Elvis, is in current release. Joe has won numerous honors including the British Fantasy Award, the American Mystery Award, the International Crime Writer's Award, the Booklist Editors' Choice Award, *The New York Times* Notable Book Award, the Edgar Allan Poe Award and six Bram Stoker awards. His latest books are *A Fine Dark Line*, a national bestseller, *High Cotton*, a collection of his best short stories, and *Zeppelins West*, an outrageous alternate history tale illustrated by Mark Nelson and designed by Tom Pomplun. Joe's next novel will be *Sunset and Sawdust*, due from Alfred A. Knopf in February 2004.

RICK GEARY (page 7)

Rick is best known for his thirteen years as a contributor to *The National Lampoon*. His work has also appeared in Marvel, DC, and Dark Horse comics, *Rolling Stone*, *Mad*, *Heavy Metal*, *Disney Adventures*, *The Los Angeles Times*, and *The New York Times Book Review*. He is a regular cartoonist in *Rosebud*. Rick has written and illustrated five children's books and published a collection of his comics, *Housebound* with Rick Geary. The fifth volume in his continuing book series A Treasury of Victorian Murder is The Beast of Chicago. More of his work has appeared in the Graphic Classics anthologies Arthur Conan Doyle, H.G. Wells, H.P. Lovecraft, Jack London, Ambrose Bierce and Mark Twain. Rick completely redrew his adaptation of The Tell-Tale Heart for this new Poe edition. You can also view his art at www.rickgeary.com.

STANLEY W. SHAW (page 25)

Stan Shaw illustrates for various clients all over the country including The Village Voice, Esquire, Slate, Starbucks, The Seattle Mariners, Nintendo, Rhino Records, Microsoft, B.E.T., DC Comics, ABCNEWS.com, Wizards of The Coast, Amazing Stories, Vibe, The Flying Karamazov Brothers and Willamette Week. His illustrations for Moxon's Master appear in Graphic Classics: Ambrose Bierce. In addition to practicing illustration, Stan teaches it; at Cornish School of the Arts, School of Visual Concepts and Pacific Lutheran University. He is now part of a group of artists advising on an illustration textbook. Stan can be reached at drawstanley@harbor-net.com.

PEDRO LOPEZ (page 39)

Born in Denmark in 1974, Pedro says he is inspired mostly by spaghetti westerns (his father's fault), Italian crime thrillers, and dark scifi movies. His passion about these movies is obvious when you read his comics. He is also inspired by French comic artists such as Tardi, Hermann, and Mézières. He claims "Dark Humor" and "Irony" as his middle names. Pedro has published comics in Denmark, and he is now adapting The Suicide Club for Graphic Classics: Robert Louis Stevenson. You can see samples of his work on his site: www.pedrolopez.dk.

LISA K. WEBER (page 50)

Lisa is a graduate of Parsons School of Design in New York City, where she is currently employed in the fashion industry, designing prints and characters for teenage girls' jammies, while freelancing work on children's books and character design for animation. Other projects include her "creaturized" opera posters and playing cards. Lisa has provided illustrations for Graphic Classics: H.P. Lovecraft, Graphic Classics: Ambrose Bierce, Graphic Classics: Bram Stoker and Graphic Classics: Mark Twain. Illustrations from her in-progress book The Shakespearean ABCs were printed in Rosebud 25. More of Lisa's art can be seen online at www.creatureco.com.

RAFAEL NIEVES (page 62)

Rafael has for fifteen years created and written numerous comics, including Hellstorm, Orlak, Nosferatu, Arianne, the critically-acclaimed Tales from the Heart (co-written with Cindy Goff), and a series based on White Wolf's Vampire: The Masquerade. His latest is Mr. Moto, a three-issue miniseries illustrated by Tim Hamilton and published by Moonstone Books. Of his imaginative interpretation of Poe's The Bells, Nieves says, "I had my work cut out for me, because the poem didn't lend itself to easy adaptation. It has a very musical quality to it, a definite rhythm that I had to preserve, at the same time wrapping a dramatic storyline around it. And of course, I had to be true to the spirit of Poe, where happy endings are few and far between." Rafael says he has another Poe adaptation in the works, this time an animated version of The Raven, and The Bells will also soon see life as a cartoon short.

JUAN GOMEZ (page 62)

Juan is a Chicago-based animator who cites Tim Burton, European comics, and Rugrats among his many influences. The illustrator of Rafael Nieves' adaptation of The Bells has also collaborated with him on Chillin's (Moonstone Comics, 1997), an anthology of horror stories about terrible tykes. Gomez's clean, simple style strikes just the right balance between humorous cartooning and more serious traditional illustration which is a perfect match for Nieves' vision of The Bells. The version presented here has been digested from the full 25-page original, published by Tome Press in 1999, and available at www.calibercomics.com. Currently, Juan is deeply involved in his creator-owned project Who? The Hex!, in collaboration with itoons, a Chicago internet animation and game studio.

ANDY EWEN (page 78)

Andy's illustrations have appeared in The Progessive, Isthmus, and The New York Times Book Review. He was the featured artist in Rosebud 10 and Rosebud 22. His personal, dreamlike drawings also appear in Graphic Classics: H.P. Lovecraft and Graphic Classics: Ambrose Bierce. In addition to his ability as a graphic artist, Andy is also a talented musician. For nearly twenty years he has been the lead singer, guitarist and songwriter for Honor Among Thieves, one of the Madison, Wisconsin area's most respected bands.

JOHN COULTHART (page 80)

John Coulthart lives in Manchester, England and divides his time as an illustrator, comic artist, and CD and book designer. Since 1989 he has worked with Savoy Books on David Britton's controversial *Lord Horror* comic series and more recently has been responsible for the packaging of their new line of prestigious book reprints. His adaptations of H.P. Lovecraft stories were collected as *The Haunter of the Dark and other Grotesque Visions* by Oneiros Books in 1999, and he adapted *An Occurrence at Owl Creek Bridge* for *Graphic Classics: Ambrose Bierce*. Future projects include Savoy's illustrated edition of *The House on the Borderland* by William Hope Hodgson, *Luvkraft vs Kthulhu*, an illustrated novella by Grant Morrison and *The Soul*, a comic series with Alan Moore.

MATT HOWARTH *(page 83)*

Matt Howarth has spent his career mixing the genres of science fiction, comic books, and alternative music. Probably best known for his *Those Annoying Post Bros.* comic book series, lately he has been doing a variety of graphic adaptations of stories by Greg Bear and Vernor Vinge. Other adaptations appeared in *Graphic Classics: Arthur Conan Doyle*, *Graphic Classics: H.P. Lovecraft* and *Graphic Classics: Jack London*. Matt continues to explore the digital genre with a variety of online comics, plus his weekly music review column (at www.soniccuriosity.com). Currently, he is working on a new *Bugtown* comic book series for MU Press, and collaborating with New Zealander electronic musician Rudy Adrain on an upcoming album. You are invited to visit www.matthowarth.com for more entertainment.

J.B. BONIVERT *(page 107)*

Jeffrey Bonivert is a Bay Area native who has contributed to independent comics as both artist and writer, in such books as *The Funboys*, *Turtle Soup* and *Mister Monster*. His unique adaptation of *The Raven* originally appeared in 1979 in *Star*Reach*, and was revised for the first edition of this volume in 2001. Jeff's art is published in *Graphic Classics: Arthur Conan Doyle*, *Graphic Classics: Jack London*, *Graphic Classics: Ambrose Bierce* and *Graphic Classics: Bram Stoker*, and he was part of the unique four-artist team on *Reanimator* in *Graphic Classics: H.P. Lovecraft*. Jeff's biography of artist Murphy Anderson appears in *Spark Generators*, and *Muscle and Faith*, his Casey Jones / Teenage Mutant Ninja Turtles epic, can be seen online at www.flyingcolorscomics.com.

ROGER LANGRIDGE *(page 114)*

New Zealand-born artist Roger Langridge is the creator of Fred the Clown, whose online comics appear every Monday at www.hotelfred.com.

Fred also shows up in print three times a year in *Fred the Clown* comics. With his brother Andrew, Roger's first comics series was *Zoot!* published in 1988 and recently reissued as *Zoot Suite*. Other titles followed, including *Knuckles, The Malevolent Nun* and *Art d'Ecco*. Roger's work has also appeared in numerous magazines in Britain, the U.S., France and Japan, including *Deadline*, *Judge Dredd*, *Heavy Metal*, *Comic Afternoon*, *Gross Point* and *Batman: Legends of the Dark Knight*. He adapted *Master*, a rare Doyle poem in *Graphic Classics: Arthur Conan Doyle*, and collaborated with Mort Castle on a comics bio for *Graphic Classics: Jack London*. Called "insanely hardworking," Roger now lives in London, where he divides his time between comics, children's books and commercial illustration.

RICHARD SALA *(page 116)*

A master of gothic humor in the tradition of Charles Addams and Edward Gorey, Richard Sala creates stories filled with mystery, adventure, femmes fatales and homicidal maniacs. Richard is the artist and author of several collections, *Hypnotic Tales*, *Black Cat Crossing*, *Thirteen O'Clock*, *The Chuckling Whatsit*, plus an homage to Gorey titled *The Ghastly Ones*. His work has appeared in *RAW*, *Blab!*, *Esquire*, *Playboy*, *The New York Times*, *Graphic Classics: Arthur Conan Doyle*, *Graphic Classics: Bram Stoker* and his current, critically-acclaimed comic series, *Evil Eye*. His illustrations for *The Black Cat* are new for this *Poe* edition. Richard also created *Invisible Hands*, which ran on MTV's animation show, *Liquid Television*. Recent projects include the children's book *It Was a Dark and Silly Night* and illustrations for a previously unpublished screenplay by Jack Kerouac titled *Dr. Sax and the Great WorldSnake*. Visit Richard's website at www.richardsala.com for "lots of wonderfully creepy things to look at."

SPAIN RODRIGUEZ *(page 124)*

Manuel "Spain" Rodriguez, born 1940 in Buffalo, New York, first gained fame as one of the founders of the underground comix movement of the 1960s. After drawing comics in New York for the *East Village Other*, he moved to San Francisco where he joined Robert Crumb and other artists on *Zap Comix*. Spain's early years with the Road Vultures Motorcycle Club and his reportage of the 1968 Democratic Convention in Chicago are chronicled in the comics collection, *My True Story*. Along with autobiographical stories and politically-oriented fiction featuring his best-known character, Trashman, Spain has produced a number of historical comics. His story of Poe's astonishing choice for a posthumous literary agent, *The*

Inheritance of Rufus Griswold, first appeared in *Arcade* in 1976. Spain's work can also be seen in the online comic *The Dark Hotel* at www.salon.com, *Graphic Classics: Jack London*, and in *Graphic Classics: Bram Stoker*.

MILTON KNIGHT *(page 127)*

Milton Knight claims he started drawing, painting and creating his own attempts at comic books and animation at age two. "I've never formed a barrier between fine art and cartooning," says Milt. "Growing up, I treasured Chinese watercolors, Breughel, Charlie Brown and Terrytoons equally." His work has appeared in magazines including *Heavy Metal*, *High Times*, *National Lampoon* and *Nickelodeon Magazine*, and he has illustrated record covers, posters, candy packaging and T-shirts, and occasionally exhibited his paintings. Labor on *Ninja Turtles* comics allowed him to get up a grubstake to move to the West Coast in 1991, where he became an animator and director on *Felix the Cat* cartoons. Milt's comics titles include *Midnite the Rebel Skunk*, *Hinkley*, and *Slug and Ginger* and *Hugo*. He has appeared in *Graphic Classics: H.G. Wells*, *Graphic Classics: Jack London*, *Graphic Classics: Ambrose Bierce*, and *Graphic Classics: Mark Twain*. Check for the latest news at www.miltonknight.net.

SPENCER WALTS *(page 140)*

Spencer is a Madison-based designer and illustrator whose award-winning work has appeared in numerous periodicals and books. He is a frequent contributor to *Rosebud*, including the "Cartoon Special", *Rosebud 18*. In 2000 Spencer founded Eyewerks Studio, where he creates animation as well as illustration and design.

TOM POMPLUN

The designer, editor and publisher of *Graphic Classics*, Tom has a background in both fine and commercial arts and a lifelong interest in comics. He designed and produced *Rosebud*, a journal of fiction, poetry and illustration, from 1993 to 2003, and in 2001 he founded *Graphic Classics*. Tom is currently working on the ninth book in the series, *Graphic Classics: Robert Louis Stevenson*, featuring *The Strange Case of Dr. Jekyll and Mr. Hyde*, *The Bottle Imp*, *The Suicide Club*, and a collection of Stevenson's poems and short fables. The book is scheduled for release in June 2004. You can see previews and much more at www.graphicclassics.com.

©1997 MAXON CRUMB